CULTURES OF THE WORLD
Angola

Cavendish
Square
New York

Published in 2019 by Cavendish Square Publishing, LLC
243 5th Avenue, Suite 136, New York, NY 10016

Library of Congress Cataloging-in-Publication Data

Names: Sheehan, Sean, 1951- author. | Bryan, Bethany, author. | Yong, Jui
Lin, author.
Title: Angola / Bethany Bryan, Sean Sheehan, and Jui Lin Yong.
Description: Third edition. | New York : Cavendish Square, 2019. | Series:
Cultures of the world
Identifiers: LCCN 2018023398 (print) | LCCN 2018031710 (ebook) | ISBN
9781502640192 (ebook) | ISBN 9781502640185 (library bound)
Subjects: LCSH: Angola--Juvenile literature.
Classification: LCC DT1269 (ebook) | LCC DT1269 .S54 2019 (print) | DDC
967.3--dc23
LC record available at https://lccn.loc.gov/2018023398

Editorial Director: David McNamara
Editor: Elizabeth Schmermund
Copy Editor: Nathan Heidelberger
Associate Art Director: Alan Sliwinski
Designer: Jessica Nevins
Production Coordinator: Karol Szymczuk
Photo Research: J8 Media

CONTENTS

ANGOLA TODAY

NOVEMBER 11 IS AN IMPORTANT DAY TO THE PEOPLE OF ANGOLA. On that day, in 1975, Angola officially became an independent nation, overthrowing the rule of the European nation of Portugal after four hundred years. On Independence Day, the Angolan people celebrate with parades and festivals. People wave the black-and-red Angolan flag, emblazoned with the cogwheel and sickle that represent the nation's industrial and agricultural workers. They celebrate with music, dancing, and traditional food and drink.

In the nation's capital, Luanda, on the fortieth anniversary of Angolan independence, in 2015, a military parade passed through Independence Square. Along the Baía de Luanda, a nearby bay, eighteen thousand paper lanterns, representing the country's eighteen provinces, were released into the sky. There was jubilant dancing and powerful speeches. But, despite this celebration, Independence Day is also a painful reminder of the fight for independence and the lives that were lost in the conflict that came next. For the twenty-seven years that followed independence, Angola was torn by civil war (1975—2002), from which the nation is still recovering.

Drilling for oil off the coast of Angola, as shown here, has increased in importance over the past decade.

The economic repercussions of the civil war continue to echo today. Angola's main export and what generates most of the nation's wealth is oil, producing about 1.8 million barrels a day. But not all Angolans benefit from this wealth because most of this income goes to the government or to oil-industry employees. Because of this, there is a steep divide between the rich and the poor, especially noticeable in the capital city of Luanda. The skyline of the capital city is made up of towering skyscrapers that overlook shacks that represent the poorer regions of the city. The Angolan capital is one of the most expensive cities in the world, partially because most food is imported from other countries.

Before the Angolan civil war, farming was a big part of the economy, and the country exported coffee, sugarcane, bananas, cotton, and other products. But during and after the war, which finally ended in 2002, many Angolans were displaced, including farmers. The farming industry is still recovering, and many of the farmers that are able to grow food are only able to grow enough to feed their families. In order to feed a nation of twenty-nine million people, food has to come from outside the country's borders, and imported food is subject to high tariffs. For comparison, a liter of milk in New York City—the most expensive American city—cost an average of $1.21 in recent years. The equivalent amount of milk cost $3.97 in Luanda. Meat in Angola sold at even more of a premium. A fast-food hamburger might cost as much as $20.38, compared to an average price of $9.52 in New York City.

Furthermore, as much as 80 percent of the food trade in Angola is handled by informal trade, through street vendors and open-air markets, but in Luanda the government is working to crack down on this type of trade, pushing for food to be sold through retail stores. This helps to prevent foodborne illness, since many outdoor markets don't refrigerate their wares, but it also makes food more expensive and harder to come by. Plus, many poorer Angolans are not comfortable shopping in a retail environment because it's not traditionally how they've made food purchases. Open-air markets and street vendors are a deeply ingrained part of Angola's culture, and many are reluctant to change their comfortable, long-standing traditions.

Access to clean water and basic resources is also an issue in modern-day Angola. Twenty-seven years of civil war often led to a breakdown of infrastructure, including access to fresh water and sanitation. Especially in rural areas, people today struggle to find potable water. Even though the country boasts a huge number of rivers flowing from the plateau region at the heart of the nation, pollution is a major problem, making river water unsafe to drink or collect for household use. Rural Angolans travel several miles to find a working tap with clean, potable water, often finding roads to be impassable.

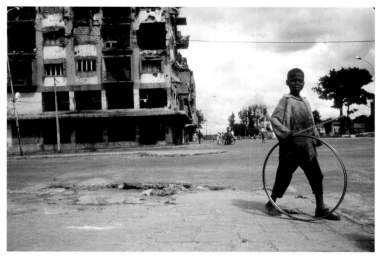

Bombed-out buildings were a common sight during Angola's twenty-seven-year civil war.

Where there isn't access to clean water, disease isn't far behind. Stagnant water leads to mosquitos, and these insects carry yellow fever and malaria. Typhoid fever and hepatitis A are spread through contaminated food and water. The average life expectancy for an Angolan citizen is around fifty-eight years for men and sixty-two for women, putting it at least twenty years below the world average. Additionally, almost one child out of five won't live to be five years of age because of disease and malnutrition.

After the civil war in Angola ended in 2002, citizens were left to pick up the pieces and rebuild. This has not been an easy task or one that could be accomplished quickly. Angola is a country in a state of redevelopment, and it's still in the early stages of that process. With time and the right resources, Angola has the potential to be one of the most powerful nations in the world. While modern life isn't easy for the poorest citizens of Angola, it remains a country rich in culture and tradition, and one that continues to persevere after hundreds of years of struggle.

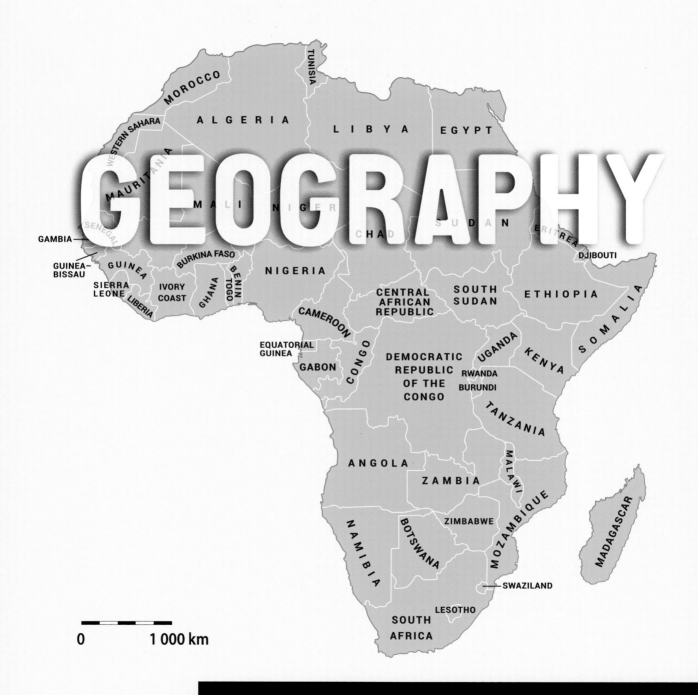

GEOGRAPHY

MOROCCO
TUNISIA
WESTERN SAHARA
ALGERIA
LIBYA
EGYPT
MAURITANIA
MALI
NIGER
SENEGAL
GAMBIA
GUINEA-BISSAU
GUINEA
BURKINA FASO
CHAD
SUDAN
ERITREA
DJIBOUTI
SIERRA LEONE
LIBERIA
IVORY COAST
GHANA
TOGO
BENIN
NIGERIA
CENTRAL AFRICAN REPUBLIC
SOUTH SUDAN
ETHIOPIA
SOMALIA
CAMEROON
EQUATORIAL GUINEA
GABON
CONGO
DEMOCRATIC REPUBLIC OF THE CONGO
UGANDA
RWANDA
BURUNDI
KENYA
TANZANIA
ANGOLA
ZAMBIA
MALAWI
MOZAMBIQUE
MADAGASCAR
NAMIBIA
BOTSWANA
ZIMBABWE
SWAZILAND
LESOTHO
SOUTH AFRICA

0   1 000 km

Angola lies on the southwestern coast of Africa.

1

THE COUNTRY OF ANGOLA CAN BE found along the western coast of Africa, north of Namibia, south of the Democratic Republic of the Congo, and sharing a border with Zambia to the east. Angola is separated from Botswana along its southern border by a 20-mile-wide (32-kilometer-wide) strip of land that is part of Namibia, called the Caprivi Strip. Cabinda, a small exclave and province of Angola, lies north of the Democratic Republic of the Congo and south of the Republic of the Congo. To the west of Angola lies the Atlantic Ocean. Covering an area of 481,354 square miles (1,246,700 square kilometers), Angola is the seventh-largest country in Africa, about twice as large as Texas.

"Any visitor to the country who drinks from the River Bengo will never want to leave."
—Angolan proverb

The name Angola comes from the word ngola, *which was the title given to kings of the historical Ndongo Kingdom of the Mbundu people, which fell to Portuguese rule in 1671. Many modern-day Angolans are descendants of these people.*

LOWLANDS AND HIGHLANDS

Most of the country lies on a large plateau that, on average, is about 3,950 feet (1,200 meters) above sea level. Some parts of the plateau rise to over 6,500 feet (2,000 m) above sea level. The highest points are Mount Moco, at 8,596 feet (2,620 m), and Mount Meco, just 121 feet (37 m) lower. Over time, erosion by water and wind has shaped the plateau. Geographers call the plateau the "Great Escarpment" (an escarpment is a steep slope or cliff) to describe the effects of this erosion.

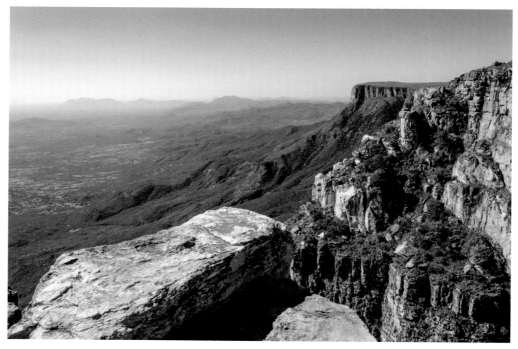

The plateau at the nation's center collects rainfall, which flows outward in the form of Angola's many rivers.

The tumboa (or Welwitschia*), which grows in the more arid regions of Angola, is sometimes referred to as a "living fossil" because it can live up to two thousand years. This plant is able to live in arid climates because it absorbs water both through a long taproot and also through its leaves when fog and rainfall are present.*

In the tropical regions of Angola, one might find the flowering herb aframmi, whose blossoms resemble flowering dill. And the grasslands of Angola are covered with the grass species Streptolophus sagittifolius, *which is native to the country. This grass species is recognizable because of its long, purplish, spiky leaves when the plant reaches maturity.*

Along the coast is a lowland area. At its widest point it extends about 100 miles (160 km) inland. Between this lowland and the main plateau is an intermediate area, known as the sub-plateau, which is 14 miles (23 km) wide in the south and around 286 miles (460 km) wide in the north.

From the eastern side of this plain, the land gradually rises toward the large plateau that occupies all but one-third of the country's total area. In places in the south of the country, however, the change from the sub-plateau to the plateau occurs abruptly, and there are dramatic escarpments of up to 3,280 feet (1,000 m) in height.

Nearly all of Angola's land is savanna—grassy plains with scattered trees. The Cabinda exclave has a small area of rain forest, and in the deep southwest, near the border with Namibia, is a stretch of desert. This desert is called the Moçâmedes Desert, and it forms the northern tip of the Namib Desert of Namibia.

From the Atlantic Ocean in the west, the desert gradually rises to a semiarid plain where African ironwood trees grow. Few people live in the desert; communities are found mainly in small fishing towns on the coast. The unique tumboa (*Welwitschia mirabilis*), a desert plant with a short, wide trunk and two gigantic leaves that can survive for one hundred years or more, is found in this desert.

EIGHTEEN PROVINCES

There are eighteen provinces that make up Angola, the largest being Moxico at 86,110 square miles (223,023 sq km), which lies along the Zambian border. The smallest province in Angola is Luanda, at 934 square miles (2,418 sq km), followed by Cabinda, at 2,807 square miles (7,270 square kilometers). Cabinda is physically separated from the rest of Angola by the Congo River and a narrow strip of the Democratic Republic of the Congo that extends to the Atlantic coast.

Before gaining independence from Portugal in 1975, Angola had a flourishing tradition of family-based farming and was self-sufficient in all major food crops except wheat. The country exported coffee and corn (maize) as well as crops such as sisal, bananas, tobacco, and cassava. By the 1990s, Angola was producing less than 1 percent of the volume of coffee it had produced in the early 1970s, while production of cotton, tobacco, and sugarcane had stopped almost entirely. Poor global market prices and lack of investment have severely limited the agricultural sector after independence. The Angolan civil war and the consequent deterioration of the rural economy and neglect of the farming sector dealt the final blow to the country's agricultural productivity. Farmers that do exist often only grow enough food for their families and local community. The farming industry makes up only about 10 percent of the gross domestic product of Angola.

The northern region of the country, made up of the three provinces of Cabinda, Zaire, and Uíge, has a typical landscape of tropical savanna. There are also areas of woodland that are good for growing cash crops such as coffee, cotton, palm oil, and sugar. Fish, both in the rivers and offshore, are a rich resource. The tsetse fly—known for carrying disease—is common in the northern region, so raising cattle is uneconomical, as disease tends to spread to the cattle through the tsetse fly. In recent years, African farmers have tended to move away from chickens, beef, and dairy cattle toward goats and sheep.

Northern Angola is largely covered by flat grasslands, typical of a tropical savanna.

To the south is a region centered around Luanda and its neighboring provinces. This is fairly rich agricultural land, with plenty of timber in Bengo province. The richest agricultural land, though, is found in the central highlands region that covers the provinces of Huambo, Bié, and Huíla. A variety of crops can be grown there, from corn and cassava to be eaten to coffee and tobacco to be sold for cash.

The two coastal provinces in the southwest, Benguela and Namibe, have a drier climate and do not support much agriculture, though some cattle are raised there. The inland provinces of Cunene and Kuando Kubango also have an arid climate that makes farming difficult; raising cattle is the main activity there. Finally there are the eastern, inland provinces of Moxico, Lunda Norte, and Lunda Sul. They are characterized by open countryside, and in the northeast, rich deposits of diamonds and other minerals.

The Angolan black-and-white colobus monkey can be recognized by its slim body and long tail.

RICH IN WILDLIFE

Angola's rich animal life includes leopards, lions, hyenas, elephants, hippopotamuses, giraffes, zebras, buffaloes, antelopes, gorillas, and monkeys. Birdlife and reptiles, such as crocodiles, are also common.

THE CUANZA, THE CONGO, AND THE CUNENE

The three most important rivers in Angola are the Cuanza at 596 miles (960 km) long, the Cunene at 587 miles (945 km) long, and the Congo at 2,900 miles (4,700 km) long, which forms part of the border with the Democratic Republic of the Congo. The Cuanza flows into the Atlantic Ocean about 40 miles (64 km) south of Luanda. Only the Cuanza and the Congo Rivers are navigable for more than a short distance.

Several other rivers and their tributaries run across the country. Together the rivers form an important potential source of hydroelectric power. However, the sector suffers from war-torn infrastructure, and blackouts occur frequently. But the government has plans to make improvements. In 2014, the African Development Bank Electricity Sector Transformation Program, which would invest $1 billion in the electricity infrastructure, set plans in motion to achieve 60 percent electrification across the country by 2025. One major new hydroelectric plant is the Lauca Station on the Cuanza River. The first of the plant's six turbines began operating in 2017 as part of the country's long-term goal of harnessing the power of water to help improve the reliability of the electrical grid. When fully operational, the plant is expected to generate around 2,070 megawatts of power.

METROPOLITAN AREAS

Luanda, on the northwest coast, is the capital of Angola. It is also the country's largest city, founded in the sixteenth century. Other important towns in the

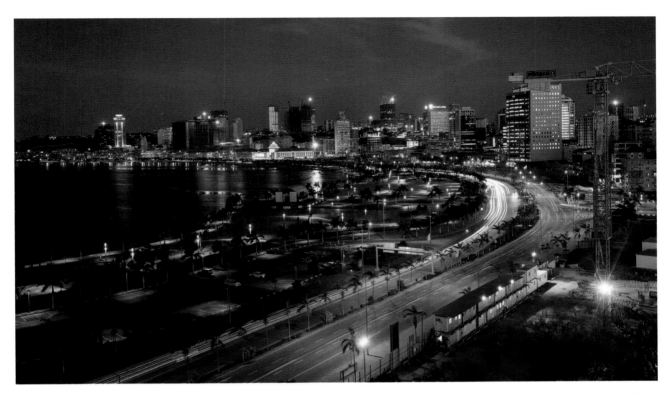

north are Cabinda, Soyo, Caxito, and Malanje. The most important urban centers in the central highlands are Huambo and Kuito. On the coast in the south, Benguela is the major town, followed by Namibe farther south. Other urban centers on the coast include Lobito and Tombua.

The inland population is small, and towns are located near sources of water, with Menongue being one of the few urban centers. In the eastern inland region, the important towns are Luena, Saurimo, and Lucapa.

MINING NATURE

Angola is the second-largest petroleum producer in Africa, after Nigeria. The oil is mostly produced in the northern exclave of Cabinda, which accounts for about 60 to 65 percent of Angola's oil. In recent years, substantial reserves of oil have also been found offshore, in both shallow and deep waters. Angola is now the seventeenth-largest producer of oil in the world.

The Luanda skyline

"Glass skyscrapers soared above the rubble of a twenty-seven-year civil war … Luanda would become, its government announced, 'a new Dubai.'"
—Kevin Sieff, from the *Washington Post*

A COMPLICATED DEPENDENCE ON OIL

Angola depends heavily on oil for economic survival. The country's current production is reaching 1.8 million barrels per day. Oil from Angola has increased so significantly that Angola is now China's second-biggest supplier of oil (after Russia) and is currently the ninth-largest exporter of petroleum to the United States. The most exciting news for the Angolan economy in recent years has been the discovery of new offshore oil reserves, many of which remain unexploited.

As much as 75 percent of the country's oil lies in the ocean, over 3,280 feet (1,000 m) deep in places, and it is only in the last fifteen years that advanced drilling techniques have been developed that can reach these deposits. Conservative estimates put Angola's oil reserves at around 9.5 billion barrels of oil. Angola is quite literally swimming in oil.

Angola is also an important supplier of diamonds for the world market, producing around 9.4 million carats of diamonds every year. Angola's state-run diamond company (Endiama) recently opened a new mine, Tcheji, on the border of the Lunda Norte and Lunda Sul provinces, the heart of the diamond-mining industry in Angola. The new mine could potentially bring in $1.5 million in revenue each month. To date, approximately one thousand kimberlites, or rock formations containing diamond-forming peridotite, have been located in the country. In 2016, a 404.2-carat diamond was found in a mine in Lunda Norte. Measuring 2.75 inches (7 centimeters) in length, the diamond is worth an estimated $20 million and is the twenty-seventh largest in history.

Angola also has substantial, largely untapped, deposits of minerals, including gold, iron ore, phosphates, manganese, copper, lead, quartz, marble, black granite, zinc, and numerous metals. Between 1950 and 1975, iron was extracted. The average amount of iron mined peaked at 5.7 million tons (5.2 million metric tons) per year between 1970 and 1974.

Natural gas resources of 11 trillion cubic feet (308 billion cubic meters) have been found in Angola, in addition to its substantial oil and mineral reserves.

INTERNET LINKS

https://www.worldatlas.com/webimage/countrys/africa/angola/aoland.htm
This site provides helpful and detailed relief maps that show the different geographic regions of Angola.

https://www.youtube.com/watch?v=_Zw9JooZhrU
This video provides a visual overview of the geography and important features of Angola.

HISTORY

The fight for independence from Portugal
raged from 1961 to 1975.

2

T O UNDERSTAND THE HISTORY OF Angola, one must understand the impact that colonization by Portugal had on the country. The history of Angola can be divided into three separate eras: before the arrival of the Portuguese; the arrival of the Portuguese in the fifteenth century followed by Portuguese rule; and after independence was achieved.

Recent Angolan history, especially the years after independence in 1975, has been dominated by a civil war that left hundreds of thousands of people dead and many more homeless.

The power struggle in the country was made worse by other, more powerful countries taking sides, hoping to use the Angolan civil war to achieve their own objectives. The United States, the Soviet Union, and South Africa armed and supported the different groups that they thought would support their own interests. But no one side managed to achieve complete victory, and the civil war took a heavy toll on the Angolan people.

After the end of the civil war in 2002, Angola's economy underwent a period of change, moving from the disarray caused by a quarter century of war to becoming a rising economy in the world market. More recently, the country has faced uncertainty because of the declining price of oil since 2014 and an economy that is dependent on natural resources.

"To our beautiful Angolan homeland our land, our mother we shall return. We shall return to liberated Angola independent Angola."
—An excerpt from "We Shall Return," a poem by Agostinho Neto, Angola's first president

HUNTERS AND GATHERERS

The land that is now Angola was inhabited from as early as 7000 BCE by hunters and gatherers as well as settled communities of fishermen. The early hunter-gatherers, known variously as Bushmen, Khoisan, or San, may have had a basic knowledge of how to make iron. Iron technology began in the Middle East and was introduced into North Africa by way of the Mediterranean. The art of smelting iron is believed to have worked its way down the west side of Africa around 300 BCE through ancient trade routes across the Sahara Desert.

How and when farming and the use of iron tools developed in Angola and other parts of southern Africa is not known for sure. What is certain, however, is that the migration of Bantu-speaking people south to modern Angola had a decisive influence on future developments. The Bantu people, who probably came from what is now Cameroon (a country located in Central and West Africa) had an advanced knowledge of iron-making, which would have given them a great advantage over the Bushmen.

The Bantu peoples are a very diverse collection of African people who share a common language: Bantu.

The migration of Bantu-speaking people into Angola may have begun as early as 1000 BCE, but it occurred gradually. There was also a later migration of Bantu speakers to Angola from eastern Africa. Much later, in the fourteenth century CE, another large movement of people to Angola took place. By the beginning of the sixteenth century, nearly all of Angola was populated by Bantu speakers.

THE KONGO KINGDOM

Very little is known about the history of the region after the first arrival in southern Africa of Bantu-speaking people. As farming developed, some family groups may have achieved positions of power based on their ownership of cattle. This was probably the origin of the various kingdoms that arose after 1000 CE. By 1200 CE, the most powerful of these kingdoms was the Kongo Kingdom, which controlled a large area that included modern Angola. To the south of this kingdom, a smaller kingdom known as the Ndongo Kingdom, which stretched inland from Luanda as far as the Lucala River, also developed. Another kingdom, the Matamba Kingdom, was based to the west of the Cuango River.

The Kongo Kingdom's success was based on its people's skill in developing metalworking and pottery. The technique of weaving cloth from raffia palm became a sophisticated art, and Kongo cloth was traded as far west as the Atlantic coast in exchange for salt. The Kongo Kingdom developed a currency based on seashells, which it also obtained in exchange for its cloth.

These kingdoms jealously guarded their territories, which were usually defined by the natural course of rivers. Sometimes they interacted with one another—in the first half of the sixteenth century, both the Matamba and Ndongo Kingdoms paid tribute to the mightier Kongo Kingdom in recognition of its superior power.

This traditional carving depicts Queen Nzinga of the Ndongo Kingdom.

However, the arrival of Portuguese explorers and traders in the late fifteenth century fundamentally affected all the kingdoms. At first, they quarreled among themselves over the benefits they thought they could gain by dealing with the Portuguese. Eventually, they united against the Europeans when they realized that the Portuguese were interested not merely in trade but in enslaving them and taking away their freedom and their land.

THE LUNDA EMPIRE

There were also other powerful states besides the Kongo. One of the most important was the Lunda Empire that developed in the sixteenth century. Lunda was a village-based kingdom whose people lived as farmers and supplemented

The Lunda title of Mwata Yamvo has continued to be used for centuries. Here, a leader called Mwata Yamvo (*right*) poses with Kosongo Niembo, another tribal leader, in 1962.

their food supply by hunting and fishing. The leaders of this kingdom originated in the south of the present-day Democratic Republic of the Congo and ruled through local chiefs who paid tribute to the king. The Lunda king was careful to appoint "advisors" in each of the chiefs' villages. These advisors ensured that the taxes that were due to him were collected. Over the next few centuries, the kingdom expanded to include portions of what are now Angola and Zambia.

The Lunda king was given the title of Mwata Yamvo ("The Lord of Vipers"). The people of the Lunda Empire benefited from the planting of new crops from America that were acquired indirectly from the Portuguese. Corn was introduced in this way, and so was cassava, which was especially valued because of its ability to withstand periods of drought and still produce a good crop. With new food sources, the Lunda Empire expanded even more. Trade with the Portuguese developed, with ivory and slaves exchanged for guns and cloth.

THE ARRIVAL OF THE PORTUGUESE

In the 1480s, the Portuguese began to arrive on the shores of Angola. Their first contact was with the king of the Kongo, and early relations between the two groups were friendly. Both sides had something to offer, and mutual trade was easily established. The Kongo king was happy to exchange some of his slaves in return for the guns that the Portuguese brought with them.

The Ndongo Kingdom was also eager to trade with the Europeans, and by the 1540s the Ndongo were dealing with the Portuguese, who had established a coastal trading post at Luanda. They even invited some of the Portuguese leaders to their capital, hoping to secure the best possible terms for future trade. This caused friction with the Kongo Kingdom, who wanted to monopolize trade with the Europeans. Fighting broke out between the two African kingdoms. By 1557, the Ndongo had broken away from the Kongo completely.

By the 1570s, the Portuguese decided to take over the territory. In 1575, the Portuguese landed in force at Luanda. The aim of the Portuguese was to conquer the interior, and in 1579 they were ready to move up the Cuanza River and attack the Ndongo capital.

PORTUGUESE COLONIZATION

The Ndongo resisted the advance of the invaders as best they could. It took the Portuguese four years to take land on either side of the Cuanza River and set up a second military base at Massangano. This would become the main interior post for the collection of slaves before they were brought downriver to the coast and shipped across the Atlantic to the Americas. The land they conquered was the beginning of what would later become the Portuguese colony of Angola.

This carving depicts the arrival of the Portuguese in Angola and the introduction of the slave trade.

The determination of the Portuguese to maintain a permanent presence in the region also brought them into conflict with the Matamba. The Kongo Kingdom, too, changed its attitude toward the Europeans, and by the end of the sixteenth century all three African kingdoms had joined forces against the common enemy. Together they managed to stop the colonizing forces.

This success was due in no small part to a new female Ndongo leader named Nzinga. Under her, the colonial advance was resisted and contained, but the Portuguese presence could not be removed entirely. A treaty was signed in 1684 and lasted until the mid-eighteenth century. By then the

Portuguese were ready to conquer more territory, and they mounted a successful invasion of Matamba territory.

During the nineteenth century, the Portuguese strengthened their hold over the country and established cotton, rubber, and coffee plantations. They abolished the export of slaves on paper in 1836, but forced labor was still widespread, so for the Angolans little changed. By 1920, the country was declared "pacified" by the Portuguese, with all effective resistance over. The country was now a full-fledged colony with a civil administration.

MOVEMENTS FOR LIBERATION

Queen Nzinga fought the slave trade during her thirty-seven-year reign.

In the 1950s, Portuguese settlers began to take over the best farmland and expel the Africans who had been working the land. Angolans were forced to work on Portuguese plantations. It was under these conditions that nationalist sentiment in Angola began to develop. The first movement to emerge was the

UPHEAVAL IN PORTUGAL

Back in Portugal, in the early twentieth century, the government was in a state of flux. On February 1, 1908, the royal family was riding in a carriage when the coach was attacked. The king, Carlos I, was assassinated, along with his oldest son, leaving his younger son, Infante Manuel Maria Filipe Carlos Amélio Luís Miguel Rafael Gabriel Gonzaga Xavier Francisco de Assis Eugénio—historically known as Manuel II—the throne. He was only eighteen years old.

But the idea of being ruled by a monarchy was quickly losing favor in Portugal. Portugal's anti-monarchy party organized a coup, attacking the royal palace. The king was forced to flee. He escaped the country aboard the royal yacht and eventually settled near London, never to return to power. The monarchy that had ruled Portugal for eight hundred years was over. The country was now a republic.

The Republic of Portugal was also short-lived, however. In 1926, the government was overthrown yet again in a military coup. In 1932, António de Oliveira Salazar came to power, establishing an authoritarian government. Salazar ruled Portugal for the next thirty-six years.

Popular Movement for the Liberation of Angola (MPLA). By the 1960s, it had developed a guerrilla force and was receiving aid from the Soviet Union.

The second movement to emerge was the National Front for the Liberation of Angola (FNLA), which was based in the Democratic Republic of the Congo (called Zaire at the time) and received aid from the United States. Later, in 1966, a splinter group from the FNLA formed the National Union for the Total Independence of Angola (UNITA).

In 1975, with the departure of Portuguese troops, the MPLA took over rule of Angola.

THE OVERTHROW OF PORTUGAL

Before independence was achieved in 1975, there was terrible loss of life in Angola. Hundreds of Portuguese settlers were killed, and twenty thousand Angolans lost their lives. The Portuguese colony of Angola came to an end as a result of a coup in Portugal in 1974 that overthrew the country's military government. The new government intended to disown its overseas colonies because maintaining control over these colonies was consuming a crippling 40 percent of the Portuguese national budget. Independence was granted to Angola in 1975. By the end of 1975, three hundred thousand Portuguese had left Angola; many deliberately destroyed factories and plantations before they left.

Unfortunately, independence was only the beginning of a new chapter in Angola's struggle to survive. The three nationalist movements—MPLA, FNLA, and UNITA—began to jostle for power, and civil war broke out.

OUTBREAK OF CIVIL WAR

The civil war that was a feature of much of Angolan life after 1975 owed much to the international conflicts of the time. The United States supported the FNLA and UNITA because it saw the struggle as a way to contain Soviet influence in Africa. South Africa, on the other hand, viewed the struggle as a way to resist radical black nationalism. Black nationalism advocates a racial definition (or redefinition) of black national identity, as opposed to multiculturalism.

Portuguese colonists first discovered oil in Angola in the late 1700s. They sent some of the oil to Lisbon and Rio de Janeiro to be used to seal leaks in their ships.

South Africa provided aid and troops to **UNITA** during the Angolan civil war.

South Africa, which had its own colony of Namibia bordering Angola, wanted to prevent the MPLA from gaining power because the MPLA supported the Namibian struggle for independence. These outside forces were already involved in Angola before independence was granted in 1975. In 1975, Cuba joined the conflict and sent troops to support the MPLA against South African troops that had invaded from the south.

ATTEMPTS AT PEACE

The Angolan civil war dragged on through the 1980s. At one point, the MPLA held the support of most of the population, but because of the MPLA's anticapitalist stand, the United States was determined to help UNITA defeat the MPLA.

This led to American support for a second South African invasion in 1981. However, South Africa withdrew from the conflict at the end of the 1980s. Cuba withdrew as well. With the collapse of the Soviet Union in the early 1990s, Soviet support for the MPLA stopped. The MPLA then began to shed its belief in Soviet-style economics and one-party rule.

A treaty was signed in 1991 between the MPLA and UNITA, and a new order seemed to be emerging, with the promise of free elections and free speech. However, there was a return to civil war when UNITA, unhappy at losing the elections that took place in 1992, took up arms again. Another peace treaty, the Lusaka Protocol, was signed in 1994, with the United Nations taking on the task of monitoring the cease-fire. Unfortunately, mutual distrust between the MPLA and UNITA, coupled with loose international monitoring, led to the collapse of the protocol. Both sides continued to build up their stockpiles of arms, and the United Nations Security Council delayed full deployment of a significant peacekeeping force in the area until late 1996. However, by December 1995 the government and UNITA were again in a state of war.

In 1998, the Angolan president, José Eduardo dos Santos asked the United Nations peacekeepers to leave, and in February 1999 they withdrew from Angola. UNITA's success in mining diamonds and selling them abroad at inflated prices allowed the war to continue even as the movement's support in the Western world and among the local populace withered away. Executive Outcomes (EO), a private military company, played a major role in turning the tide for the MPLA. One US defense expert called the EO the "best 50 or 60 million dollars the Angolan government ever spent." Executive Outcomes trained four thousand to five thousand troops and thirty pilots in combat in camps in Lunda Sul, Cabo Ledo, and Dondo.

The Angolan military found and killed Jonas Savimbi, the leader of UNITA, on February 22, 2002. After that, the military commanders of UNITA and MPLA signed a memorandum of understanding, and UNITA's new leadership declared the rebel group a political party and officially demobilized its armed forces in August 2002. That same month, the United Nations Security Council replaced the United Nations Office in Angola with the United Nations Mission in Angola—a larger, nonmilitary, political presence.

"We must not face a future in which we can no longer help our friends, such as Angola, even in limited and carefully controlled ways. We must not lose all capacity to respond short of military intervention."
—Gerald Ford's 1976 State of the Union address

THE ONGOING LEGACY OF WAR

The civil war spawned a disastrous humanitarian crisis in Angola, internally displacing 4.28 million people, one-third of Angola's population. The United Nations estimated in 2003 that 80 percent of Angolans lacked access to basic medical care, 60 percent lacked access to water, and 30 percent of Angolan children would die before the age of five, with an overall life expectancy for Angolans of less than forty years of age. Human Rights Watch, an organization that works to defend and protect human rights, estimates that UNITA and the Angolan government employed more than nine thousand child soldiers during the war. Human rights analysts found five thousand to eight thousand girls under the age of twelve married to UNITA militants. Some girls were ordered to forage for food for the troops. If the girls did not bring back enough food, as judged by their commander, then the girls were not allowed to eat. After victories, UNITA commanders would be rewarded with women, who were often abused.

Many believe that the future of Cabinda is one free from Angolan rule.

THE FIGHT FOR CABINDAN INDEPENDENCE

With an area of 2,807 square miles (7,270 sq km), the northern Angolan province of Cabinda is unique because it is separated from the rest of the country by a 37-mile- (60 km) wide strip of the Democratic Republic of the Congo along the lower Congo River. The exclave of Cabinda is best known for its oil, which has given it the nickname "the Kuwait of Africa"—it provides around 60 to 65 percent of Angola's oil. Since Angola achieved independence, the territory of Cabinda has been a site where separatist guerrillas fight to oppose the government of Angola.

In 2010, during the Africa Cup of Nations, Cabindan separatists attacked a bus carrying the soccer team from Togo, killing the Angolan driver and injuring nine others. The Front for the Liberation of the Enclave of Cabinda (FLEC) took responsibility for the attack.

NEW LEADERSHIP FOR ANGOLA

José Eduardo dos Santos, a former nationalist member of the MPLA, had been the president of Angola for thirty-eight years when he finally stepped down in 2017, naming João Lourenço, then the MPLA vice president and Angolan defense minister, as his successor. On August 23, 2017, 76 percent of registered Angolan voters headed to the polls and elected Lourenço in a landslide victory for the MPLA party. The MPLA held on to a majority in the National Assembly (the Angolan parliament), winning 150 out of 220 seats. One of the first issues that Lourenço vowed to address after the election was the pending health crisis. Falling oil prices and the continued recovery from the Angolan civil war created a shortage of medication. This led to dangerous epidemics of yellow fever and malaria.

João Lourenço appears here on election day in 2017, casting his vote.

INTERNET LINKS

http://www.buala.org/en/to-read/memories-of-the-angolan -slave-trade
This site provides some historical insight into the slave trade in Angola under Portuguese rule.

https://www.facebook.com/amadeu.sansao/about
This is the official Facebook page of the president of Angola, João Lourenço.

GOVERNMENT

With the overthrow of Mobutu Sese Seko, Zaire became the Democratic Republic of the Congo.

3

ONE OF THE LARGEST TURNING points on the road to peace in Angola occurred in 1997, when Mobutu Sese Seko of Zaire was overthrown and Zaire became the Democratic Republic of the Congo. Mobutu was a supporter of UNITA, but the newly founded Congolese government aligned with the MPLA.

In April 1997, UNITA joined the MPLA to form a new Angolan government, called the Government of Unity and National Reconciliation. A few months later, the People's Assembly, which was first elected in 1992, began to function, and for the first time representatives from both parties sat together in the National Assembly.

But UNITA broke away from the Lusaka Protocol in 1998, claiming that the MPLA had violated it. The following year, in 1999, Angolan armed forces destroyed 80 percent of UNITA's militant wing and captured 15,000 tons (13,600 metric tons) of military equipment, essentially destroying UNITA as a conventional military force and forcing UNITA to return to more traditional guerrilla tactics. The Angolan civil war ended only after the death of Jonas Savimbi, who was killed in an ambush on February 22, 2002. His death shocked Angolans, many of whom had grown up during the Angolan civil war and witnessed Savimbi's ability to successfully evade efforts by Soviet, Cuban, and Angolan troops to kill him.

"Forward, Angola! Revolution through the power of the people! A united country, freedom, one people, one nation!"
—The Angolan national anthem

Angola is a member of international organizations such as the United Nations, the World Bank, the International Monetary Fund, the World Trade Organization, and the African Development Bank, which works to fund economic development and reduce poverty across Africa.

The home of Jonas Savimbi was destroyed in 2002, the year of the **UNITA** leader's death.

Six weeks after Savimbi's death, in April 2002, UNITA agreed to a cease-fire with the government. Under an amnesty agreement, UNITA soldiers and their families—a total of about 350,000 people—were gathered in thirty-three demobilization camps under the Program for Social and Productive Reintegration of Demobilized and War Displaced People. In August 2002, UNITA officially gave up its armed wing and put all of its efforts into the development of its political party. Despite the cease-fire, deep political conflict between UNITA and the MPLA remains. Today, UNITA and the MLPA are the two most influential political parties in the Angolan government.

HOW THE ANGOLAN GOVERNMENT RUNS

Angola is a presidential republic, where the president is both head of state and head of government, and is in charge of a multiparty system. The head of state is a person who represents an independent state. The head of government is the chief officer of an executive branch of government. In a parliamentary

Within months of entering office, João Lourenço fired José Eduardo dos Santos's daughter Isabel from her position as head of Sonangol, Angola's state-run oil company. He went on to then fire Dos Santos's son José from the Angolan Sovereign Wealth Fund. Lourenço said that his actions were part of his plan to tackle corruption. These aggressive actions left many Angolans referring to their new president as "the Terminator."

PRESIDENT JOÃO LOURENÇO

Angola's current president, João Lourenço was born in 1954 in the town of Lobito in the Benguela province of Angola. His father worked in medicine, and his mother was a seamstress. Lourenço went to school at the Industrial Institute of Luanda and then joined the MPLA. Under longtime Angolan president José Eduardo dos Santos, Lourenço served as vice president of the National Assembly and then defense minister starting in 2014. When Dos Santos announced his plans to step down after thirty-eight years as president, he announced Lourenço as his successor. Lourenço was officially elected in August 2017. Angolans playfully nicknamed him JLo.

system, they are often the same person. Executive power is exercised by the government. Legislative power is vested in both the government and parliament. Government includes the political direction and control exercised over the actions of the citizens of a state. Parliament plays more of a lawmaking role in the state.

Angola changed from a one-party Marxist-Leninist system ruled by the MPLA to a formal multiparty democracy following the 1992 elections. President José Eduardo dos Santos won the first-round election with more than 49 percent of the vote, compared with Jonas Savimbi's 40 percent. In the next parliamentary election, held in 2008 (long delayed due to the civil war), the MPLA won 81.64 percent of the vote and 191 out of 220 seats. The next presidential election took place in 2012, with Dos Santos claiming 74 percent of the vote. The MPLA won 74.46 percent of the vote, hanging on to 175 of the 220 seats and maintaining the majority. In the 2017 elections, the MPLA held on to 150 of the seats.

The executive branch of the government is made up of the president and the council of ministers. The council of ministers, all of whom are government ministers and vice ministers, meets regularly to discuss policy issues. The president appoints governors of the eighteen provinces. The constitution of 2010—which replaced the earlier constitution of 1992—establishes the broad outlines of government structure and identifies the rights and duties of citizens. The legal system is based on Portuguese and customary law, but it is weak

José Eduardo dos Santos

"No one is so rich and powerful that they cannot be punished and no one is so poor that they cannot be protected."
—João Lourenço

In 2010, a new constitution was voted into law in Angola, replacing the 1992 version. In the new constitution, the post of prime minister was eliminated, giving those powers over to the president. These changes also established the post of vice president, which would handle the day-to-day state affairs. Importantly, these changes to the constitution also made the role of president no longer electable through direct voting. Under the new constitution, the head of the party that wins the majority becomes president. Finally, these changes gave the president the power to appoint judges to the high courts, including the Constitutional Court and Supreme Court. Many believed that these changes were made to keep Dos Santos in power and strengthen the hold of the MLPA over the government.

and fragmented. Courts operate in only 12 of more than 140 municipalities. Legal fees are also very high in Angola, so disputes often won't go to court to avoid the cost.

ANGOLA'S POLITICAL PARTIES

MPLA stands for the Movimento Popular de Libertação de Angola (Popular Movement for the Liberation of Angola). Formed in 1956 under the leadership of Agostinho Neto, it was the first political group to seek independence from Portugal. Support for the party came mainly from the Mbundu people, and the MPLA primarily developed in Luanda and other large towns.

Both the MPLA and UNITA were nationalist parties that called for independence from Portugal, but there was an important political difference between the two groups. The MPLA was attracted to communism as an alternative to capitalism. UNITA, on the other hand, was seen as an anticommunist party. It was this crucial difference in political ideology that led the United States and South Africa to support UNITA, while communist Cuba and the former Soviet Union sided with the MPLA.

In 1977, the MPLA added Partido Trabalhista (Party of Labor) to its name and became the MPLA-PT. In the 1980s, the MPLA-PT developed into a tightly controlled party that sought to govern Angola through one-party rule. Corruption became common within the party, and people of Ovimbundu origin found it very difficult to obtain official positions, even if they were well qualified. In the early 1990s, the MPLA-PT abandoned its Marxist past in favor of democratic socialism and endorsed multiparty elections in the wake of a peace settlement with UNITA. It also dropped the PT from its name. Socialism favors a society characterized by equal opportunities for all people. Communism promotes the establishment of an equal, classless, stateless society based on common ownership. The MPLA is currently a member of the Socialist International, a worldwide organization of democratic socialist, social democratic, socialist, and labor political parties.

The Broad Convergence for the Salvation of Angola—Electoral Coalition (CASA-CE), founded in 2012, is another party on the rise in Angola. The party

Lourenço supporters gathered for a campaign rally on March 4, 2017.

After the 2017 election, unhappy members of UNITA, CASA-CE, PRS, and FNLA protested the results, calling them unconstitutional. Their argument was that only three of the provinces—Cabinda, Uíge, and Zaire—had followed electoral law when processing the election results. They also alleged that ballot boxes and votes had disappeared. Maka Angola, an anticorruption website, argued that votes hadn't been completely officially tallied before the National Electoral Commission announced that the MPLA, and therefore João Lourenço, had won.

Even if election results were corrupted, they showed that the MPLA was slowly losing support across Angola. Unemployment around the time of the election was at around 20 percent, and prices of goods were skyrocketing because of inflation. Many blamed younger voters who didn't live through the Angolan civil war for looking for leadership outside of the ruling party.

received 6 percent of the vote in 2012, which grew to 9.5 percent in 2017. The CASA-CE's goal is to fight corruption in the Angolan government and find a foothold among younger voters who feel disenfranchised by UNITA and the MPLA. The three remaining seats after the 2017 election went to the Social Renewal Party (PRS) and the FNLA.

SAVIMBI, LEADER OF UNITA

Jonas Savimbi, the founder of UNITA, was born in 1934. His father worked on railroads under the Portuguese, and this helped Savimbi attend both elementary and secondary school. Savimbi won a scholarship to study medicine in Portugal, and he gradually become more interested in politics. In 1966, he established UNITA and built up its support in eastern and southern Angola among the Ovimbundu people. When an MPLA government was established in 1975, Savimbi organized military resistance, and with substantial help from South Africa and the United States, UNITA launched a civil war.

Savimbi became the best-known figure in Angolan politics during the 1980s. His fluent English and support from the United States helped establish his presence on the international stage. After surviving more than a dozen assassination attempts, Savimbi was killed on February 22, 2002, in a battle with Angolan government troops. Six weeks after his death, a cease-fire between UNITA and the MPLA was signed, but Angola remains deeply divided politically between MPLA and UNITA supporters.

The death of Jonas Savimbi brought a tentative peace to Angola, but deep divides remain.

INTERNET LINKS

https://www.aljazeera.com/topics/country/angola.html
Al Jazeera is a global news network for keeping up on news from around the world, including Angola.

https://www.constituteproject.org/constitution /Angola_2010.pdf?lang=en
The Constitution Project makes constitutions from around the world, including Angola's 2010 constitution, available for anyone to read.

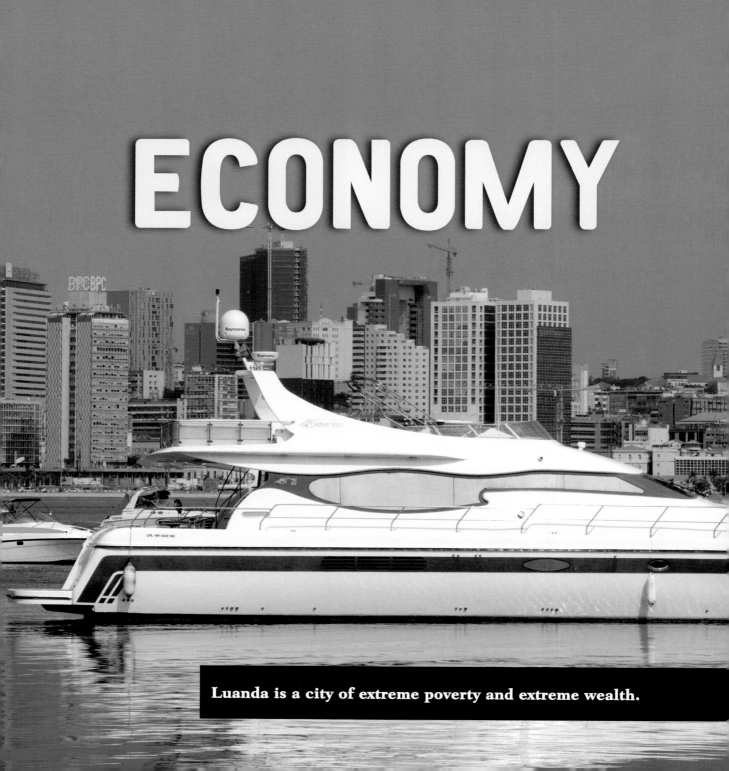

ECONOMY

Luanda is a city of extreme poverty and extreme wealth.

4

THE ECONOMY OF ANGOLA IS ONE that is complicated and fragile, and has been since 2002, when twenty-seven years of civil war came to an end. Angola is rich in oil, natural gas, and diamonds, and it has begun to harness hydroelectric energy and farm vast agricultural regions, but the country continues to struggle under the weight of a damaged infrastructure and unstable government.

Oil accounts for over 90 percent of Angola's exports, 50 percent of the country's gross national product, and 70 percent of government revenue. But the oil market is one that fluctuates frequently, and sinking or unsteady oil prices in an economy that depends on oil sales can be disastrous. In 2002, the average price of a barrel of oil was $22.81, or $31.02 after being adjusted for inflation. The price in 2005 was $50.04 ($62.66 with inflation). The price continued to climb, and in 2008 the price reached $91.48 ($103.67 with inflation). The Angolan economy was flourishing in 2008, despite years of struggle, because oil prices were high. But 2015 and 2016 saw a significant drop in the average price of a barrel of oil: $41.85 ($43.22) and $36.34 ($37.02), respectively. In short, the higher the price of a barrel of oil in an economy that depends on the oil trade, the better. So when the prices drop, so does the standard of living for the Angolan people.

"Next to the sleek skyscrapers and luxury apartments, ramshackle shantytowns and crowded slums spread for miles in every direction, housing millions of people living on less than $2 a day."
—Victoria Eastwood and David McKenzie

Many in Luanda are still struggling, even years after the end of the war.

Although Angola is now technically a middle-income country, 67.4 percent of its population still lives below the poverty line, especially in rural regions, where the poverty rate is 94 percent. Average life expectancy is just 60.2 years. Agriculture makes up only 10 percent of Angola's GDP, with 85 percent of the labor force working as farmers. Meanwhile, those working in industry and services account for the other 15 percent.

INVESTING IN THE ECONOMY

Since 1996, the Angolan government has sold dozens of small- and medium-sized businesses that were once owned and run by the central government to private companies. The production of coffee is an example of this change. After independence, the coffee industry was taken over by the government, and more than thirty different state-owned companies were formed. All these companies are now being sold to private investors. In 2015, the coffee company Liangol was sold to a Portuguese investment group for around $1 billion. The hope is that allowing outside investors ownership of the companies will help revitalize certain industries in Angola that were damaged by war.

In another important change, foreign banks are being invited to set up branches in Angola. Even Portuguese companies are returning to the country as private investors. The largest private investors in Angola (outside of the oil industry) are Portuguese.

In the early years following the end of the Angolan civil war, many international banks and construction companies lined up to take advantage of Africa's mineral wealth, and Angola was a prime target. Europe's banks opened lines of credit with Angola worth 1 billion euros (US $1.329 billion). But as the price of the Angolan kwanza—Angola's main currency—fell with oil prices after 2014, so did investments. The election of João Lourenço was actually good news for investors, because new leadership can often revitalize a struggling economy.

In addition to oil and diamonds, Angola is rich in agricultural land and was once a major exporter of coffee, sisal, cotton, sugar, and tobacco. But the civil war caused a huge upheaval for farmers, the majority of whom can only grow enough to feed their families and communities. Since distribution of the oil industry's wealth has been lopsided, industries like farming continue to struggle. Oil money is flowing into Angola, even when prices are lower, but there is no guarantee that it will be used for the public good. Its main effect at the moment is to strengthen those in power and in the oil industry. But many Angolans and investors from around the globe hope that a change in leadership will help all Angolans to prosper.

The main products that farmers are able to produce in Angola include bananas, sugarcane, coffee, sisal (or agave), corn, cotton, and cassava.

Much of Angola's economic recovery has been because of loans and investments from China. Here, President Dos Santos meets with Chinese leader Xi Jinping in 2015.

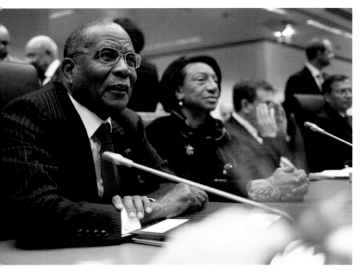

Angola's minister of petroleum, José Maria Botelho de Vasconcelos, attended this OPEC meeting in 2013.

Banco Nacional de Angola was established as Angola's central bank in late 1996 as part of governmental financial reforms. One of the bank's roles is to provide financial advice and information to the government.

ANGOLA'S OIL

With growing instability in the Middle East following the United States—led "war on terror," Africa has become increasingly important for global oil and natural gas supplies. Over the last decade, Angola and Nigeria have run neck and neck as Africa's largest oil producers. In 2008, Angola passed Nigeria to become Africa's largest and the world's eighth-largest oil producer, but Nigeria reclaimed the top position in 2017.

Angola is now producing more than 1.8 million barrels per day of high-quality crude oil from onshore and nearshore fields. As mentioned previously, the oil sector produces half of Angola's gross domestic product (GDP) and over 90 percent of its exports, and the government is in the process of expanding this by taking advantage of the country's ultra-deep offshore oil fields, located 4,921—9,843 feet (1,500—3,000 m) below the ocean. Currently, 75 percent of Angola's oil production comes from offshore fields. In 2007, Angola joined the Organization of the Petroleum Exporting Countries (OPEC). OPEC is a global organization made up of some of the world's top oil-producing countries, like Iraq, Algeria, and the United Arab Emirates. OPEC helps to regulate the price of oil so that a high-producing country can't lower prices and cause economic damage to a country that produces less oil and therefore can't charge the same low price. By joining OPEC, Angola positioned itself as a global power in the oil industry.

As the price of oil in Angola remains in flux, it continues to rely heavily on its top investors, China and Portugal. China was one of the first countries to secure a major stake in Angola's oil production. In 2004, China promised a $2 billion package of loans and aid, including funding for roads, railroads, bridges, schools, hospitals, and a fiber-optic network. Today, loans from China total around $20 billion. In addition to oil, China also imports timber, aluminum, copper, nickel, iron ore, and diamonds, much of which it hopes to get from Africa—Angola being one of its main suppliers.

THE DIAMOND INDUSTRY

Angola is Africa's third-largest diamond producer, after Botswana and the Democratic Republic of the Congo. Angola's diamond production is controlled mainly by the state-owned Empresa Nacional de Diamantes de Angola (Endiama) and produced about 9.21 million carats in 2016, worth around $1.079 billion. This price was around $130 million less than in 2015 because even though Endiama produced around the same amount, overproduction drove the prices down. Some of the revenues from the sale of diamonds, which once helped fund the war between the government and the UNITA rebel movement, are being used to fund Endiama's expansion and exploration program to look for more diamond deposits.

The Angolan diamond industry has also been the subject of global criticism since the 2011 publication of *Blood Diamonds: Corruption and Torture in Angola* by

This diamond miner in Angola shows off a large diamond he found.

journalist Rafael Marques de Morais—the founder of the Maka Angola website. The book alleges numerous cases of torture and executions of mine workers and villagers living near diamond mines at the hands of security and military forces. One story involves forty-five miners being buried alive by soldiers who deliberately caused a cave-in at the mine's entrance, tearing down supports using crowbars. The book was immediately banned in Angola, and Marques de Morais was convicted of slander in 2015. He received a six-month suspended sentence, provided he remove books from circulation and the internet.

GROWTH OF AGRICULTURE

In the last decade of the colonial period, Angola was a major African food exporter, but it now imports almost all its food. The war brought agricultural activities to a near standstill. Today, agriculture in Angola is in the process of redevelopment. For example, coffee production, although at only a fraction of its pre-1975 level, is nonetheless sufficient for domestic needs and some exports.

Many Angolans keep livestock to help feed their families and provide a small income.

BEEF AND CHICKENS

Meat is at a premium in Angola, available mostly through import, resulting in high prices. Currently, Angola is the fifth-largest importer of chickens from the United States, importing 396,832 tons (360,000 metric tons) of chicken in 2015, and spending around $500 million to import 100,000 tons (91,000 metric tons) of beef each year. Chickens and cattle are expensive to raise. Cattle, in particular, require lots of food and land to graze. The chickens currently in Angola require about 400,000 tons (362,874 metric tons) of corn and soybeans each year to eat. Therefore, for many of the same reasons that crop growth is struggling to bounce back in the Angolan economy, the livestock industry is struggling as well. Farmers just don't have the land and means to raise cattle and chickens, so importing has become the simplest solution.

But work is being done to help increase self-sufficiency. The Angolan government has begun to invest in livestock production, spending millions to import 340,500 live cattle for breeding in 2015 in an initiative meant to improve production over the next several years. Similar work is being done to increase egg and chicken production as well. By the end of 2016, Angola was producing enough eggs to provide seventy eggs per person for a year.

Angola has fertile soil, a favorable climate, and about 146 million acres (59.2 million hectares) of agricultural land (land that can be used to produce food), including more than 12 million acres (5 million ha) of arable land (land that can be used to grow crops). Large areas of agricultural land still cannot be cultivated because of the presence of land mines. Functioning infrastructure in rural areas is limited, and there are few incentives for people to return to farming, hence the mass migration to cities such as Luanda to find work.

It takes a lot of capital to rehabilitate the agriculture industry in a nation of poor, displaced farmers who are still feeling the effects of the Angolan civil war. The World Bank, a global bank that provides loans to developing nations, is working on an agricultural development program to help farmers, which will include land rehabilitation and providing access to irrigation.

Agriculture's contribution to GDP—including forestry and fisheries—has been about 10 percent. Yet much of the population still depends on agriculture for food and income. Subsistence agriculture provides the main livelihood for 85 percent of the workforce. About 90 percent of farms throughout the country are small to medium in size. Smallholder farms are very small plots of land that farmers use to grow enough to feed their families and share with their local communities.

THE SLOW RETURN OF MANUFACTURING

The manufacturing industry is slowly returning to Angola after the economy's industrial capacity was looted, destroyed, or fell into disrepair during the civil war. Many factories closed down due to lack of local skill, the absence of spare parts, and dropping local demand. Today, up to 90 percent of Angola's consumer goods are imported. Thanks to the arrival of big foreign investors in the oil and diamond industries and the end of the war, however, industry may eventually reach prewar levels. Angola's potential to develop and boost its economy through manufacturing is enormous. Light industry survived the war years in a variety of areas—including textiles and clothing, footwear, soaps and detergents, and paint. Angola also has the ability to manufacture foods such as soft drinks, bakery products, and beer. In 1999, the Coca-Cola Company built a $36 million bottling factory southeast of Luanda, and in 2008 South African breweries pledged $6 million for the construction of a second Coke plant in the southern town of Lubango. In March 2002, the Benguela sugar factory was opened after a $5 million Angolan government—financed restoration by an Anglo-American consortium. The company Fabrimetal, founded in 2010, provides 40 percent of the metal needed in Angola today for construction and to fix the country's infrastructure. Rather than mining for it, the company converts scrap metal into rebar. The scrap metal industry has helped to decrease the need for steel imports. In 2015, Angola imported around 81,318 tons (73,771 metric tons) of steel. By 2016, steel imports dropped to 34,862 tons (31,627 metric tons). The company relies on metal collectors who travel around searching for scrap left behind after the war, including cars and tanks.

One of the most successful industries to survive the ravages of the civil war is cement. In 2017, in the Luanda province, a new cement plant opened with the capacity to produce 7.7 million tons (7 million metric tons) of cement every year. In a nation recovering from a war, building materials are a necessity. Until Angola can become self-reliant in manufacturing, importing products will continue to be the norm.

Tanks and other items left behind after the war have led to many earning a living through selling scrap materials.

MINING MATERIALS

Once one of the country's major exports, iron ore was no longer mined in the late 1980s because of security and transportation problems. From the mid-1950s until 1975, iron ore was mined in Malanje, Bié, Huambo, and Huíla provinces, and production reached an average of 5.7 million tons (5.2 million metric tons) per year between 1970 and 1974. Now that the war is over, Angola is working to reopen the Cassinga Mines and explore the vast iron ore deposits of Cassala Kitungo. The deposits might contain up to 16.5 million tons (15 million metric tons) of iron, and the mines could produce 1.7 million tons (1.5 million metric tons) per year. The Angolan iron and steel company Ferrangol and some companies in foreign countries are negotiating to take on the task. Angola is also rich in several other mineral resources, such as iron ore, phosphates, copper, bauxite, and uranium.

ANGOLA'S CENTER OF INDUSTRY

Luanda is the capital and the largest city of Angola. It is both Angola's chief seaport and administrative center. It has a population of about 5.5 million. It is also the capital city of Luanda province. The city is currently undergoing major reconstruction, with many large developments taking place that will change the cityscape significantly. Luanda's new international airport is expected to begin operation in 2019 or 2020. Luanda has passed Zurich, London, and Hong Kong to become the world's most expensive city.

During the civil war, slums called *musseques* ("MUS-seek") stretched for miles beyond Luanda's former city limits. This was partly due to large-scale migration of civil war refugees from other parts of Angola. For decades, Luanda's infrastructure did not expand enough to handle this massive increase in the city's population. After 2002, with the end of the civil war and high economic growth rates fueled by the wealth provided by the increasing oil and diamond production, major reconstruction started. Luanda has recently seen an increase in violent crime, particularly in the shantytowns that surround the urban core established during the colonial years. Major affordable housing

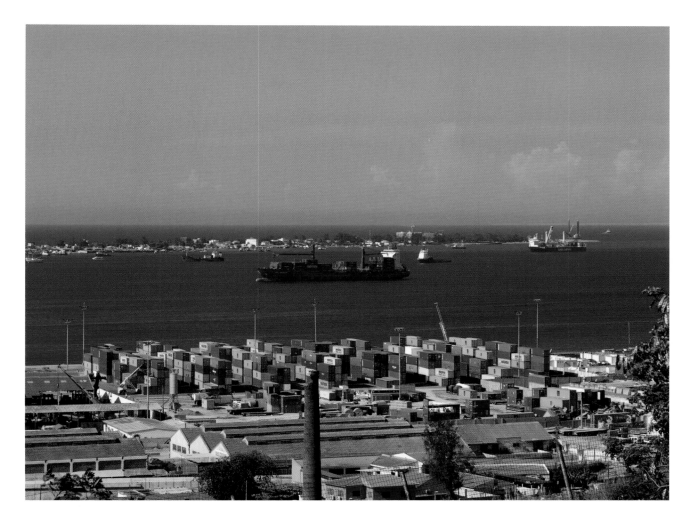

has been constructed by the government to give a place to live to those who currently reside in the slums that dominate the landscape of Luanda. A large Chinese firm built much of this housing.

Luanda has an excellent natural harbor. Its chief exports are petroleum, coffee, cotton, sugar, diamonds, iron, and salt. The city also has a thriving building industry—an effect of the nationwide economic boom that has been going on since 2002, when political stability returned with the end of the civil war. Economic growth is largely supported by oil extraction activities, although massive diversification in economic activities is taking place.

The harbor in Luanda is often backed up for days with ships waiting to dock.

The Angolan civil war created one of the world's most serious land mine legacies, threatening lives and causing the suffering of more than 70,000 survivors of land mine accidents. Militant forces laid approximately fifteen million land mines by 2002. The problem continues to be severe— over 155 square miles (400 sq km) have been damaged by up to four million land mines, affecting 2.4 million people. This has been a particularly big issue in the city of Cuito Cuanavale, where the MPLA and their Cuban and Soviet allies met UNITA and their American and South African allies in a battle that lasted from March 1987 to June 1988. Several international nongovernmental organizations (NGOs), like the Halo Trust, have made clearing minefields to protect local communities their focus, and the *government has cooperated by destroying its own stockpile of land mines. The Halo Trust has destroyed around ninety-three thousand mines, more than a third of which were in Cuito Cuanavale.*

The impact of land mines on agriculture, economic development, and voter registration has impeded national objectives. Around 32,000 acres (12,950 ha) of mine fields still need to be cleared, and around 88,000 acres of land (35,612 ha) suspected to contain land mines still needs to be declared safe. But progress is slow. Funding cuts have reduced the size of the Halo Group's staff by hundreds in recent years. A global treaty banning land mines required that Angola be cleared by 2018, but at the current rate, the work may not be completed until 2025, according to Angolan officials. Others estimate that the work will not be completed until after 2040.

RAILWAYS AND ROADS

The Portuguese colonial rulers developed transportation networks in the country by building railways and roads to help move produce bound for Europe. The most important railroad line, known as the Benguela Railway, linked Angola with Zambia and the Democratic Republic of the Congo. It fell into disuse as a result of the civil war, but it has been repaired through the help of a loan from the Chinese government.

Travel on highways outside of towns and cities in Angola (and, in some cases, within towns and cities) is often not easy for those without four-wheel-drive vehicles. Although a reasonable road infrastructure has existed within Angola, the war took a toll on the road surfaces, leaving many with severe potholes and littered with broken asphalt. In many areas, drivers have established alternate tracks to avoid the worst parts of the road surface, although careful attention must be paid to land mine warning markers by the side of the road.

The Angolan government has made plans to restore many of the country's roads. Companies have come into the country from China and surrounding nations to help improve road surfaces. The road between Lubango and Namibe, for example, was completed in 2003 with funding from the European Union, and is now comparable to many European main routes. In 2016, repairs started on roadways connecting the cities of Uíge and Negage. Complete rehabilitation to Angola's roadways will take years.

The current port system along Angola's coast cannot cope with the number of vessels arriving. In 2005, in Luanda, ships were waiting up to thirty days to dock and unload cargo. But work is being done to improve wait times and streamline railroads for moving cargo more quickly and efficiently. Similar work is being done at Lobito and Namibe.

INTERNET LINKS

https://www.halotrust.org
This organization works to clear land mines from nations damaged by war across the globe.

https://tradingeconomics.com/angola/crude-oil-production
This statistics-based website shows up-to-date information on oil production and prices from all of the oil-producing nations in the world.

ENVIRONMENT

The savanna regions of Angola have a wide
variety of wildlife, including lions.

5

ANGOLA IS MADE UP OF MANY different types of habitat. The northwest region and Cabinda are made up of tropical coastal forest. But farther to the west, along the coastline, you'll find a drier savanna region with tall trees surrounded by grasses and dotted with a few swampy areas. The largest ecological region of Angola, at its center, is a wooded savanna with a tropical climate. Along the southern border lies a dry, arid region.

Population pressures and inadequate infrastructure have led to many environmental problems in Angola. Drinking water is scarce, especially in rural areas. Because food production has not kept pace with the country's rapid population growth, much of Angola's food must be imported. Poor agricultural practices have led to widespread soil erosion and desertification. Siltation of rivers and dams is a serious related problem. Deforestation, especially to supply the international tropical timber market, is rapidly eliminating the rain forests in the north and threatening biodiversity.

A protected system of parks and nature reserves exists but lacks funding. Only about 62,740 square miles (162,500 sq km) of land (around 13 percent of the country) is protected on paper, and logging, poaching,

"I was a soldier but, after peace, I was demobilised and now we are rangers—as we call it 'nature soldiers.' We are dealing with poachers who have firearms. When we find them, we fight them. It is not an easy job, but I have my weapon, so I am not concerned."
—Former soldier Elias Kawina

and agricultural encroachment are continuing threats. The civil war caused tremendous damage and brought environmental programs to a halt.

Most of Angola is covered with dry woodland, savanna, and grassland. The total forest cover as 46.4 percent as of 2015. Angola has signed agreements to protect the sea and biodiversity, and to combat climate change and desertification. Soldiers are being trained as park wardens through a collaborative project between the International Union for Conservation of Nature (IUCN) and the Ministry of Agriculture and Rural Development. There are also extensive protected areas that remain relatively undisturbed.

DROUGHT AND DESERTIFICATION

The harvesting of wood for use as fuel has contributed to the problem of desertification. Desertification refers to the loss of soil fertility and structure, making it hard for the land to support plant life. In Angola, forest areas are often cleared in order to harvest fuel wood for agricultural use. Traditional farming practices, which tend to be inefficient and land-intensive, significantly

Deforestation can lead to drought and loss of habitat for many animal species.

Storms dropped 3.15 inches (8 cm) of rain, over a period of twenty-four hours, on the Luanda province on March 21 and 22, 2017, causing severe flooding. The floods killed eleven people, injured others, and left thousands of people homeless when over seven hundred homes were destroyed and thousands were damaged.

degrade scarce arable land—the single most important natural resource in Angola. Desertification can lead to downstream flooding, reduced water quality, and sedimentation in rivers and lakes. Because of all the dust produced during the desertification process, it also can lead to dust storms, air pollution, and health problems such as respiratory illnesses and allergies. But work is being done to combat drought and desertification. Currently, Angola celebrates World Day to Combat Drought and Desertification on June 17 every year, and programs like Integration of Climate Resilience in Agricultural and Pastoral Production Systems (IRCEA) work to enact conservation practices in drought-afflicted regions.

DIAMOND MINING'S ENVIRONMENTAL CONSEQUENCES

At present, the major environmental damage resulting from diamond mining is the diversion of rivers to allow for the mining of alluvial diamond deposits. After the mining is completed, the rivers are not redirected to their original course. This leads to pollution of the water and the destruction of flora and fauna. The mining activities also degrade the surrounding land by increasing air pollution, contaminating surface and groundwater, and increasing soil erosion and leaching. The pollution, in the most extreme cases, leads to desertification and permanently rules out agricultural use of the land, making it useless to traditional inhabitants in the long run, after the diamonds have all been mined. In the short run, the inhabitants of the region are suffering from sickness and diseases related to contaminated drinking water supplies. Many have been forced to relocate.

It can be difficult to find clean water in areas of Angola.

"It is hard … We have to wake up early in the morning. We then go to search for a place that has clean running water. We buy it from places that have running water in town." —Adriano Correia, Luandan water vendor

POLLUTED WATER

In some areas of Angola, the water is contaminated with raw sewage and industrial discharge from oil and mining operations. Safe drinking water is available to 75.4 percent of the urban population and only 28.2 percent of rural dwellers. Not surprisingly, Angola's disease risk is among the worst in the world. Angola's government and a number of nongovernment programs are working to improve water infrastructure.

WASTE AND SANITATION

Most of the country, including Luanda, has no basic infrastructure, such as water distribution and waste and water treatment. Many residents bathe and drink from water that is thick with trash and waste from some of Luanda's bays. Right now about 88.6 percent of the urban population have access to sanitation facilities, while only 22.5 percent have access in rural areas. Without clean water, safe dwellings, and waste disposal, it will be difficult for Angolans to address many of the challenges to their country's quality of life and education. But the government, with the help of the World Bank Water Sector Institutional Development Project, is working on a $545 million strategy to improve water supply and sanitation by building more water treatment facilities.

RECYCLING PROGRAMS

Collect-a-Can, a recycling initiative that aims to reduce litter and save the environment, has set up a partnership with Coca-Cola in Angola. Collect-a-Can optimizes the cost-effective recovery of used beverage cans in the African region. Collectors form their own collection networks and deliver their cans directly to one of the company's branches for a fee. Angolans now can collect cans to exchange for cash in order to improve their lives. Many steel mills make products from scrap metal, including weapons left behind after the civil war. And in 2017, a recycling plant opened in Luanda to help reduce the amount of waste going to landfills.

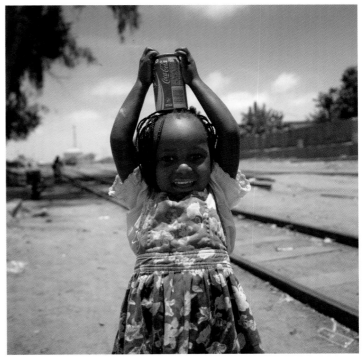

The Collect-a-Can initiative urges Angolans to aid in the recycling effort.

PLANT AND ANIMAL LIFE IN ANGOLA

The exceptional biodiversity in Angola is due to the combination of a number of factors: the vast size of the country, its intertropical geographical location, the altitude variation, the biome types, and its 1,025-mile- (1,650 km) long coastline. Biomes range from dense tropical forests to deserts. Of the estimated 5,000 plant species that are believed to exist in the country (without mentioning the vast floral wealth of Cabinda province), 1,260 are native to Angola—making Angola the second-richest country in Africa in terms of endemic plants.

Angola's diversity of mammals is also one of the richest on the continent, with 275 recorded species. Angola is also an important center of marine biodiversity and a productive area in fish resources. Wide estuaries such as

Angolans celebrated World Forest Day on March 21, 2018, by planting trees in forests all over Angola, including five hundred in the Benefica forest in Luanda. Illegal logging has become a serious issue, especially in Uíge, Cabinda, Moxico, and Kuando Kubango, the country's main wood-producing regions.

The gray-striped francolin is similar to a pheasant or grouse and can be found only in Angola.

those of the Congo, Dande, Cuanza, and Cunene Rivers support important food chains that are essential to the livelihood of the people that live there. Mangroves occur along the Angolan coastline and form important ecosystems, providing harbors and nurseries for crustaceans and fish, and economic and tourist opportunities for the country.

Around 120 plant species are listed as endangered, many of them occurring in protected areas. Trees such as the avicennia and combretum, which are important parts of the vegetation that protects the Angolan coast, are also listed as highly endangered species. Threats to biodiversity include uncontrolled bush burning to clear the land for agriculture, poaching of animals, logging, and illegal trade in animals.

BIRDS

Over 90 percent of the bird species of southern Africa live in Angola, with around one thousand known species. These include fourteen endemic species of birds, such as the gray-striped francolin and the Gabela helmetshrike. Both species are threatened because of habitat loss due to deforestation.

ANGOLA'S ENDANGERED SPECIES

Endangered species in Angola include the black rhinoceros, the western gorilla, the chimpanzee, the fin whale, and the African elephant. Additionally, in 2016,

National Geographic announced that only 7,100 cheetahs remained in the wild, down from around 14,000 in 1975. Overfishing, deforestation, and poaching continue to threaten Angola's wildlife.

Cheetahs are a vulnerable species because of the impact of humans on their habitat.

ELEPHANTS AND THE IVORY TRADE

The bloody plight of the country's elephants is getting worse as a result of the illegal ivory trade. During the 1980s, sometimes known as the "elephant holocaust," the population of African elephants is estimated to have dropped from one million to four hundred thousand. The international ivory trade was banned in 1989, but this has only slowed poachers down. An estimated twenty thousand African elephants were killed in 2015 alone. Within southern Africa, Angola, Mozambique, Nigeria, and the Democratic Republic of the Congo have the largest illegal trades in elephant ivory. Angola's wild elephant population has not been accurately surveyed for decades, and due to the lack of information, the International Union for the Conservation of Nature's African Elephant Database (AED) estimates around 3,396, with a 1,562-elephant margin of error. But this estimate covers only 13 percent of the known and possible elephant range of Angola.

Change is happening in Angola, though. In 2013, the country signed the Convention on International Trade in Endangered Species of Wild Fauna and Flora (CITES, which entered into force in 1975 and now has 183 member countries). CITES is an international agreement that international trade involving animals will not damage their survival.

SURVIVAL OF THE BLACK RHINO

The black rhinoceros weighs 1,760 to 3,080 pounds (800 to 1,400 kilograms), and its height varies from 4.3 to 5.9 feet (1.3 to 1.8 m). The black rhino has two horns and poor eyesight, but its hearing is good. Black rhinos often have a mutually beneficial relationship with birds called "oxpeckers." The birds eat parasites found on the rhinos' skin, and the birds' acute eyesight helps warn the rhinos of potential danger. The black rhino is unpredictable and can be dangerous, sometimes charging when it comes across a disturbing sound or smell. Mortal combat is recorded to take place more often between black rhinos than any other mammal. It results in the death of about 50 percent of male black rhinos and 30 percent of females due to fight-related wounds.

The black rhino population suffered a huge reduction during the twentieth century. In the early 1900s, there were probably several hundred thousand rhinos; by the early 1990s, there were fewer than 2,500. However, since 1995, numbers of black rhinos throughout Africa have started to increase again. There are estimated to be around 5,042 to 5,455 today. Hunting and clearance of land for settlement and agriculture were the major reasons for the decline of black rhino populations in the twentieth century. The situation facing the black rhino is still critical. The demand for rhino horn in Asia (for traditional medicines) and in the Middle East (for dagger handles) persists, and the threat of a return to large-scale poaching is still present.

This sable antelope lives in captivity, but in the wild the giant sable antelope is critically endangered.

THE REEMERGENCE OF THE GIANT SABLE ANTELOPE

The giant sable antelope, also known in Portuguese as the *palanca negra*, is a large, rare subspecies of sable antelope that is native to the region between the Cuango and Luando Rivers in Angola. Both males and females have horns. In fact, males and females are strikingly similar in appearance until they reach three years of age, when the males become darker and develop majestic horns. The horns are massive and more curved in males, reaching lengths of 2.7 to 5.4 feet (0.8 to 1.6 m), while females' horns are only 2 to 3.3 feet (0.6 to 1 m) long. The male antelope weighs an average of 525 pounds (238 kg), with a height of 3.8 to 4.7 feet (1.2 to 1.4 m). Females weigh 484 pounds (220 kg) and are slightly shorter than males. Like all antelopes, they are shy by nature, but they can also be very aggressive. The males can be especially dangerous when they are hurt, attacked, or approached.

Long thought to have been wiped out during the civil war, the giant sable antelope reappeared in 2004, but it is still in grave danger of extinction. This species of antelope is greatly respected by the people of Angola. This may be one of the reasons the animals survived the long civil war. In African mythology, just like other antelopes, these creatures symbolize vivacity, speed, and beauty. The giant sable antelope is a national symbol of Angola and is portrayed on numerous stamps, banknotes, and even passports of the nation. The Angolan national football team is fondly known as the Palancas Negras in honor of the antelope. Today, there are fewer than one hundred of the giant sable antelope in Angola.

NATIONAL PARKS OF ANGOLA

Cameia National Park is situated in the Moxico province of Angola, located about 3,609 feet (1,100 m) above sea level. It shares its name with the nearby municipality of Cameia. The Cameia-Luacano Road forms the northern boundary of the park, with the Chifumage River forming the southern portion of the eastern boundary and the Lumege and Luena Rivers forming the southwestern boundary. Much of the park consists of seasonally flooded plains that form part of the Zambezi River basin, with the northern half of the park draining into the Chifumage River. Two lakes, Lago ("lake" in Portuguese) Cameia and Lago Dilolo (the largest lake in Angola), lie outside the park boundaries. Both have extensive reedbeds and grassy swamps that are rich in aquatic birds. The wildlife was almost completely wiped out after the civil war, uncontrolled poaching, and the destruction of infrastructure devastated the park. There is a serious lack of staff, resources, and support for the park.

Cangandala National Park is a national park in Malanje province. It is situated near the Cuanza River, with the towns of Culamagia and Techongolola found on the edges of the park. It is the smallest national park in Angola and covers an area of 230 square miles (600 sq km). Cangandala was originally founded to protect the giant sable antelope, which was discovered in Cangandala in 1963.

THE OKAVANGO WILDERNESS PROJECT

The Okavango River Delta in northern Botswana is home to 530 species of birds, 160 species of mammals, 155 species of reptiles, and 1,500 species of plants, and what makes it unique is that, unlike most river deltas, this one doesn't open to the sea. Instead, it simply fans out, creating enormous wetlands. The river itself is the fourth longest in Africa at around 1,000 miles (1,600 km) in length, and almost all of the water comes from Angola, in the rainy highlands at the country's center (in Angola, the Okavango River is called the Kubango). Therefore, although the Okavango River Delta isn't in Angola, Angola is indispensible to its survival. However, work is being done in Angola to harness the power of its rivers for hydroelectricity. Dams slow or stop the flow of these rivers, eventually causing harm to the Okavango River Delta.

The Okavango Wilderness Project, led by Dr. Steve Boyles, sent a group of scientists into this region to explore and study ways to protect it. One of the first expeditions of the project took scientists through the Kubango and Cuito River basins in Angola. They hope that their findings will help to engage discussion with the governments of Angola, Namibia, and Botswana to work together to preserve the river delta region.

Iona National Park (Parque Nacional do Iona in Portuguese) is a national park in Namibe Province. It is about 124 miles (200 km) from the city of Namibe and, at 5,850 square miles (15,150 sq km), is the largest in the country. Before the Angolan civil war, Iona was an animal paradise, rich in big game. However, as is true for most Angolan national parks, illegal poaching and the destruction of infrastructure have caused considerable damage to the once rich park. The park is also known for unique flora and incredible rock formations.

Quiçama National Park, also known as Kissama National Park, is the only fully functioning national park in all of Angola. The others remain in disrepair after the Angolan civil war. The park is approximately 43 miles (70 km) from Luanda, the Angolan capital. The park covers 4,630 square miles (12,000 sq km)—more than twice the size of the US state of Rhode Island.

The park once was home to many large game animals, such as elephants and giant sable antelopes, but after wide-scale poaching during twenty-seven years of civil war, the animal population was virtually eliminated.

In 2001, the Kissama Foundation, a group of Angolans and South Africans, initiated Operation Noah's Ark to transport animals, especially elephants, from neighboring Botswana and South Africa to repopulate Kissama National Park. The animals adapted well to the move from overpopulated parks in their homes countries. Noah's Ark was the largest animal transplant of its kind in history, and it has given the park momentum to be restored to its natural state.

Mupa National Park is in Angola's Cunene province. It is significant for its wide variety of birdlife. Many Angolans reside within the park, which, along with nomadic pastoralists and mineral prospecting, threatens to destroy the park's birdlife.

The baobab tree, which is referenced in African folklore, can be found in Kissama National Park.

INTERNET LINKS

https://www.nationalgeographic.org/projects/okavango
The Okavango Wilderness Project is an ongoing research effort to find ways to protect the Okavango River Delta.

https://rhinos.org
The International Rhino Foundation conducts research and works toward protecting the rhino from extinction.

ANGOLANS

Pope Benedict XVI's visit to Angola drew hundreds of thousands of Angolans.

6

CURRENTLY, THE POPULATION OF Angola stands at between 28.4 million and 29 million people, according to 2017 estimates. Angola's birthrate is one of the highest in the world, at an average of 6.2 children per mother, but the infant mortality rate is also high because of inadequate water supplies and disease.

ANGOLAN IDENTITY

In Angola, a regional or tribal sense of identity is often more important than a national one. Someone's sense of identity as an Ovimbundu may be far stronger and deeper than his or her sense of being an Angolan. There are historical reasons for this—the Portuguese never tried to create a sense of national identity, and after independence in 1975, the country was plunged into civil war, which pitted people against one another along ethnic lines.

Although the Portuguese did not adopt apartheid in the form it took in South Africa, Europeans were treated as superior to the native inhabitants of the country. Angolans—classified as "natives"—were only allowed to hold menial jobs. They were obliged by law to carry special *caderneta* ("KAD-er-ne-ta;" identity cards) that confirmed their status. As holders of the caderneta, Angolans were subject to special laws and regulations that limited their economic opportunities. In the 1950s, only 5 percent of "native" children attended elementary or secondary school, and the

The designs on the cheeks of this Ovimbundu figure represent the movement through birth, life, and death.

vast majority of older teenagers were unable to read or write. The only way for an Angolan to escape this fate was to learn Portuguese, turn his or her back on traditional culture, and apply for the special status of *assimilado* ("ass-sim-ill-AD-o").

This was what many people of mixed African and European ancestry did. By the 1970s, there were about thirty Angolans of mixed blood for every one hundred white Portuguese. Because most Portuguese colonists were male, those of mixed descent were likely to have a black mother and a white father. In practice, this also meant that these Angolans of mixed race tended to identify themselves with the white Portuguese rather than with the black majority.

ANGOLA'S ETHNIC GROUPS

Angolans are members of various ethnic groups, and these groups tend to be concentrated in different parts of the country. Each group has its own language and shares a sense of common descent and a separate history—this is what works against a sense of national identity.

The largest ethnic group is the Ovimbundu, which makes up about 37 percent of the population and lives mainly in the central highland areas, covering the provinces of Huambo, Bié, Benguela, and northern Huíla. The most important subgroups of the Ovimbundu are the Bailundu, Bieno, Dombe, Ganda, and Wambu. The Ovimbundu were important long-distance traders in the past, and although trade is still a traditional means of livelihood, most Ovimbundu people now engage in agriculture.

The next largest ethnic group is the Mbundu (sometimes known as Kimbundu) people, making up 25 percent of the population. There are three major subgroups—the Mbaka, the Ndongo, and the Dembos. The Mbundu traditionally inhabit Luanda province, which includes the capital city. They have been exposed to the influence of the Portuguese more than any other ethnic group.

The Chokwe, a branch of the Lunda-Chokwe ethnic group, originally came from a highland region about 300 miles (483 km) southeast of Luanda. They were hunters, and when the Portuguese arrived they began to collect ivory and beeswax to exchange for guns with the Portuguese. They formed groups up to a thousand strong and began to expand their territory to collect more ivory and

beeswax. In this way they spread both to the north and to the east. In the nineteenth century, by which time there were few elephants left to hunt, the Chokwe became involved in the production of rubber because of the increasing European demand for this material. Chokwe women became adept at collecting the sap from the rubber trees that produced latex and rolling it into large hardened lumps that could be easily carried to the nearest trading post.

The people living in the northwest provinces of Zaire and Uíge belong mostly to the Bakongo group that is also found in the neighboring countries of the Republic of the Congo and the Democratic Republic of the Congo. In Angola, they make up about 13 percent of the population. The main subgroups of the Bakongo group are the Bashikongo, Sosso, Pombo, Sonongo, and Zombo. Other groups include the Chokwe (or Lunda), Ganguela, Nhaneca-Humbe, Ambo, Herero, and Xindunga. In addition, mixed race—European and African—people amount to about 2 percent, with a small (1 percent) population of whites, mainly ethnically Portuguese.

PORTUGUESE ANGOLANS

Given that the Portuguese were in Angola for nearly five hundred years, one might think that a significant proportion of Angolans would be of Portuguese descent, but this is not the case. Although the Portuguese first arrived in 1480, it was not until the nineteenth century that they established themselves in the plateau region of the interior. It was only in 1880 that northern Angola officially became a part of their colony.

For most of their five hundred years in the area, the Portuguese who lived in Angola tended to remain in a small number of coastal settlements. Even by 1940, there were only some 40,000 Portuguese living in Angola. By 1975, when independence was won, there were 340,000 Portuguese in Angola. As the war of independence escalated in the 1970s, an increasing number of Portuguese chose to leave and return to Portugal, and this process was accelerated in the months following independence. In 2010, however, Portugal found itself in a debt crisis, and many Portuguese people flooded into Angola—30,000 people in 2013 alone made the move, and many through illegal means. Just a few years after the debt crisis in Portugal began, the Angolan government began to build a detention center to house the undocumented migrants.

These Angolans had to flee to the Democratic Republic of the Congo and are ready to finally return home.

"We're nothing without land. Land is our mother, a tool to survive and evolve as people." —Teresa Quivienguele, director of Action for Rural Development and Environment

A NATION OF DISPLACED PEOPLE

The civil war spawned a disastrous humanitarian crisis in Angola, internally displacing 4.28 million people—one-third of Angola's population. The government spent $187 million settling internally displaced persons (IDPs) between April 4, 2002, and 2004. After that, the World Bank gave $33 million to continue the settling process. The United Nations Office for the Coordination of

Humanitarian Affairs (OCHA) estimated that fighting displaced 98,000 people between January 1, 2002, and February 28, 2002, alone. Many stayed in Angola, but around 550,000 fled to Zambia, the Democratic Republic of the Congo, the Republic of the Congo, and South Africa. Around 73,000 of them are still living in exile.

Simply moving back to the land they once owned or occupied is virtually impossible for many who were displaced. Some who lived in rural areas never had ownership paperwork. It was simply understood that the land was theirs. Struggles with rights to land and areas made uninhabitable by land mines continue to plague those displaced by the war.

Signs that alert people to the dangers of nearby landmines are common in Angola.

INTERNET LINKS

https://www.cnn.com/2016/04/04/africa/angola-refugees-the-most-important-thing-unhcr/index.html
This gallery of photographs shows Angolan refugees posing with the treasured possessions they refused to leave behind and plan to take back with them.

http://www.unhcr.org/en-us
The Office of the United Nations High Commissioner for Refugees is a UN-run organization that helps refugees around the world to relocate to safety.

In 2017, conflict in the Kasai province of the Democratic Republic of the Congo sent tens of thousands of Congolese fleeing over the Angolan border for safety.

LIFESTYLE

Armed UNITA forces in Angola rose
up against the ruling MPLA.

7

FOR THE PEOPLE OF ANGOLA, LIFE has consistently been in a state of upheaval since 1961, when rebels first rose up against the Portuguese, fighting against four hundred years of oppression. The fight for independence continued until 1975, when Angola was granted its independence. But conflict was not at an end. Opposition forces grasping for control of the newly liberated Angolan government ignited a civil war. Those years of living in a state of upheaval continue to affect the people of Angola today.

The United Nations has estimated the number of people killed in fighting at over half a million, with a similar number—mostly young children—dying from preventable diseases and malnutrition brought about by the civil war. Another two million people lost their homes, and about fifty thousand children lost their parents. Today, while work has been done to rebuild, issues still remain that prevent a sense of normalcy in Angola.

"March 15, 1961, began like almost any other day in the north of Angola. Africans throughout the region arose, as usual, with the first light of dawn, lit their breakfast fires and warmed themselves against the chill of the early morning mist. Many who worked the nearby Portuguese coffee plantations began sharpening their machetes."
—Lloyd Garrison, the *New York Times*, 1964

The 2014 downturn
of oil prices in
Angola may have
led to an increase
in kidnappings for
ransom, leading
many Chinese
businesses to ask
for protection of
their employees
by the Angolan
government
in 2015.

THE MUSSEQUES OF LUANDA

The term shantytown—known as a musseque in Luanda—describes a poor part of town, where people live in crudely built shacks. The name comes from the characteristic red sand found in coastal Luanda that forms the floor of the makeshift compounds that make up a musseque. About 70 percent of Luanda's residents live in the musseques (around 3.9 million people)—most of whom were not born in the city. Families fled to the capital city from their village communities in fear for their lives during the war, and the shanties where they now live give many a feeling of safety. Many don't have homes outside of Luanda to go back to, so the musseques have become their permanent residences.

A musseque is usually built around small compounds of about 270 square feet (25 square meters) with up to six single-story houses inside. The compound itself is usually surrounded by a wall of corrugated iron sheets or concrete blocks.

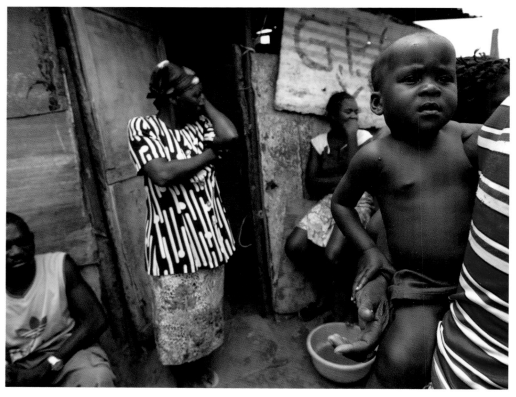

Families live in overcrowded conditions with limited access to water in the musseques of Luanda.

The day in a musseque begins at dawn. Often a woman starts the day's work by boiling water for coffee and breakfast. Clothes that have been left out to dry overnight need to be taken down and put away. The washing of clothes is a daily activity, and clean garments are folded and kept in plastic bags. Water is always needed, and getting it often involves a trip on foot with buckets to the nearest standpipe. Even then, the supply is irregular and cannot be relied on. Poor people are often forced to buy water from private contractors at prices that can be as much as ten thousand times more than what people pay for piped water in the comfortable suburbs. The risks of this form of water supply, together with nonexistent sanitation and waste disposal, led to serious outbreaks of cholera in both 2006 and 2007. Some homes have access to a water tank that holds 1,400 gallons (5,000 liters) or more and can be refilled by a tanker. The family washes each morning, using cold water, no matter what time of year it is. In Luanda, winters are relatively mild, reaching an average minimum temperature of 71.6 degrees Fahrenheit (22 degrees Celsius).

People who see Luanda as their permanent home are more likely to take part in one of the many self-help projects designed to improve the quality of life. Establishing running water and a regular supply of electricity, the proper disposal of garbage, and the provision of public toilets are all major concerns. In rural areas, limited access to safe water and sanitation has led the government to promise major investments in a "water for all" program, which has made slow progress since it was introduced in 2007. Today, 71.8 percent of the rural population of Angola have not seen any improvement to their water access.

LIFE IN THE CITIES

Many young people who travel to the nearest large town hoping to find employment and a better life are greatly disappointed. Life in a musseque is hard, and in Luanda, which attracts the majority of young people from the countryside, 68 percent of the population live in extreme poverty. Jobs are scarce, and there is always an urgent need to earn enough money to buy food. Obtaining fresh water is a constant problem. It has been estimated

The poorest citizens of Luanda often line up for hours to fill buckets with clean water.

that the average family in the capital spends the equivalent of almost a day every week traveling to a source of fresh water, lining up for their turn, and then returning home. Poor families live on whatever food they can afford, sometimes fish, vegetables, and beans.

Street children who have been left to fend for themselves are a common sight in Luanda. They survive by begging for food and a few coins, and they may be tempted to engage in illegal activities. In recent years, crime in the cities has increased significantly. Desperate people have been driven to burglary, theft, and other more serious crimes.

LIFE OUTSIDE THE CITIES

In rural areas, most Angolans live in village communities. The typical family is extended, with grandparents and other relatives living with the husband and wife and their children. Most children will only spend their younger years in the family home because the lure of the city is powerful, especially for young men. The city offers the possibility of employment and the chance to receive some form of education.

Angolans who live in the countryside depend on their farms for their livelihood. They may own some land, or a small group of families may rent a plot from the Ministry of Agriculture. Growing beans and cassava sustains many small farms. Toward the end of each year, the fields are weeded and prepared for a new planting of crops. The December rainfall provides a good start for the new crop, as November to April is the rainy season.

In many rural areas, there are more women than men. This often results in families being headed by a woman, a significant change from traditional rural life, in which the male figure was the customary head of the family. But whether the woman is the head of the household or not, women usually do more work than men in the fields, looking after the crops and harvesting them.

Around 71.1 percent of Angolans over the age of fifteen can read and write. However, only 60.7 percent of girls are literate, compared to 82 percent of boys

This farmer and his team of oxen plant a crop of potatoes in 2009.

Men are more likely to take charge of the family's cattle, following an age-old tradition across many parts of Africa. The average extended family may have a herd of about twenty cattle. Each year one or two of these cattle may be sold for cash to buy necessities that the family cannot grow or produce themselves.

Another way rural families may earn some extra cash is by working in traditional crafts, such as making household and kitchen items. There is always a demand for cooking utensils and farming tools, and many women earn a small but valuable income this way. For centuries, women in African societies have been known for making pottery.

BUYING AND SELLING GOODS

In Angola, buying and exchanging goods at the open-air market is part of culture and tradition. Many of the nation's poorest depend on the informal market economy to buy and sell the things they need. This type of market still exists today in rural regions, but in Luanda, markets are being closed as formal supermarkets are taking over.

Luanda was once home to an enormous open-air market, the Roque Santeiro, which was one of the largest in the country and one of the largest

Open-air markets are an important part of Angolan culture and community.

LIFE UNDER PORTUGUESE RULE

Under Portuguese rule, the Angolan people were classified as "natives" and were not allowed to enjoy the "benefits" of European civilization until they had undergone the process of assimilado, or assimilation. To be assimilated means to be absorbed into a larger group, and in Angola this meant that an African had to abandon his or her traditional culture and adopt European customs and habits. Those who completed the process were given a higher level of rights than those who didn't. Assimilado has been compared to the apartheid rules of South Africa.

Only a limited number of Angolans were allowed to complete assimilado. Strict rules laid down the conditions: a minimum age of eighteen, fluency in the Portuguese language, a clean police record, and a job that paid a salary. Beyond these rules lay a clear understanding that an Angolan had to be prepared to turn his or her back on traditional village culture and adopt the manners and dress of the Portuguese. An Angolan had to apply to become an assimilado, and if he or she was successful, a special identity card was issued to show that the holder had adopted a new cultural identity. Special rights afforded to the assimilado were freedom to travel, the ability to vote, and access to the right to trial, among other rights Portuguese citizens enjoyed. The modern generation of Angolans no longer have to undergo this process.

in Africa. The Roque Santeiro market was far more than just a food market. It was the African equivalent of a huge shopping mall where everything that a family might need could be found, especially during the 1980s when formal shops were facing shortages. For many of Luanda's poor, the market provided a living. The Roque Santeiro was shut down in 2010 to reclaim the area, allegedly because of the poor slum-like conditions and because food products were not stored in a sanitary manner, but many believe it was because the land is prime real estate. A new market was opened soon after in Panguila, about 12 miles (20 km) north of the city, but the expense of transportation makes it hard for many vendors to justify traveling the distance. Plus, the road to Panguila is in need of repairs.

The majority of the population prefers open-air markets or smaller grocery stores because they're simply more comfortable in a traditional environment, so grocery stores are creating strategies to attract shoppers who used to rely on informal trade. The Nosso Super chain opened stores near traditional market places. Other stores play loud Angolan music to make customers feel more comfortable.

Angola's first-ever shopping mall, Belas Shopping, opened in Luanda on December 14, 2008, with one hundred stores, eight movie theaters, a restaurant area, banks, travel agents, attractions, and nine hundred parking spots. The huge consumer palace, made possible by foreign investors and a quickly growing Angolan middle class, gave many hope that postwar Angola was gradually getting back to normal, but high prices do little to attract the city's poor.

EDUCATION IN ANGOLA

During the Angolan civil war (1975—2002), nearly half of all schools were reportedly looted and destroyed, leading to current overcrowding. The high dropout rate limited net enrollment to only 56 percent in 2005. In provinces hardest hit by the war, gross enrollment rates averaged less than 40 percent.

Many schools were damaged and destroyed during the Angolan civil war.

Teachers tend to be underpaid, inadequately trained, and overworked (sometimes teaching two or three shifts a day). Teachers also reportedly demand payment or bribes directly from their students. Other factors, such as the presence of land mines, lack of resources and identity papers, and poor health, also prevent children from attending school regularly.

At Primary School 200, in João de Almeida, in 2011, there were 7,348 students and 138 teachers (around 53 students per teacher), and only eight classrooms. In early April 2017, Angola's teachers went on a three-day strike to fight for fair wages.

HEALTH AND HEALTH CARE

Under colonial rule, health care in Angola was left mainly to religious missions and, in the towns, to privately run clinics. After independence, the government took over the responsibility of providing its citizens with basic health care but failed to allocate sufficient funds. With the outbreak of civil war, health care received even less attention. Over 60 percent of primary health-care

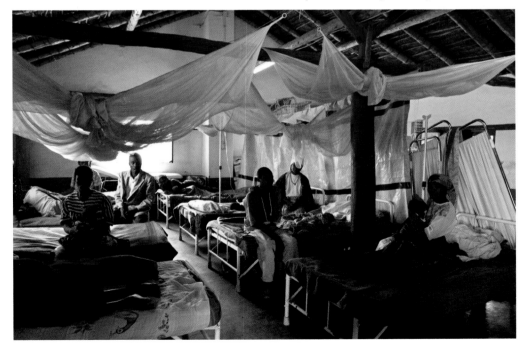

Well-supplied and staffed hospitals remain at a premium in Angola.

Vaccines, like this one for polio, are necessary for children in rural regions of Angola.

centers were destroyed in the civil war, and many doctors were forced to flee the country. Today there is about one doctor per ten thousand people, with the majority of doctors working in cities.

The low level of health care available and the poverty that affects most Angolans means that many children born in Angola never have a chance to grow up. For every one thousand children born, about sixty-eight will die before they reach one year of age, and one in five will die before they reach the age of five. The lack of health-care centers, doctors, and trained nurses and midwives also means that for every mother who goes to a hospital to give birth, another mother will deliver at home without even the help or advice of a midwife. The maternal mortality rate in Angola is 477 per 100,000 pregnant women.

In many other countries, children are immunized against diseases that can prove fatal in their early years. In Angola, until recently, only about one in three children received injections to protect them against diseases such as measles and polio. In 2011, however, then vice president Fernando de Piedade Dias dos Santos announced an initiative to administer the polio vaccine to all children under the age of five. By December 2015, Angola was declared polio-free by the World Health Organization (WHO). Work is also being done to protect children from measles. In March 2018, seven thousand children in Luanda were vaccinated against the disease. In 2013, children in Angola began receiving the pneumococcal vaccine, which protects against pneumonia.

However, the ability to continue administering these types of vaccines comes down to the vaccines' availability and doctors and nurses with the training to provide them. Budget cuts due to falling oil prices since 2014 have dropped Angola into a health crisis as basic supplies have begun to run low.

In rural areas, people depend on clinics run by religious organizations. Many also still rely on traditional healers, who use spells and magical potions to rid the body of unhelpful spirits that are believed to be the cause of certain health problems. According to 2016 findings by the CIA World Factbook, Angola shows the rate of HIV/AIDS infection to be only 1.9 percent of the population, which is considerably lower than in neighboring countries. One interesting explanation for this is that there is an unusually high percentage of circumcised men in Angola, which may lower the risk of infection.

INTERNET LINKS

https://borgenproject.org
The Borgen Project is a nonprofit organization that works against poverty and disease in developing nations, including Angola.

http://www.unaids.org/en
UNAIDS is an organization working on a global level to wipe out AIDS by collecting data and working to inspire policy in the most at-risk regions.

RELIGION

This church was built during Portuguese
rule of Angola and still stands today.

8

RELIGIOUS BELIEFS ARE IMPORTANT to many Angolans. Around 41.1 percent of the population are Roman Catholic; another 38 percent are Protestant; 8.6 percent of Angolans practice another religion, and the remaining 12.3 percent are nonpracticing.

All religion was discouraged by the left-wing government in Luanda after independence was achieved in 1975. Religious institutions lost their schools, clinics, and properties. But when the MPLA abandoned communism, religious organizations regained influence, especially the Roman Catholic Church. As of 2015, there were eighty-three legally recognized religious groups in Angola. Today, in order for religious groups to be legal in the eyes of the government, they must have one hundred thousand registered members, and they must be active in at least one-third of the country's eighteen provinces.

A FUNDAMENTAL BELIEF

The term "living dead" may sound like something from a horror movie, but it refers to the fundamental belief in Angola and other parts of Africa that the meaning of a person's life does not end with the death of his or her body. This belief is not the Christian idea of the resurrection of the soul or the notion that people will ultimately be judged according to their life on earth.

"The state shall recognize and respect the different religious faiths, which shall be free to organize and exercise their activities, provided that they abide by the Constitution and the laws of the Republic of Angola."
—Angola's Constitution

An Angolan funeral procession

There is also no sense of heaven and hell in traditional religions in Angola. Even the idea of an all-powerful God—so central to Islam, Judaism, and Christianity—is not linked to the tremendous reverence that a person may receive after death. When people die, they may be remembered by name for one hundred years or more, with their memory being passed down through three generations through word of mouth. A family shrine may even contain remnants of their bones to revere them and keep their memory alive.

In a sense, the dead remain members of their families long after they have died. If misfortune befalls a family member, the family may consult an expert in these matters—a "diviner," sometimes also called a witch doctor—to find out if a deceased person is unhappy about something. In Angola, the diviner is known as the *kimbanda* ("kim-BAN-da"). If the deceased is deemed to be unhappy, the kimbanda will perform a ritual to placate the spirit.

The Seventh Day in the Light of the World is an illegal religious group in Angola, founded by leader Jose Julino Kalupeteka in the early 2000s as an offshoot of the Seventh Day Adventist Church. The three thousand members of the group believed that the world would end on December 31, 2015, and gave up their worldly belongings in order to move to a secluded camp on Mount Sumi in the Huambo province in central Angola.

In a crackdown on illegal religious groups and in an attempt to capture Kalupeteka, the Angolan government ordered a raid on the Light of the World's compound in April of 2015. Thirteen members of the group were killed in the raid, along with nine police officers. Kalupeteka was arrested, along with other members of the group.

But what exactly went on during and after the raid has been fiercely contested. The thirteen dead sect members were said to be snipers who opened fire, according to the police, but details are sketchy because freedom of the press is limited in Angola. The Huambo province is a stronghold of the UNITA party, who accused the police of hundreds of revenge killings on sect members following the raid. The violence stirred up the old conflict between UNITA and the MPLA, who blamed UNITA for unrest following the raid. Nine members of the sect and Kalupeteka later received jail sentences between sixteen and twenty-eight years.

DIVINERS

In Angolan society, a diviner is someone who uses special means to find out something about the world of the supernatural. In larger villages, the diviner is a specialist who usually works with his own divination basket. The basket contains a number of small ritual objects, such as clay figurines, pieces of polished metal, carved pieces of bone, and the teeth or horns of animals.

Special prayers are made to the ancestors of the clients, and the diviner shakes up the basket as part of the ritual. Then the diviner studies the arrangement of the objects once they have settled and gives his or her interpretation. Many diviners also have knowledge of herbal medicine.

"The problem is that the men in government believe that Angola is a Catholic country."
—Elias Isaac of the Open Society Initiative for Southern Africa

Diviners are usually consulted when an individual has an illness or complaint of some kind that is thought to have a spiritual cause. The diviner hopes to identify the cause and fix the problem with the appropriate prayers. Some diviners specialize in certain illnesses. The more respected a diviner is, the larger the fee he or she is able to charge for his or her services.

CHRISTIANITY

Christianity began in Angola with the arrival of the Portuguese toward the end of the fifteenth century. Their first contact inland was with the Kongo Kingdom, and there was a difference of opinion within the kingdom over the best way to deal with the European presence. The king at the time, Nzinga a Nkuwu, was an early convert to Roman Catholicism and changed his name to King João I. He was the first African Christian to wield power in Angola, and through his influence the new religion spread with the help of Portuguese priests.

Baptême du ROY de CONGO.
DOOPING DES KONINGS VAN KONGO.

This 1780 engraving depicts King João I being baptized by Portuguese missionaries.

In the late nineteenth and early twentieth centuries, missionaries introduced Protestantism. Several Christian societies, including Protestant societies from North America, sent missionaries to Africa, and they eventually reached Angola. Initially, the process of conversion was slow. For a long time, missionary stations were confined to the coastal region. In the early twentieth century, however, missionaries began to make an impact. A major reason for this was that a missionary station often offered some elementary education and basic health services. Over time, these services attracted large numbers of people who had no other way of acquiring literacy or gaining access to health care. Jonas Savimbi, the founder of UNITA, was a student at the school run by Canadian and US Congregationalists.

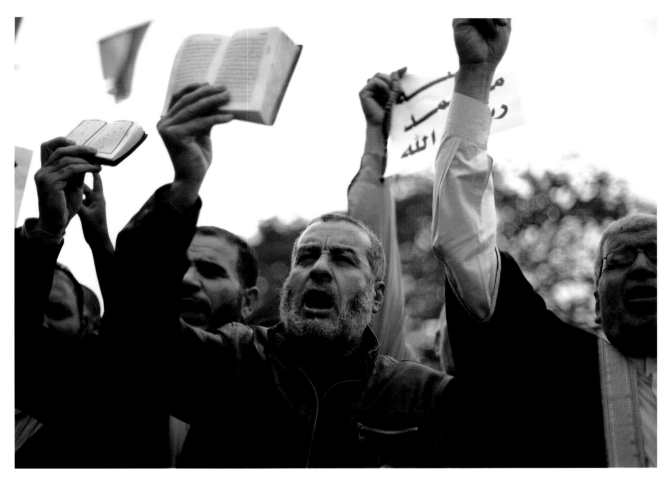

Throughout the years of civil war, Christian churches were never banned outright. However, the power of the Catholic Church diminished in the decade after independence, partly because the MPLA government did not want to encourage any organization that might rival its own power. Today, Christian missions continue to operate in Angola.

Palestinians protest the closing and destruction of many mosques around Angola in 2013.

ISLAM IN ANGOLA

Islam is one religion that has struggled to find a foothold in Angola. In 2013, news spread that Angola had banned the practice of Islam, shutting down and destroying mosques across the country. The Islamic community of Angola claimed that eight mosques had been destroyed between 2011 and 2013 and

Christian missionaries established the first schools in Angola for the non-Portuguese. They needed converts who would agree to become Christian teachers. In return, they offered free education. They performed a valuable role in opening the door for black Angolans to educate themselves. Missions also established a rudimentary health service that benefited many people.

However, despite these benefits, the first missionaries in Angola actively supported the slave trade. They argued that they were saving the souls of the godless Africans. As late as 1870, a marble chair on the docks at Luanda was reserved for the bishop who baptized Angolans by the hundreds as they were rowed in chains on their way to the slave ships that would transport them across the Atlantic Ocean.

The missionaries who first spread Christianity in Angola did not understand or respect traditional African forms of belief. They dismissed what they viewed as childish superstition and worked to replace it with their own beliefs and cultural values. Traditional African cultural practices were condemned by missionaries who did not understand their role within African society.

almost all had been shut down, but Angolan officials denied that any such ban had been imposed.

There were ninety thousand Muslims living in Angola in 2013, short of the one hundred thousand members needed to be legally recognized by the government. The government claimed that mosque shutdowns were due to them being unlicensed. Because Islam is not legally recognized, Muslims are prevented from building places of worship, schools, or clinics. Today, Angolan Muslims live in fear of religious persecution, and anti-Muslim sentiments only continue to rise.

Many of Angola's Christian churches have been around for centuries. Our Lady of Muxima Church in the Bengo province was built between 1641 and 1648. It's now a national monument and receives thousands of visitors every year.

INTERNET LINKS

https://www.state.gov/j/drl/rls/irf/2016/af/268616.htm
The US State Department provides a summary of religious freedoms and restrictions in Angola.

http://www.welcometoangola.co.ao/_churches_in_angola
The *Welcome to Angola* website is the go-to information hub for tourists. It lists all of the historical church sites across Angola.

A man displays Angolan newspapers in Portuguese.

9

BECAUSE OF THE LONG PERIOD OF living under Portuguese rule, 71.2 percent of Angolans speak Portuguese, making it the country's official language. But Angolans value their regional and ethic identities, which is why 23 percent of Angolans speak Umbundu, the language of the Ovimbundu. Other languages spoken frequently in Angola are Kikongo (8.2 percent); Kimbundu (7.8 percent); Chokwe (6.5 percent); Nhaneca (3.4 percent); Nganguela (3.1 percent); Ibinda (2.4 percent); Kwanhama (2.3 percent); Muhumbi (2.1 percent); Luvale (1 percent); and other languages (3.6 percent). Many Angolans speak more than one of these languages.

Many people do not learn to read or write their non-Portuguese African language. Indeed, before European colonization spread across Africa, most cultures with their own languages did not have a written form. Europeans often mistook the absence of a written language as evidence of underdevelopment, failing to understand that a culture can have a

"When the Portuguese colonized Angola, they tried to diminish the value of Kimbundu and other local languages. Suppressing the culture made it easier to colonize us."
—Toty Sa'Med, Angolan singer

sophisticated form of communication that can transmit information across generations without the need for a written form. In such cultures, what is important is the oral tradition, and this is very true of Angolan society.

STORYTELLING TRADITION

In the mid-1970s, during the civil war, one faction arrived in a village and tried to gain the support of the villagers. The following story was told as a way of communicating with the people:

One day there was a rabbit who wanted to marry the daughter of a bear. The rabbit went to the bear and asked for his permission, but the bear refused and told the rabbit that only someone who could build a house in one day would be a suitable match for his beautiful daughter. The rabbit went away and gathered from his large family all the rabbits who looked like him. Then, making sure that the bear only ever saw one rabbit at any one time, they all worked together and succeeded in building a house in just one day. The bear, suitably impressed, gave permission to the clever rabbit to marry his daughter.

This story was readily understood by the villagers as a parable promoting the idea of working together for a common end. Angolans would have been taught through stories and fables from early childhood.

THE NATIONAL LANGUAGE OF ANGOLA

Portuguese is the national language, and more people speak Portuguese in Angola than in any other African nation. In the towns and cities, daily life is conducted in Portuguese. Portuguese is more commonly spoken in urban areas and by younger people, while tribal languages are more common in rural areas and among older Angolans.

Portuguese is still widely spoken today because of historical reasons. It was the language of the ruling class who colonized the country, relegating the various ethnic languages of Angolans to an inferior role. The mother tongues of the ethnic groups were not acknowledged and were not used in any dealings between the colonial powers and the ordinary people. Any Angolan who wanted to receive an education and get a job outside of farming had little choice but to learn Portuguese.

The need for Angolans to learn Portuguese was an essential aspect of the assimilado process. A formal language test required an Angolan to show fluency in both speaking and writing Portuguese.

The Portuguese language spoken in Angola today is called Angolan Portuguese, as it has been influenced by the several African languages spoken in Angola, especially Kimbundu.

In 2008, the textbook publisher Pearson, the Angolan government, and the Moreno Institute for Language and Literacy worked together on a project to publish textbooks in seven indigenous Angolan languages (and Portuguese) in order to give educational materials for students a wider reach.

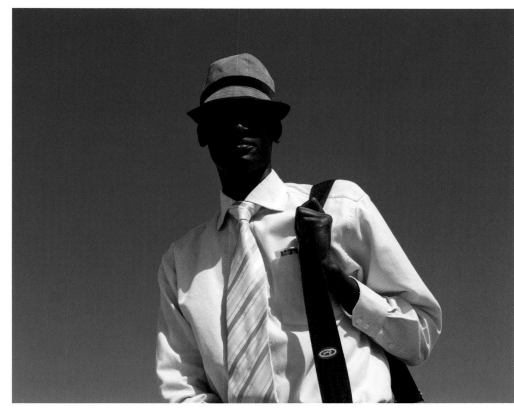

Many Angolans dress in more of a European style today because of Portuguese influence on culture.

Here are some common phrases in Kimbundu.

Please: . . . . Nga ku diondo.

Thank you: . . . . Ngasakidila.

Hello, how are you?: . . . . . Wazekele kyebi?

What is your name?: . . . . . Dyjina dye?

My name is _____.: . . . Eme [your name].

Goodbye: . . . . Nde kimbote

LANGUAGE AND IDENTITY

Angolans have a strong sense of ethnic and regional identity. One main reason for this is that the different ethnic groups have their own languages. The Ovimbundu people, the largest group in the country, speak Umbundu—the language most commonly used and understood in central and southern Angola. Kimbundu, the language of the second-largest ethnic group, the Mbundu, is spoken mainly in the provinces of Luanda, Cuanza Norte, and Malanje.

Historically, Luanda province is the area that has been most influenced by the Portuguese, and so, not surprisingly, the legacy of colonization on language has been most keenly felt by the Mbundu who live there. They generally speak Portuguese and, in many cases, the use of Angolan Portuguese is more prevalent than the native language.

In the northwest of Angola, in the provinces of Zaire and Uíge, the Kikongo language is spoken by the Bakongo people. This language is also spoken by people who belong to the same ethnic group in the neighboring countries of the Republic of the Congo and the Democratic Republic of the Congo. In Cabinda, younger generations are starting to embrace their own sense of identity by referring to themselves and their common language as Ibinda, which is derived from the Kikongo language.

THE LANGUAGE OF THE OVIMBUNDU

In its traditional form, Umbundu, the language of the Ovimbundu, uses various proverbs and sayings that are rooted in the lives of the people who speak the language. Two examples are expressions that translate as "We have roots in the fields of our ancestors" and "The advocate speaks, the king decides." In an Umbundu conversation, the speaker who uses one of these sayings will do so within a particular context, and usually the person being spoken to would interpret the remark in the light of that context.

Angolans have a strong sense of ethnic and regional identity.

For example, if there were a disagreement over who owned a plot of land and someone made the remark about roots in the fields of ancestors, this might be understood in terms of a claim to ownership based on a family relationship. If the other speaker replied by quoting the remark about advocates and kings, this might be understood as a way of saying that the matter needs to go to arbitration.

In 2003, many Angolans gathered around televisions and radios to wait for news of missing loved ones.

THE MEDIA IN ANGOLA

In Angola, the government controls all media with nationwide reach, including radio, which is the most influential medium outside of the capital. Television, the private press, and internet access are very limited outside of Luanda. In 2016, around 13 percent of Angolans had internet access. There is one state-run national daily, the *Jornal de Angola*, and Luanda has several weekly newspapers. The official government newspaper is the *Diario da Republica*. Regional newspapers are also published in several towns.

The state-owned Rádio Nacional de Angola (RNA) broadcasts in Portuguese, English, French, Spanish, and several tribal languages, including

Kimbundu, Umbundu, Kikongo, and Chokwe. Private stations operate in the main cities, including the Catholic station Radio Ecclesia, but RNA is the only available broadcaster across much of the country. Pay TV services are operated by MultiChoice Angola and TV Cabo; they carry some Brazilian and Portuguese channels. The TV service TPA is state-owned and rarely criticizes the government.

INTERNET LINKS

https://freedomhouse.org/report/freedom-press/2016/angola
Freedom House studies the status of the freedom of the press in countries around the world. Read their report about Angola here.

https://www.justlanded.com/english/Angola/Angola-Guide /Language/Languages-in-Angola
The Just Landed website offers a basic primer on the languages of Angola for visitors to the country.

http://www.nalrc.indiana.edu/brochures/kimbundu.pdf
The University of Indiana offers a language program for students interested in learning Kimbundu.

https://www.omniglot.com/writing/portuguese.htm
This page from Omniglot, an online language encyclopedia, outlines the Portuguese language, including the alphabet and a pronunciation guide.

ARTS

Angolan people keep centuries of traditional folk dance alive through continuing to learn and practice it.

A RT IN MODERN-DAY ANGOLA IS A mix of tradition and contemporary art. Angolan artists have long enjoyed sculpture and mask-making as traditional mediums, as well as basket-weaving and pottery. Traditional styles of dance and music continue to be popular forms of expression. But contemporary art forms, like photography, film, and modern painting styles, are slowly growing in popularity.

AN EARLY ART FORM

Sculpture is one of Angola's oldest art forms. The earliest sculptures were done with wood and ivory, but modern sculptors also use metal as a base material. The designs that inspired sculptors had their origins in traditional religious beliefs and were often abstract in form. The arrival of Europeans in the fifteenth century exposed Angolans to Christian imagery, and this had an important influence on Angolan artists.

Another important influence that still plays a part in contemporary Angolan sculpture has been European and North American interest in ethnic African art. This has had the effect of introducing non-African

Chokwe art typically features large upturned hairstyles on figures.

pictorial ideas as subjects for sculptors. For instance, a traditional subject often portrayed by Angolan artists is that of the disgruntled ancestor who bewails the fact that he has not been shown the proper respect by his living relatives. Small carved objects of such figures are familiar items in the diviner's basket of ritual objects.

THE ART OF THE CHOKWE

Chokwe art is renowned for the quality of its wooden sculptures. The best examples were made between the sixteenth and mid-nineteenth centuries, when the Chokwe were under Lunda rule. After 1860, the Chokwe rose up against the Lunda and even dominated them, but the sculpture of this period is not considered as good.

A feature common to Chokwe art is the large upturned hairstyles on figures, possibly a reflection of what was once a fashion among the leading chiefs and their families. Chokwe sculptures often portray their leaders with hands and feet on a clearly exaggerated scale—a pair of hands, for example, would be significantly larger than the figure's head. This signifies the great power and strength of the rulers.

MASKS AS AN ART FORM

Mask painting brings together the art of sculpture and the art of painting. The mask itself is usually made of wood or by using a wicker frame and lining it with bark cloth. The cloth or wooden surface is then painted. Masks are used in rituals and ceremonies, such as those to mark the transition from childhood to adulthood or the celebration of a new harvest.

The start of the hunting season may also be marked by a mask ceremony, with some masks painted to represent the animals that the community hopes to hunt successfully.

MACHETE AS MEDIUM

Painter Francisco Vidal grew up in Portugal, but his ties to Angola, his father's home country, are strong. He has worked to grow the art scene in Luanda, building an artists' collective and studio complex with project spaces for other artists. He also runs an art education program there. In 2015, he gained notoriety for an art series where he painted colorful flowers directly on machetes using oil paint.

PAINTERS

In the second half of the twentieth century, a number of Angolan artists achieved international recognition for their paintings. One of the earliest and most famous is José zan Andrade, more familiarly known as Zan. He was born in 1946 and taught himself how to paint. He first became known for his work in Chinese ink painting and gouache, a method of painting that uses opaque pigments ground in water and mixed with a glue-like substance. Contemporaries of Zan who have been influenced more by modern art movements include Tomas Vista (born in 1957) and Paulo Jazz (born 1940).

MODERN ART

Modern art in Angola is spread across a variety of mediums and is growing in popularity. Artist Nástio Mosquito works in video, performance art, music, installation, and digital art to make political and social statements. His work has been displayed at the Museum of Modern Art in New York.

"My motivation creates the work but from then on the work is the work, it should have a life of its own."
—Nástio Mosquito

Many Angolans sell their art in open-air markets; bright colors and traditional subjects are evident here.

Perhaps the most famous artist in Angola today is António Ole, filmmaker, painter, and sculptor. Ole was self-taught, first learning to paint and later working to develop his skills as a sculptor. He studied filmmaking at the Center for Advanced Film and Television Studies in Los Angeles. His work digs deep into Angola's turbulent past, as well as life in modern urban Luanda.

WEAVING: TRADITION AND ART

The art of weaving first developed as a practical skill, mainly to produce mats for use in the home. When imported machine-made textiles became more readily available, the art of weaving in Angola went into decline. Only recently, beginning in the 1980s, have Angolan women revitalized the art. Today, weaving has emerged as a specialized art that caters to an international market, although weavers still draw on traditional motifs for their designs and ideas. Modern designer Eneida Tavares uses Angolan weaving methods and ceramics in her work.

DANCE AND MUSIC

Song, dance, and music are all fundamental aspects of traditional African culture. Regions that are widely separated geographically may have surprisingly similar forms of song and dance, and although no one has been able to explain these similarities, they can presumably be traced back to an earlier time when these art forms were first being developed. For example, in parts of eastern Angola, there is a form of multipart singing that uses exactly the same tone as that found among an ethnic group in Côte d'Ivoire in West Africa.

Nevertheless, some forms of Angolan dance are unique to the country. In the southwest of Angola, for example, the Nkili dance uses a pair of dancers to very dramatic effect. At the climax of the dance, the male dancer leaps into the air, landing with his hands on the shoulders of the female dancer, who balances him on her shoulders. Such a dance requires constant practice and strong shoulders on the part of the woman.

One attempt to understand and classify the great variety of African dance styles is based on the idea that different styles use different parts of the body. European dance, by comparison, is said to treat the body as a single whole. According to this system, many of the Angolan dance forms revolve around the movement of the pelvis to create a characteristic form.

This street performer is doing the Tchingange traditional dance for tourists in Lobito.

Derived from the masemba *and inspired by Brazilian and Caribbean dance styles, the kizomba ("ki-ZOM-ba") is a popular dance and music style in Angola that has been making a comeback in recent years. The kizomba was first created in the 1980s. Like disco in the United States, kizomba clubs grew in popularity, especially in Luanda. It is known for the sensual nature of the dance and the focus on the intense connection between dance partners.*

Learning the steps is fairly easy. There are only four to five moves that a dancer needs to practice to learn kizomba. The tricky part is learning to master those moves with a partner and conveying emotion through those dance steps. Today, kizomba communities and classes exist on several continents as the kizomba craze continues to grow.

Slavery brought African dance forms to both North and South America. The Brazilian dance known as the lunda *is related to an Angolan dance. When it returned to Africa, it became one of Luanda's most popular dances. Now called the* masemba *("MASS-m-ba"), it is a type of belly dance, where a pair of dancers thrust their stomachs toward one another. The word* lunda *comes from the Bantu word* kilunda *("KILL-un-da"), meaning "spirit," which suggests that the dance has its origin in a religious ritual.*

Another type of Angolan dance is characterized by the use of masked dancers, who use a greater variety of movements. Each set of movements, using a particular part of the body, has its own name in the local language.

MASKS AND DANCE

Dances based on the use of masks are fairly unique to west and west-central Africa. The region bounded by eastern Angola and parts of Zambia and the Democratic Republic of the Congo is one of the richest sources of masked dancing on the continent. There are a wide variety of masks, and each ethnic group has its own colors and designs. Just as important is the function or meaning attached to a particular mask, because this helps convey the story behind the mask or the significance associated with a specific mask.

Many Angolan masks represent ancestral members of a prestigious royal family. Some masks represent officials and servants of the court. Masked dances thus perform a function similar to that of oral tradition—they help preserve a sense of history and identity that is not dependent on books and writing. When performing a dance, the person wearing the mask also uses gestures and pantomime-like actions to convey the character represented by the mask.

PRESIDENT AND POET

Agostinho Neto, the first president of independent Angola, was widely recognized as an accomplished poet. Born in 1922 in Bengo province, Neto studied medicine in Lisbon. He first became known at the age of twenty-six when he published a volume of poems and joined a national cultural movement aimed at rediscovering indigenous Angolan culture. Neto died in Moscow in 1979. The following lines are taken from one of Neto's poems, "Fire and Rhythm":

> *Rhythm in light*
> *rhythm in color*
> *rhythm in movement*
> *rhythm in the bloody cracks of bare feet*
> *rhythm on torn nails*
> *Yet rhythm*
> *rhythm.*
> *Oh painful African voices.*

PERCUSSION AND STRINGS

Angolan music is produced using a rich variety of traditional musical instruments. A typical example of a percussion instrument is the *saxi* ("SAR-ki"), more commonly known as maracas. In Angola, these are made from the dried fruit known as *maboque* ("MA-boo-ker") and are filled with dried seeds or glass beads.

Drums, known as bongos or tam-tam, vary in size from one region to another, but they are often a popular instrument for accompanying dancing. In the past, drums were used to send messages. Other traditional instruments include the marimba, a type of xylophone, and the *xingufos* ("SING-U-fos"), which are large antelope horns that have been cleaned and dried.

A rare Angolan instrument is the *sagaya* ("sar-GA-ya") of the Humbi people in the southwest of the country. An ordinary hunting bow is fitted with a mouth brace, and the player breathes through the brace while stroking the bow's string with a fine twig-like strip of leather. As the player changes his breathing and the position of his mouth, the tone produced by playing the string changes.

Another, more common string instrument is the *hungu* ("HUNG-go"). A small stick, held in the right hand, plays the bow, which is held at stomach level. The hungu was taken to Brazil in the days of slavery, and it is now known in South America as the *berimbau* ("bur-IM-ba").

This Brazilian musician plays a berimbau with the Capoeira Angola Palmares ensemble in 2000.

INTERNET LINKS

https://africa.uima.uiowa.edu/peoples/show/Chokwe
The University of Iowa has a virtual gallery of Chokwe art and explains where it can be seen in person.

http://www.kizombacommunity.com
Kizomba Community is a good resource for semba and kizomba dance styles, with information on safety and etiquette, and locations of dance communities across the globe.

http://nastiomosquito.com
Nástio Mosquito's works are available to view on his website.

LEISURE

Angolan children play soccer on a Bengula beach.

11

FOR CENTURIES, LEISURE TIME HAS been at a premium for many Angolans. Twenty-seven years of civil war following four hundred years of life under colonial rule have greatly complicated the lives of Angola's citizens, and they are still recovering. But what leisure time they do enjoy is rooted in tradition and community. Angola is a fairly young country. The median age is around sixteen years old, meaning half the country's population is age sixteen or younger. Young people in Angola are finding new ways to enjoy leisure time in a liberated country in a way that their parents and grandparents couldn't.

The years of civil war disrupted family life and forced many people to rely on themselves. The massive drift of population to Luanda and other urban centers has also caused overcrowding, widespread unemployment, and a general sense of insecurity. But it's also brought people together, centralizing elements of culture and building a larger community.

"Leisure in Angola is a world of endless possibilities."
— *Welcome to Angola* website

Capoeira is a combination of dance and martial arts, with origins in both Angolan and Brazilian tradition. Many believe that Angolan slaves who were brought to Brazil used capoeira, and it soon became a Brazilian tradition as well. Today, young people in Angola are practicing capoeira again as a way to express themselves and work through their aggressions.

Even though many families are still living with the aftermath of war, they have managed to find times to come together and enjoy one another's company. This is part of the rebuilding of Angola.

ANGOLA'S BEACHES

Some of the most majestic beaches in Angola can be found in Benguela.

Luanda has a beautiful, natural bay with a sandy beach. This bay was where the Portuguese first landed and where, in the centuries that followed, thousands of poor Portuguese arrived to start a new life in Africa. Today, the same beach is open to everyone and provides relaxation and recreation for the poor people of the city. On the weekend especially, the beach is crowded with families.

On one side of the bay is a narrow peninsula of land that stretches into the sea, called Mussulo. On the weekends, both sides of this peninsula are crowded with Angolans enjoying picnic lunches. During the week, people also come to the beach to relax after work and to escape from the drudgery of shantytown life. Nearby islands attracts weekend visitors who are able to organize the boat ride there and back. Farther down the coast, Benguela is also famous for its beautiful beaches. Baía Azul, which translates to "Blue Bay," is considered to be one of the best beaches in Angola.

EVENING IN THE MUSSEQUE

During the week, leisure time in one of Luanda's musseques revolves around the evening meal. With family members leaving for work at different times, the evening meal is an occasion for everyone to come together and talk about their

This is a folktale of the Mbangala people of Angola that goes back centuries to the time when the Lunda Kingdom was first established by people from another kingdom—the Luba—in what is now the southeastern part of the Democratic Republic of the Congo.

A young prince named Chibinda Ilunga came to the Lunda Kingdom because he had an argument with the Luba king, who had accused Chibinda of being afraid to fight in war. The truth was that the Luba king was secretly jealous of Chibinda's great skill as a hunter. The queen of the Lunda people, named Lueji, was down by the riverside one morning when she met Chibinda for the first time. She was struck by his great beauty and natural manners. Before the day was over, they had fallen in love.

In time they married, and in due course, Lueji announced to her court that Chibinda was now their king. He made a speech to the court and promised that as a hunter he would continue to kill animals, but that he would never shed the blood of another human being. This was accepted, but a problem arose when Lueji was unable to bear children. The difficulty was solved when Lueji found another woman, named Kamonga, who also became Chibinda's wife and bore him children.

day. The father may have some good news, even if it is only a rumor that new water pipes are going to be laid down or that the electricity station that used to provide power to the musseque is finally being repaired. The mother may announce that she has sold more than the usual amount of food at the market that day. After the meal, oil lanterns and perhaps a fire in the yard outside will be lit. The family may gather around and continue their conversation.

Before going to bed, some chores may be completed—water may need to be collected for the morning, or wet clothes may need to be hung out to dry.

LEISURE OUTSIDE THE CITIES

A traditional form of leisure in the countryside is for a small group of friends or neighbors to gather and talk around an open fire, especially when a full moon provides plenty of light. An interesting or amusing story, perhaps first brought to the village by someone who has been working in Luanda, will be told more than once. A more traditional story may be told by one of the respected elders

Rural families spend their leisure time together.

of the village. Sometimes such a story is accompanied by someone playing a kalimba, made by attaching strips of bamboo or metal to a board that acts as a resonator. The board is held in both hands and played with the thumbs.

Some rural areas are visited regularly by a traveling movie group that brings its own equipment and movies. If there is no movie theater in the town and a suitable blank wall is not available to show the movie on, a large white sheet is hung over a wall as a substitute.

On the weekends, dances are held regularly in the rural areas, perhaps accompanied by a live drum band. Smaller parties are held at home for special occasions, such as the birth of a child, and a radio broadcast provides music for dancing.

PLAYING SPORTS AND SPORTING EVENTS

Angolan footballer Dolly Domingos Menga (*left*) fights for the ball in this qualifying match for the 2018 World Cup.

Sports are very popular in Angola. The sports that attract the most participants and spectators are soccer, basketball, handball, swimming, and roller hockey. The Angolan basketball team has won eleven Federation of International Basketball (FIBA) Africa Championships, the first in 1989 and the most recent in 2013. They also won the basketball tournament at the All-Africa Games several times, including in 2015.

In track and field, Angola has also enjoyed success. José Armando Sayovo was the first person to win a Paralympic medal for Angola, at the 2004 Summer Paralympic Games in Athens, when he won three gold medals, in the 100-, 200-, and 400-meter sprints. In 2012, he won the bronze medal for the 200-meter and the gold for the 400. Sayovo retired in 2015. That same year, Buya Befilia, who is vision impaired, placed second in the 800-meter at the Paralympic World Championship.

Soccer is very popular, in part because it only requires one ball for twenty-two people to enjoy a game. Angola has a professional soccer league, but the players are often lured away to Portugal because of the higher wages players can earn there. Still, Angola's national soccer team qualified to play in the 2006 World Cup, despite being ranked 78th in world soccer. In 2018, they were ranked at 141 going into the World Cup in Russia. In large towns, it is not

The Portuguese card game sueco *(su-E-co) is played frequently in Angola, along with the gambling game* sete e meio *(SE-te e MEHJ-u).*

Ware *is a game similar to mancala that is popular among children. The game is sometimes played using a board and game pieces, but players can simply use seeds, shells, or rocks and small holes dug into the ground.*

Chess has also grown in popularity since 1987, when Angolan Manuel Mateus was certified a chess master. Since then, over a dozen Angolans have also been named chess masters. In 2016, the men's chess team rose from ninety-sixth to seventy-fifth in the International Chess Federation ranking.

unusual for seventy-five thousand spectators to fill the stadiums if one of the top soccer clubs is playing.

Handball is also a widely played sport. The Angolan women's team won the African championship in handball in 2008 and 2016 while hosting the tournament. They also took eighth place in the 2016 Olympic Games in Rio.

INTERNET LINKS

http://www.angop.ao/angola/en_us/noticias/desporto.html
Angop has all of the latest news about sports from around Angola.

http://capoeira-connection.com/capoeira/about
Capoeira Connection has all of the information a person needs to learn more about capoeira and where to find groups near you.

https://library.si.edu/digital-library/book/folktalesofango00chat
The Smithsonian website provides the complete text of *Folk-Tales of Angola*, a book published in 1894.

"When ... Angola's national team hits the pitch on Sunday, it will be the most important game in the country's history. Facing Portugal, its erstwhile colonial master, more will be at stake than just winning."
—Oliver Lück, as Angola prepared to play Portugal at the 2006 World Cup

FESTIVALS

The Angolan Carnival in Luanda is a yearly tradition that attracts Angolans and tourists alike.

12

LARGE FESTIVALS THAT SOMETIMES last several days, or even weeks, are an important part of life in Angola's cities. Angolan people use festivals to celebrate art, tradition, holidays, religion, and even just pride over living in certain parts of their home country. Festivals bring people together, but they also help to attract tourism. Smaller festivals and parties are often held in rural regions to help celebrate family events and holidays. Food and dance are a big part of Angolan festivals and events.

FAMILY EVENTS

In Angola, communities enjoy the often impromptu social festivals that take place for occasions such as the birth of a child. The birth of a child is always a cause for celebration, and even among poor families, the occasion is marked in some way. A special meal is usually cooked at the earliest opportunity, often for the evening of the day when the child is born. Even if the mother travels to a clinic for the actual birth, she usually comes back home the same day.

> "A great sense of imagination and humor is used to make peculiar costumes, which makes carnivals in Angola spectacular."
> —ThisIsAfrica.me

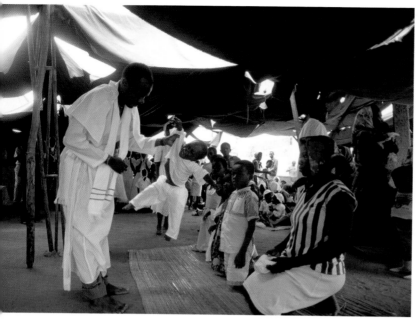

A chicken or a duck is often considered a necessary part of the special meal. Sometimes a family member may give a gift of one of their chickens or ducks, and it will be killed and prepared within an hour. Neighbors will almost certainly pay a visit to wish the newborn a prosperous and happy future, and a small amount of money will be given as a gift for the child. The home needs to be cleaned up and made as presentable as possible for the visitors. If there is money for beer, a few bottles are bought and offered to guests.

Baptisms are a time for friends and family to gather together and celebrate a new life.

The baptism of a child, a Christian ceremony marking a spiritual stage in a child's life, is often followed by a small private celebration for family and neighbors. Parents and neighbors may also celebrate the first birthday of a child. When a daughter reaches the age of eighteen, her parents may present her to the community in a "coming out" party. In a small village, this celebration might include nearly all of the villagers, although in a town the party would only be attended by family, friends, and neighbors.

RELIGIOUS HOLIDAYS

Christmas Day is usually celebrated in Angola with a special meal. Families try to gather as many members of the family as possible for the meal. Often beef, goat, or chicken that has been saved up for a special occasion will be served, along with vegetables, rice, and fish. For dessert, Angolans will often enjoy pieces of *bolo-rei* ("BO-lo ray"), a cake similar to the king cake eaten in New Orleans during Mardi Gras. The cake has a small fava bean or candy hidden inside. According to lore, the person who finds the gift is awarded with luck and wealth for the following year. After midnight on Christmas Eve, Angolans might have a small gift exchange.

Christians celebrate Christmas for its religious significance because the day is traditionally regarded as the birthday of Jesus Christ. Even non-Christians are likely to regard the day as a time for general goodwill and merriment. For the average Angolan, Christmas is more of a family occasion than a religious event.

Easter, which celebrates the belief that Christ was resurrected after his crucifixion, is the most important festival for Roman Catholics. Easter Sunday takes place between late March and early April, depending on the date of the first full moon after the spring equinox. The weeks before Easter are known as Lent, and they are traditionally observed as a period of abstinence to commemorate Christ's forty-day fast in the wilderness. In Angola, this tradition of abstinence is reflected in the practice of not eating meat during Lent.

The *bolo-rei* is a colorful Christmas cake rumored to award luck to the person who finds the prize inside.

CELEBRATING WEDDINGS

Wedding traditions vary from tribe to tribe in Angola, but that a wedding is a cause for celebration is standard across the country. In the countryside, it is not uncommon for Angolan parents to suggest a possible partner for their son or daughter. In some rural areas, this goes a step further, with arranged marriages still taking place regularly. However, in urban areas this practice is in decline, and it is more common for parents to simply pass on to their daughter a compliment that a man may have made about her. Such a compliment is made on the understanding that this might be interpreted as the first stage in a proposal of marriage. It is a common practice for the groom to officially ask for the bride's hand in marriage—this practice is called *alambamento* ("al-LAM-bi-man-jo"). The groom sends a letter asking for the bride's hand, often along with some money. If he is employed full time, he is also expected to provide gifts as determined by the bride's uncle, sometimes beverages, a goat, clothes, shoes, or other goods. A groom who isn't employed full time might meet his

The Lubango Festival in the city of Lubango takes place every year in August and lasts thirty days. It includes music, parades, sports, motorbike races, fashion shows, and a beauty pageant.

The following are the public holidays celebrated in Angola:

New Year's Day	*January 1*
Martyrs of the Colonial Repression Day	*January 4*
Luanda's Day	*January 25*
Liberation Day	*February 4*
Carnival	*February, date varies*
International Women's Day	*March 8*
Peace and Reconciliation Day	*April 4*
Good Friday	*Friday before Easter*
Easter Monday	*Monday after Easter*
Labor Day	*May 1*
Africa Day	*May 25*
International Children's Day	*June 1*
National Heroes' Day	*September 17*
All Saints' Day	*November 1*
All Souls' Day	*November 2*
Independence Day	*November 11*
Christmas Day	*December 25*

gift demands by performing labor for the bride's family, working in the field or on the family's farm. He might help the bride's mother around the house. A wedding consultant is an important part of the event. The consultant traditionally carries the bride to the groom's house—or simply walks her there, if necessary.

Marriage is always a cause for celebration. Once the compulsory registration in a government office has taken place, there may be a church ceremony. The couple might wear a European-style white dress and tuxedo, or they may choose more traditional clothing with brighter colors, or a combination of these styles. A special meal will be prepared, drinks will be available, and a party atmosphere will turn the event into a festive occasion. Singing and dancing always accompany the party.

Many Angolan brides choose a more traditional style of dress.

THE PRACTICE OF CIRCUMCISION

The masked figure of the Ndzingi is one of the most popular figures at circumcision festivals, called *mukanda* ("MU-kan-da"), among the Mbwela people. The Ndzingi first instills fear because of his frightful appearance, characterized by his large red-colored mouth, but this fear turns to laughter when he falls to the ground because his head is too large for his body.

Young boys in the audience run up and help him stand upright—but he soon collapses again. The combination of feelings evoked by the dance—first fear and then the relief of laughter—matches the emotions of many boys who take part in the circumcision ceremony.

"The alambamento is a traditional ceremony in the Angolan culture and (is) required when young people love each other and want to live together."
— *Welcome to Angola* website

After the Angolan civil war, there were fewer men than women, especially in rural regions of Angola. Therefore, the practice of polygamy became common. Polygamy is illegal and frowned upon, but many families live this way, with the woman as the head of the household, caring for her children, while the man has a number of families to provide for. There is even a popular song about the practice of polygamy called "The Other."

THREE DAYS OF CARNIVAL

Carnival is the most popular festival in Angola. During the Angolan civil war, Carnival faced restrictions by military police, but today Angolans are free once again to celebrate. Carnival used to take place at the end of March each year, marking the anniversary of the expulsion of invading South African troops. Carnival has now been moved to February. In Luanda, Carnival is celebrated

A funeral, known as a komba ("KUM-ba") in Angola, is not always as somber an affair as it is in the West. In traditional rural areas, it is believed that the deceased will be happy if everyone celebrates. The komba is organized by close relatives and friends, and together, they cover the cost of the food and drink that is served to those who attend the funeral. Often the close friends are neighbors of the deceased, because in Angolan villages neighbors can become very close and may be regarded almost as part of the family.

on the streets with processions, food, masemba and other kinds of music, and lots of colorful costumes. The colorful and elaborately decorated floats that make up the main procession are one of the most striking aspects of the festivities.

A prize is awarded for the most impressive float, and various groups spend a lot of time designing and decorating their floats, hoping to win the prize. Carnival is so popular in Luanda that troupes drive to the capital from rural areas in trucks, bringing their floats fully or partly made. When the main procession through the streets is over, the Carnival spirit continues until late in the night.

INTERNET LINKS

http://familyfoodie.com/bolo-rei-the-king-of-christmas-desserts
Learn to bake a Portuguese bolo-rei Christmas cake here.

https://www.youtube.com/watch?v=LNwSBxOsyYY
See Carnival 2017, including parades and costumes, in action on YouTube.

COMÉRCIO INTERNO

FOOD

In urban areas, supermarkets are beginning to take off, but rural dwellers rely on the open-air market for food.

13

FOOD IS AN IMPORTANT PART OF Angolan culture, and also one of the biggest challenges facing the country today. Food is at a premium both in rural regions and the cities because of the lack of a strong agricultural industry in the years since the Angolan civil war. Farmers tend to only be able to raise enough crops to sell locally and feed their families. Therefore, in the cities, food is mostly available via import, and imported food is very expensive. Even if locally grown goods make it to the cities to be sold, the cost of transporting the items is high, making goods more expensive.

Even with these limitations plaguing the people of Angola, they manage to maintain a sense of food culture, influenced by Portuguese cuisine and deeply rooted in tradition.

"In the countryside, a box of one hundred mangos sells for around ten dollars. By the time the fruit has reached Luanda, a single mango can be five dollars."
—*Our Africa* website

Yams can frequently be found on dinner tables across Angola.

FARM STAPLES

Corn is a crop that provides a rich source of starch as well as protein. However, growing corn requires regular weeding, lots of water, and a degree of care on the part of the farmer. Postwar conditions have made growing corn more difficult, even impossible in some areas. Angolans have responded to these conditions by using land that was traditionally reserved for corn to grow millet, cassava, sweet potatoes, and sorghum. Millet is also a grain grass, but it grows faster than corn and needs less weeding. Sorghum is far more resistant to drought than corn, so it requires less watering. Corn is still an important part of the Angolan diet, however. Around 1,800 tons (1,633 metric tons) of corn are produced annually, but the demand is much higher, at around 4,500 tons (4,082 metric tons). Therefore, corn is typically imported for both human and livestock consumption.

In central and eastern Angola, people fish in streams or lagoons. Along the coast, seafood is found in more abundance. Tilapia and prawns are popular. In the past, fishing for food was regarded as a secondary activity for women, but it is now practiced by all members of the family. Along the coast, industrialized fishing is an important source of income.

In Luanda and other large towns, a limited form of agriculture has developed in the musseques. Pigs are a familiar sight in Luanda, and children are often tasked with keeping a watchful eye on this valuable source of food. Wherever possible, a family keeps a few chickens or goats, and the care of these animals often falls to the women and children. Cattle are also raised in Angola, but are more expensive to feed and need land to graze. Therefore, they are typically only found in the rural regions. Beef has become the second-largest agricultural product in Angola, after cassava. However, for poorer Angolans, meat is generally reserved for special occasions.

ANGOLA AND WHEAT

Wheat is one of the few crops that never dominated prewar Angolan agriculture, but the country is working to begin producing and milling enough of the grain to slow the need for wheat imports, especially in the form of milled flour. In 2015, Angola imported around $177 million worth of wheat flour from Turkey and Europe. Angola would save money by growing wheat and milling it in their own country, and bolster the agriculture industry. Therefore, in 2017, Angola opened a wheat flourmill in Lobito. A second mill was expected to open in Luanda.

THE MANY USES OF CASSAVA

Cassava is the most important food crop in Angola. It can be made into a variety of foods—cassava flour, bread, tapioca—and even a laundry starch. An alcoholic brew can also be made from cassava. The raw root of the cassava is poisonous—it contains a cyanide-based sugar—and must be prepared carefully before it is safe to be eaten.

Traditionally, the cassava root is processed by women. The first stage involves soaking the root and letting it dry completely. It is then pounded into flour using a mortar and pestle. Before the root is harvested, the leaves of the plant can be removed and used to make *kizaka* ("kiz-AH-ka"), an Angolan dish made from vegetables. Another popular and inexpensive meal based on cassava is *fuba* ("FOO-bar"). Untreated cassava, known as *bombom* ("BOMB-bomb"), can be bought in towns by the bucketful.

"Cassava, also known as manioc and yuca, is a staple food for about 700 million people worldwide." —Kathryn Harkup, the *Guardian*

MEALS AND MEALTIMES

Breakfast usually consists of bread or *funje* ("PHON-jee"), a porridge made from cassava. Coffee is a popular drink. Although good-quality coffee is cultivated in Angola, most people drink instant coffee imported from abroad because it is easier to get than the superior local coffee. Young children may be fed milk made from imported milk powder. Poorer families drink plain water.

Lunch is often quick and informal, especially for those who work, and may consist of bread with some cheese. The evening meal, on the other hand, is an occasion for most of the family to be together. It is often delayed until everyone has returned home.

Funje is a good multipurpose dish. It can be eaten plain or with meat or fish.

Because meat is at a premium, vegetables, beans, rice, and sometimes fish are more commonly eaten. In the towns, meals and hot drinks are prepared using a stove fueled with bottled gas. Many homes in urban areas do not have a separate kitchen; the stove is found in the living room.

Some families also have a space outside their home for a small open fire, built using wood and charcoal, which saves the expense of bottled gas. Some people earn their living by collecting firewood in the countryside and then selling it in towns. A small supply of paraffin is usually kept to sprinkle over the wood to make it easier to light. In the countryside, stoves are usually fueled by charcoal or coal, and the cooking often takes place outside the home in the open.

ABUNDANCE OF BREAD

In Luanda, one seldom needs to walk far before finding a bakery. Bread forms the basis of a quick lunch for many working people. Some people bake bread in their own homes and sell it by the roadside or in a market.

FOREIGN INFLUENCES

Because Angola was a colony of Portugal for many years, the Portuguese influence upon Angolan cuisine was subtle but pervasive, bringing the European sense of flavoring with spices and techniques of roasting and marinating to traditional Angolan foods. These influences blended with the local cuisine and produced interesting new recipes. There are some differences between the ingredients used in the cuisine of the coast of Angola and those used in European cuisine.

While Angola is a large country with many regional flavors and ethnic cultures, one of the elements these different regions have in common is the fact that Angolans like their food spicy. Angolan cuisine is varied and tasty, with local dishes based mainly on fish, cassava products, and spicy stews. The cuisine of Angola can be called a "rainbow cuisine" because it has integrated influences from India, Malaysia, and Europe. The food is a blend of many cultures in most regions of Angola.

One bag of flour makes around five hundred rolls, and a baker needs to know how many fresh rolls he hopes to sell before baking a new day's supply. In smaller towns and in the countryside, a popular type of bread is *pao burro* ("pow BORE-o"; donkey's bread), which can be baked inexpensively at home in a simple wood-burning oven.

THE HIGH COST OF FOOD

The prices of basic foods have increased rapidly over the past decade. Due to climate change, the main grain-producing area in Angola has been hit by both

Bananas are gaining momentum as an important cash crop for Angola's economy. In May 2016, Portugal imported 17 tons (15 metric tons) of bananas from Angola. It was the first shipment of fruit going from Angola to Europe in over forty years.

drought and flood in recent years. El Niño took a toll in 2015—2016, leading to drought conditions. In addition to drought, the oil crisis has led to spending cuts in agriculture and a lower value of the kwanza. Because of this, poorer families are spending a large proportion of their income on food.

Fuel is also needed to cook food. The cheapest fuels are firewood and charcoal, and the prices of these gradually increase as it becomes necessary to travel farther away from the city center to find a suitable supply.

INTERNET LINKS

http://allafrica.com/stories/201710120390.html
The *All Africa* news site has some information on current president João Lourenço's plans to cut back on food imports.

http://infoangola.blogs.sapo.ao/1194.html
Info Angola lists some of the most famous, flavorful dishes to be found in Angola.

https://www.shoprite.co.ao/en/recipes.html
The website for the Angolan Shoprite grocery chain has some well-curated recipes for several of Angola's best dishes.

CALDEIRADA DE CABRITO

Caldeirada de cabrito is a popular dish to be served on Angolan Independence Day. It traditionally uses goat meat, but this recipe has been adapted for lamb.

1 pound (0.5 kilograms) lamb meat
1 tablespoon (15 milliliters) olive oil or bacon fat
1 tablespoon (14 grams) piri piri sauce
8 ounces (0.25 kg) cooked bacon or chorizo
4 cloves garlic, whole
2 white onions, chopped
2 large tomatoes, chopped
1 bell pepper, diced
1 cup (240 mL) vegetable stock
1 pound (0.5 kg) potatoes, sliced or cut into wedges
1 teaspoon (4 g) paprika
Salt to taste

Cut goat meat into bite-sized pieces and place in a bowl or large container. Season with olive oil (or rendered fat from cooking bacon), piri piri sauce, and garlic. Let meat marinate for 3—4 hours.

Sauté meat in a pan with the marinade for 2—3 minutes.

In a large bowl, sprinkle potatoes with salt and paprika.

In a large saucepan, layer ingredients starting with onions, peppers, goat, and tomatoes. Sprinkle with chorizo or bacon and garlic cloves.

Pour vegetable stock over the prepared dish.

Cover the pan with a lid and cook for 30-35 minutes on medium heat, stirring frequently to keep it from sticking.

Serve in bowls.

ARROZ DE COCO E PAPAIA

This common dessert is delicious, but not very sweet. It can be sweetened with honey if desired.

1 cup (185 g) white or jasmine rice
½ teaspoon salt
½ teaspoon cinnamon
2 cups (473 mL) coconut milk
¼ cup (59 mL) water
2 cups (350 g) fresh chopped papaya
Honey, to taste

In medium saucepan, mix coconut milk and water.

Add rice, salt, and cinnamon.

Bring mixture to a boil over medium-high heat. Then cover and turn heat to low. Let simmer for 20 minutes, or until rice is tender.

Fluff rice with a fork, cover pan, and let stand for 10 minutes.

Mash 1 cup (175 g) of papaya. Leave the other cup chopped as before.

Add papaya to rice mixture and heat over low heat until papaya is warm.

You may add honey to sweeten this dessert, if desired.

REPUBLIC OF THE CONGO

Maiombe Forest

CABINDA

Cabinda

Noqui

Soyo · Congo

ZAIRE

UÍGE

Uíge

Ambriz

Cuango

DEMOCRATIC REPUBLIC OF THE CONGO

Dundo

Lucapa

LUNDA NORTE

Lucala

Malanje Highlands

Dande

CUANZA NORTE

LUANDA
Caxito

LUANDA

BENGO

MALANJE

Malanje

Cuanza

Cuango

Saurimo

LUNDA SUL

CUANZA SUL

Sumbe

HUAMBO

Bié Plateau

Moco ▲ (8,596 ft / 2,620 m)

BIÉ

Kuito

Lunda Divide

Luena

Zambezi

Cazombo

Lobito
Benguela · **BENGUELA**
Catumbela

Huambo

Cuanza

MOXICO

HUÍLA

Cubango

Capelongo

Menongue

Cuando

Lubango

Huíla Plateau

Cuito

Cuito

NAMIBE

Namibe

Tombua

Moçâmedes Desert

Cunene

CUNENE

Ondjiva

Ruacana Falls

KUANDO KUBANGO

Cubango

Cuito

Mavinga

ZAMBIA

Zambezi

N

NAMIBIA

● Capital city
● Major town
▲ Mountain peak

Feet	Meters
16,500	5,000
9,900	3,000
6,600	2,000
3,300	1,000
1,650	500
660	200
0	0

MAP OF ANGOLA

Ambriz, A2
Atlantic Ocean,
  A1—A5

Bengo province,
  A2—A3
Benguela, A4
Benguela province,
  A3—A4, B3—B4
Bié Plateau, B3
Bié province, B3—
  B4, C3—C4

Cabinda, A1
Cabinda province,
  A1
Capelongo, B4
Catumbela River,
  A4, B4
Caxito, A2
Cazombo, D3
Congo, Democratic
  Republic of the,
  A1, B1—B2, C1—
  C2, D1—D3
Congo River, A1
Cuando River, C4,
  D4—D5
Cuango River, B1—
  B2, C2—C3
Cuanza Norte
  province, A2, B2

Cuanza River, B3—
  B5, C5
Cuanza Sul
  province, A2, B3
Cuito, C4
Cuito River, C4—C5
Cunene province,
  A5, B4—B5
Cunene River, A5,
  B4—B5

Dande River, A2,
  B2
Dundo, C2

Huambo, B4
Huambo province,
  B3—B4
Huíla Plateau, B5
Huíla province,
  A4—A5, B4—B5

Kuando Kubango
  province, B4—
  B5, C4—C5, D5
Kuito, B3

Lobito, A3
Luanda, A2
Luanda province,
  A2
Lubango, A4
Lucala River, B2

Lucapa, C2
Luena, C3
Lunda Divide, B3—
  B4, C3—C4
Lunda Norte
  province, B2, C2,
  D2
Lunda Sul province,
  C2—C5, D2—D3

Maiombe Forest,
  A1
Malanje, B2
Malanje Highlands,
  B2—B3, C3
Malanje province,
  B2—B3, C3
Mavinga, C5
Menongue, B4
Moçâmedes Desert,
  A5
Moco (mountain),
  B3—B4
Moxico province,
  C3—C5, D3—D5

Namibe, A4
Namibe province,
  A4—A5
Namibia, A5, B5,
  C5, D5
Noqui, A1

Ondjiva, B5

Republic of the
  Congo, A1, B1
Ruacana Falls, A5,
  B5

Saurimo, C3
Soyo, A1
Sumbe, A3

Tombua, A5

Uíge, A2
Uíge province, A1—
  A2, B1—B2

Zaire province,
  A1—A2, B1
Zambezi River,
  D3—D5
Zambia, D3—D5

133

ECONOMIC ANGOLA

Agriculture
- Bananas
- Sugarcane
- Coffee
- Corn
- Tobacco
- Sisal
- Cotton

Natural Resources
- Copper
- Diamonds
- Gold
- Granite
- Hydroelectricity
- Iron
- Petroleum
- Phosphate
- Quartz
- Uranium

Services
- Airports
- Tourism
- Ports

ABOUT THE ECONOMY

OVERVIEW

Angola's high growth rate is driven by its oil sector, which makes up about 50 percent of the country's GDP. Increased oil production supported growth averaging more than 17 percent per year from 2004 to 2008, but lower oil prices led to the GDP falling 0.7 percent in 2016. A postwar reconstruction boom and resettlement of displaced persons has also led to high growth rates in construction and a slow recovery to the agriculture industry. Much of the country's infrastructure is still damaged or undeveloped due to the twenty-seven-year-long civil war, and remnants of the conflict, such as widespread land mines, still mar the countryside. Subsistence agriculture provides the main livelihood for 85 percent of the people, but half of the country's food must still be imported. In 2005, the government started using a $2 billion line of credit, now around $20 billion, from China to rebuild Angola's public infrastructure, and several large-scale projects have been undertaken since then, including dams for producing hydroelectricity, railways, and the new airport in Luanda.

GROSS DOMESTIC PRODUCT (GDP)
US $192 billion (2017 estimate)

GDP GROWTH
1.5 percent (2017 estimate)

CURRENCY
Kwanza
US $1 = 216.85 kwanzas (April 2018)

WORKFORCE
12.51 million (2017 estimate)

UNEMPLOYMENT RATE
6.6 percent (2016 estimate)

INFLATION
30.9 percent (2017 estimate)

EXTERNAL DEBT
$27.34 billion (December 31, 2017, estimate)

MAJOR EXPORTS
Crude oil, diamonds, refined petroleum products, coffee, sisal, fish and fish products, timber, cotton

MAJOR IMPORTS
Machinery and electrical equipment, vehicles and spare parts, medicines, food

MAIN TRADE PARTNERS
China, India, United States, South Africa

NATURAL RESOURCES
Petroleum, diamonds, iron ore, phosphates, copper, feldspar, gold

AGRICULTURAL PRODUCTS
Bananas, sugarcane, coffee, sisal, corn, cotton, cassava (tapioca), tobacco, vegetables, plantains, livestock

CULTURAL ANGOLA

M'banza-Kongo
M'banza-Kongo is the capital of Zaire province. It sits on top of an impressive flat-topped mountain and is also known for the ruins of its sixteenth-century cathedral, which many Angolans claim is the oldest church in sub-Saharan Africa.

Luanda
Luanda, the capital of Angola, retains its heritage as a Portuguese colonial city, and there are several buildings of historical significance, such as the Museum of Armed Forces. Luanda is also adjacent to a beautiful bay.

Mussulo Peninsula
Mussulo Peninsula is an extension of land located in the south of Luanda famous for its natural beauty. One can try aquatic sports and sample some of the local food, or simply relax under the numerous palm trees.

Quiçama National Park
Quiçama is Angola's most accessible and well-stocked wildlife park. This huge swath of coastal savanna punctuated by gnarly baobab trees is home to elephants, water buffalo, indigenous palanca antelopes, and a precarious population of nesting sea turtles.

Benguela-Lobito Railway
Rattling and bumping through Benguela's rural hodgepodge is a unique and unforgettable Angolan experience. The railway line roughly follows old trade routes between the ancient trading center of Benguela and its hinterland of the Bié plateau.

Namibe
This province is the land of the tumboa (*Welwitschia mirabilis*), a carnivorous desert plant that resembles a giant octopus. The Namib Desert offers excellent hunting, and Namibe is one of the main fishing centers in Angola.

Calandula Falls
Located in the large central Angolan province of Malanje, the Calandula Falls in the Lucala River tumbles more than 328 feet (100 m) down and is Africa's second-largest waterfall after Victoria Falls. Work is being done to construct a nearby hotel to increase tourism to the region.

Iona National Park
Iona National Park is the largest natural game reserve in the country. Illegal poaching and the destruction of infrastructure have caused considerable damage to the once rich park. However, work is being done to bring back the "Big Five" animals: springbok (gazelle), kudu (antelope), ostrich, oryx (antelope), and the cheetah. The park is also known for unique flora and incredible rock formations.

Lubango
Lubango is the capital of the province of Huíla. It is surrounded by mountains, and one of them has a statue of Jesus Christ with a fantastic view of the city. Lubango also provides access to the beautiful beaches of Namibe.

Cameia National Park
There is flora and fauna in Cameia National Park that cannot be found anywhere else in Angola. Two lakes lie outside the park boundaries, and both have extensive reed beds and grassy swamps that are rich in aquatic birds.

ABOUT THE CULTURE

OFFICIAL NAME
Republic of Angola

CAPITAL
Luanda

POPULATION
29,310,273 million (2017 estimate)

MAIN CITIES
Cabinda, Huambo, Lobito, Benguela

LANGUAGES
Portuguese (official), Umbundu, Kikongo, Kimbundu, Chokwe, Nhaneca, Nganguela, Ibinda, Kwanhama, Muhumbi, Luvale

AREA
481,354 square miles (1,246,700 square kilometers)

NATIONAL FLAG
Two equal horizontal stripes of red and black, with a five-pointed star, half a cogwheel, and a machete superimposed in the center in gold

HIGHEST POINT
Mount Moco (8,596 feet/2,620 m)

ETHNIC GROUPS
Ovimbundu, 37 percent; Kimbundu, 25 percent; Bakongo, 13 percent; mestico (mixed European and native African), 2 percent; European, 1 percent; other, 22 percent

MAIN RELIGIONS
Roman Catholic, 41.1 percent; Protestant, 38.1 percent; other, 8.6 percent; none, 12.3 percent (2014 estimate)

LAND USE
Agricultural land, 47.5 percent; forest, 46.5 percent; other, 6 percent (2014 estimate)

RIVERS
Cuanza, Congo, and Cunene

CLIMATE
Semiarid in south and along coast; north has cool, dry season (May—October) and hot, rainy season (November—April)

PROVINCES
Bengo, Benguela, Bié, Cabinda, Cuanza Norte, Cuanza Sul, Cunene, Huambo, Huíla, Kuando Kubango, Luanda, Lunda Norte, Lunda Sul, Malanje, Moxico, Namibe, Uíge, Zaire

BIRTHRATE
44.2 births per 1,000 (2017 estimate)

DEATH RATE
9.2 deaths per 1,000 (2017 estimate)

TIMELINE

IN ANGOLA	IN THE WORLD
	116–117 CE The Roman Empire reaches its greatest extent, under Emperor Trajan (98–117 CE).
1300 The Kongo Kingdom consolidates in the north.	**1206–1368** Genghis Khan unifies the Mongols and starts conquest of the world. At its height, the Mongol Empire under Kublai Khan stretches from China to Persia and parts of Europe and Russia.
1483 The Portuguese arrive.	
	1530 The beginning of transatlantic slave trade organized by the Portuguese in Africa.
1575 The Portuguese found Luanda.	**1789–1799** The French Revolution
1836 Slave trade is officially abolished.	**1869** The Suez Canal is opened.
1885–1930 Portugal consolidates colonial control over Angola.	**1914** World War I begins.
	1939 World War II begins.
	1945 The United States drops atomic bombs on Hiroshima and Nagasaki. World War II ends.
1956 The early beginnings of the socialist guerrilla independence movement, the Popular Movement for the Liberation of Angola (MPLA).	
1961 The guerrilla war begins.	
1974 Revolution in Portugal; colonial empire collapses.	
1975 Angola gains independence, but a power struggle ensues between the MPLA and the FNLA plus UNITA.	**1975** The Vietnam War ends.
1979 MPLA leader Agostinho Neto dies. José Eduardo dos Santos takes over as president.	
1989 Dos Santos and UNITA leader Jonas Savimbi agree to a cease-fire. It collapses soon afterward, and guerrilla activity resumes.	

IN ANGOLA	IN THE WORLD
1991	**1991**
Dos Santos and Savimbi sign peace deal that results in a new multiparty constitution.	Breakup of the Soviet Union
1992	
Presidential and parliamentary elections are certified by United Nations monitors as generally free and fair. Dos Santos wins more votes than Savimbi, who rejects the results and resumes guerrilla war.	
1994	
The Angolan government and UNITA sign the Lusaka Protocol peace accord.	
1996	
Dos Santos and Savimbi agree to form a unity government and join forces into a national army.	
1997	**1997**
Unified government is inaugurated, with Savimbi declining a post in the unity government. Tension mounts, with few UNITA troops having integrated into the army.	Hong Kong is returned to China.
1998	
Full-scale fighting resumes.	**2001**
2002	Terrorists crash planes into New York,
Savimbi is killed by government troops. The government and UNITA sign a cease-fire.	Washington, DC, and Pennsylvania.
2008	**2008**
President Dos Santos's governing MPLA party scores a landslide victory in the first parliamentary elections in sixteen years.	The first black president of the United States, Barack Obama, is elected.
2015	
Angola celebrates its fortieth anniversary as an independent nation.	
2016	**2016**
Yellow fever epidemic breaks out in DRC and Angola.	Donald Trump wins the US presidential election.
2017	**2017**
João Lourenço is elected president, the first new president since 1979.	Rohingya Muslims flee Myanmar following attacks that kill thousands.
2018	**2018**
Angola faces a health crisis due to drug shortages.	Winter Olympics in PyeongChang, South Korea

GLOSSARY

assimilado (ass-sim-ill-AD-o)
Special status given to Angolans who adopted the Portuguese way of life during colonial rule.

bark cloth
A soft, thick, slightly textured fabric so named because it has a rough surface like that of tree bark.

biome
A large community of plants and animals occupying a distinct region.

bombom (BOMB-bomb)
Untreated cassava.

caderneta (KAD-er-ne-ta)
Special identity cards carried to Angolans during Portuguese colonial rule.

desertification
A process by which land becomes a desert region because of drought or deforestation.

exclave
An area of land that is part of another country but separated physically from that country.

gouache
Method of painting that uses opaque pigments ground in water and mixed with a glue-like substance.

hydroelectric
The generation of electricity using flowing water.

intertropical
Occurring between the Tropic of Cancer and the Tropic of Capricorn.

kimbanda (kim-BAN-da)
Diviner or witch doctor.

kimberlites
Shafts of volcanic rock known for containing diamonds.

komba (KUM-ba)
Funeral.

masemba (MASS-m-ba)
A type of dance popular in Luanda where a pair of dancers thrust their stomachs toward one another.

musseque (MUS-seek)
Shantytown.

pao burro (pow BORE-o)
Bread popular in smaller towns and in the countryside.

standpipe
A vertical pipe into which water is pumped.

tariff
A tax paid on certain imports and exports.

tumboa
A plant species endemic to Angola that grows in dry regions.

FOR FURTHER INFORMATION

BOOKS

Birmingham, David. *A Short History of Modern Angola*. New York: Oxford University Press, 2016.

Cleveland, Todd. *Diamonds in the Rough: Corporate Paternalism and African Professionalism on the Mines of Colonial Angola, 1917—1975*. Athens, OH: Ohio University Press, 2015.

Gleijeses, Piero. *Visions of Freedom: Havana, Washington, Pretoria, and the Struggle for Southern Africa, 1976—1991*. Chapel Hill, NC: University of North Carolina Press, 2013.

Heywood, Linda M. *Njinga of Angola: Africa's Warrior Queen*. Cambridge, MA: Harvard University Press, 2017.

Orenstein, Ronald. *Ivory, Horn and Blood: Behind the Elephant and Rhinoceros Poaching Crisis*. Richmond Hill, ON, Canada: Firefly Books, 2013.

Scholz, Leopold. *The Battle of Cuito Cuanavale: Cold War Angolan Finale, 1987—1988*. Solihull, UK: Helion & Co., 2016.

Soares de Oliveira, Ricardo. *Magnificent and Beggar Land: Angola Since the Civil War*. New York: Oxford University Press, 2015.

Stuart, Chris, and Mathilde Stuart. *Stuarts' Field Guide to Mammals of Southern Africa: Including Angola, Zambia & Malawi*. Cape Town, South Africa: Struik Nature, 2015.

WEBSITES

Al Jazeera: Angola, https://www.aljazeera.com/topics/country/angola.html

CIA World Factbook: Angola, https://www.cia.gov/library/publications/the-world-factbook/geos/ao.html

The *Guardian*: Angola, https://www.theguardian.com/world/angola

Welcome to Angola website, http://www.welcometoangola.co.ao

FILMS

Gamboa, Zézé. *The Hero*. David and Golias, DVD, 2004.

MUSIC

Kizomba de Angola, Vol. 2, Stick Music, 2012

Marcas de Angola: Angolan Sound Experience, Semba Comunicação, 2015.

Music of Angola, Manuel Benedito Diogo, ARC, 2015.

BIBLIOGRAPHY

BOOKS

Alden, Chris. *China in Africa: Partner, Competitor or Hegemon?* African Arguments. London, UK: Zed Books, 2007.

Berkeley, Bill. *The Graves Are Not Yet Full: Race, Tribe, and Power in the Heart of Africa.* New York, Basic Books, 2001.

Chabal, Patrick, et al. *A History of Postcolonial Lusophone Africa.* Bloomington: Indiana University Press, 2002.

Clapham, Christopher. *Africa and the International System: The Politics of State Survival.* Cambridge Studies in International Relations. Cape Town, South Africa: Cambridge University Press, 2008.

Ghazvinian, John. *Untapped: The Scramble for Africa's Oil.* Orlando: Harvest Books, 2008.

James, W. Martin, III. *A Political History of the Civil War in Angola, 1974—1990.* Abingdon, UK: Routledge, 2011.

Maier, Karl. *Angola: Promises and Lies.* London, UK: Serif Publishing, 1996.

McKissack, Patricia. *Nzingha: Warrior Queen of Matamba, Angola, Africa, 1595.* The Royal Diaries. New York: Scholastic Inc., 2000.

Moorhouse, Karin, and Wei Cheng. *No One Can Stop the Rain: A Chronicle of Two Foreign Aid Workers During the Angolan Civil War.* London, UK: Insomniac Press, 2000.

Moorman, Marissa J. *Intonations: A Social History of Music and Nation in Luanda, Angola, from 1945 to Recent Times.* Athens, OH: Ohio University Press, 2008.

Schubert, Jon. *Working the System: A Political Ethnography of the New Angola.* Ithaca, NY: Cornell University Press, 2017.

Weigert, Stephen L. *Angola: A Modern Military History, 1961-2002.* New York: Palgrave Macmillan, 2011.

INDEX

INDEX

THE ILLUSTRATED NATURAL HISTORY

Scientific Consultants to the Serie

OF CANADA The Arctic Coast DOUGLAS WILKINSON

Earth Science Consultant WALTER TOVELL, Curator, Department of Geology, Royal Ontario Museum. *Life Science Consultant* J. MURRAY SPEIRS, Department of Zoology, University of Toronto

Publisher: Jack McClelland
Managing Editor: Michael Worek
Art Director: Peter Moulding
Visual Editor: Bill Brooks

Editorial Consultant: Pierre Berton

THE ARCTIC COAST

Art Director: Peter Moulding
Artists: Vlasta van Kampen
Gordon McLean/Huntley Brown
Gus Fantuz/Jerry Kozoriz/Roy Irwin

Page 1: *A solitary bull walrus.*
Pages 2/3: *Spear-fishing in the glow of the midnight sun near Pelly Bay.*
Pages 4/5: *Glacial majesty on Axel Heiberg Island.*

Contents

Prologue

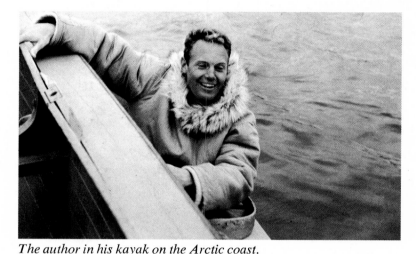

The author in his kayak on the Arctic coast.

A WORLD FOR DREAMERS

The Arctic coast of Canada is a world for dreamers, a land few Canadians have ever seen or will ever see, a region about which we have come to know much but, as yet, understand little.

Natural history is a contemporary record of events that have occurred in the earth's past as seen through the probing, but biased, eye of literate man. Biased for many reasons; with few exceptions man is a creature of the mid-latitudes of earth. Throughout his long evolution he has lived in a world of regular rhythms—from the beginning of time he has watched the sun rise above the horizon in the east and set again in the west; night has followed day, followed by night again in endless sequence; season has followed season in uninterrupted pattern of cold and warm, or wet and dry. Beneath his feet man has usually felt soft soil supporting an abundant growth of grasses, flowers, trees, and an endless variety of mammalian life. Most important of all, in his mid-latitude world, man has always viewed the normal state of H_2O, as liquid water and not as crystalline ice.

Can there then be any wonder that modern man is biased in his view of his Arctic regions—a land where the darkness of the cold winter night can last for two months or more, where the summer day can be a full five months long while the sun circles endlessly around the horizon to north and south each cloudless day, a land where ice and cold covering land, lake and sea is the normal condition for at least nine months of every year? Can there be any wonder that man has come to regard the cold climate of the Arctic coast as the sign of a disordered land, and the basic condition of cold as one of his greatest enemies?

Yet on the Arctic coast of Canada there are many areas where, during July and August, temperatures rise into the mid-sixties; where flowers bloom in clusters in the valleys and fields of Arctic cotton grass flutter and dance in the wind; where birds nest and insects buzz; where water is everywhere on the surface of the rolling land. But this brief period of summer warmth only serves to heighten the fact that, in the Arctic, winter is the main season of the year and the ice is never far away.

Yet in terms of extremes of cold, the Arctic coast must take second place to areas further south. The record low for the Arctic coast region is −63° Fahrenheit, a figure often equalled by points in northern Ontario and in the northern United States. The record low temperature for North America is −81.4° Fahrenheit, recorded in the sub-Arctic interior of the Yukon District, over 500 miles south of the Arctic coast. As well as not being the coldest place on earth the Arctic coast region doesn't have much snow; it is a desert area with a combined rain and snowfall averaging slightly under ten inches per year, about the same as that of the Sahara Desert in Africa. Although the winter snowfall in the Arctic piles into drifts that can be fifteen to twenty feet deep, the snow cover over most of the land amounts to only a few inches, a foot or so at best, per year. All winter long, on the windswept hilltops there is often no snow at all.

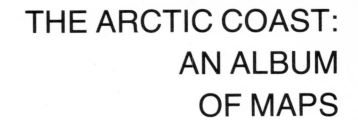

THE ARCTIC COAST:
AN ALBUM
OF MAPS

The full colour maps on the following pages of this album were especially commissioned for the series to illustrate the most important aspects of the natural history of the Arctic Coast region.

The photograph on the next two pages shows the area as seen from a satellite high above Greenland, facing westward.

The top of the world

Four times, some geologists say five, glacial ice has crept out of the far north to inundate northern North America, Europe and much of Asia. Today we are still emerging from the last of these glacial assaults, the ice of which melted away from southern Ontario a mere ten thousand years ago, and which still covers sections of the Arctic coast region. Is the Arctic coast getting warmer or colder? Is the Arctic Ocean on the way to becoming free of ice, or will the ice begin to grow again to bury all the coast region under an icy mantle? Scientists are not sure and recent history provides only meagre clues. Pack ice issuing from the Arctic Ocean is dropping slightly in quantity; the southern limit of permafrost in Russia is slowly creeping north. But the Arctic coast is still a cold, cold land and will likely remain this way for some time to come.

Physiographic zones

- Innuition region (mainly highlands)
- Lowlands and plateaux
- Canadian shield
- Arctic mountains
- Interior plains
- Hudson Bay lowlands

Vegetation

- Glaciers
- Rock desert
- Stony sedge, moss, lichen, tundra
- Dwarf shrub, sedge, moss, lichen, heath
- Subarctic forest, tundra

Sea ice and climatic zones

- Permanent ice
- Pack ice, August minimum
- Pack ice, Feb/Mar minimum
- Ice cap zone
- Tundra zone
- Subarctic zone
- Mean annual number of days with a minimum temperature of 0°F or lower
- Permafrost, southern limit of continuous permafrost zone

60°W

140°W

C A N A D A

Living and breeding in a far northern land

Note: In this illustration, the breeding ranges of birds are shown, along with the habitats of mammals.

Ringed seals are found everywhere along the Arctic coast, but rarely in open waters of big seas.

Rock ptarmigans live everywhere on the tundra and mountains, from lower Hudson Bay to Ellesmere Island.

Whistling swans are inhabitants of the lower Arctic in summer, but a few move far north to Baffin Island.

Polar Bears are found east to west, north to south; wherever there are ringed seals, there are polar bears.

Barren ground caribou, one of the very few mammals to migrate over great distances, live in open tundra.

Snowy owls are often seen in the south of Canada when food is scarce in their normal range of the north.

Red-throated loons, a summer only visitor, will nest as far north as there is land in the Arctic islands.

Musk ox are tundra dwellers found on many of the Arctic islands, and on the mainland at Thelon Sanctuary.

Arctic foxes live everywhere north of the tree line, on the treeless land in summer, wintering on the ice.

Gyrfalcons, during their white phase, can live in the Arctic all winter. Preys on birds and rodents.

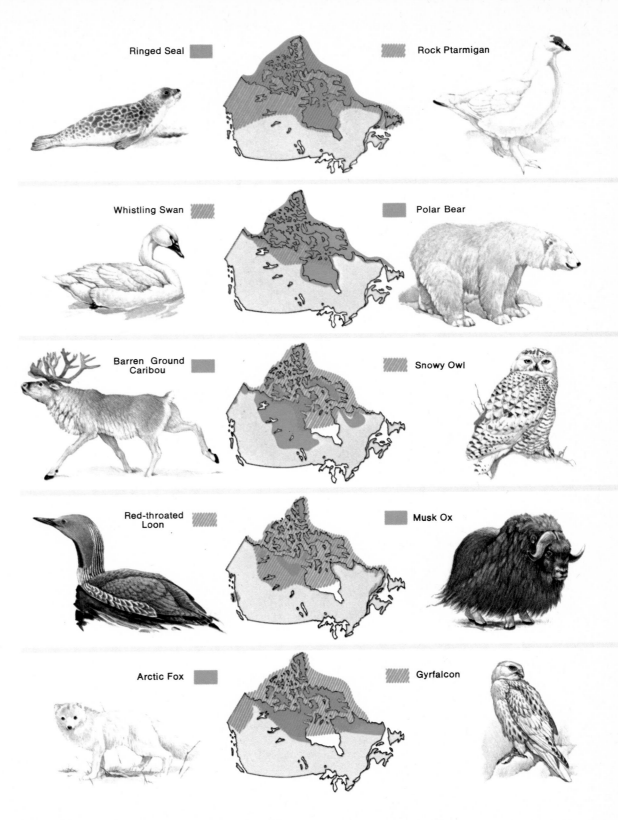

Ringed Seal • Rock Ptarmigan • Whistling Swan • Polar Bear • Barren Ground Caribou • Snowy Owl • Red-throated Loon • Musk Ox • Arctic Fox • Gyrfalcon

Take a train to the Arctic coast

Non-commercial forest

Forest   Tundra

Rankin Inlet •

Churchill •

• Moosonee

Churchill to Rankin Inlet

200 MILES

Seal River

CHURCHILL •

Churchill River

Churchill River

White Whale

Hudson Bay

Railway

River

Port Nelson •

Nelson

Winnipeg / Churchill

River

Walrus

MANITOBA

Provincial Boundary

ONTARIO

Snow Goose

Polar Bear

Cape Henrietta Maria

Polar Bear Provincial Park (shaded)

Ptarmigan

Ekwan River

Attawapiskat River

Float plane to Polar Bear Park from Moosonee

Trout

River

James Bay

Caribou

Sturgeon

Canada Goose

Alba

MOOSONEE •

• Fort Rupert

• Moose Factory

Tidewater Provincial Park

ONTARIO

Moose River

Cochrane / Moosonee Railway

QUEBEC

Camera Stops (along railway to Cochrane/Moosonee)

Brown Bear

Churchill, our only Arctic seaport

Would you like to stand on the stone ramparts of Fort Prince of Wales at the very spot from which Samuel Hearne set out on his epic walk across the northern barrens to become the first European to reach the northern Arctic coast? Then travel by rail, north from Winnipeg to Churchill on Hudson Bay. C.N.R. runs summer excursion trains to Canada's only Arctic seaport.

Moosonee via the Polar Bear Express

Moosonee is not a true Arctic coast community, but you can camp near Arctic tidewaters and find many examples of Arctic flora and fauna in a nearby provincial park. An interesting visit may be paid to the museum which houses artifacts telling of the fur-trading history of the region. A short plane trip will take you to the vast Polar Bear Park, where Arctic wildlife roams free.

PART ONE / THE REGION

1 THE LOWLAND ARCTIC

Because it spreads across such a huge area of northern North America it will be apparent that the Arctic coast region is not one land, but several. In the northeast it is a land of high mountains, much of it covered by glacial ice. On the west coast of Hudson Bay it is a land so low that each incoming tide inundates miles of soggy mud and sand. On the north central coast it is a land of low rock hills; in the northwest it is a delta area; in the northwest islands it is a low, rolling land of mud and shale, and broken rock hills that, in very few places, rise more than a thousand feet above the level of the sea. Based on physiography the Arctic coast can be divided into a number of provinces. However, based on how it looks to the human eye and mind, the Arctic coast can be split into two main divisions—the lowlands, plains and plateaux Arctic; and the mountains and ice cap Arctic.

The lowland, plains and plateaux Arctic, hereafter called the lowland Arctic, makes up the bulk of the Arctic coast region –all the mainland Arctic coast, all the lower Arctic islands with the exception of the northeast coast of Baffin and Bylot Islands, all the central and western high Arctic islands, excluding only eastern Devon Island, Axel Heiberg Island and Ellesmere Island. Within this huge lowland area all land is generally less than two thousand feet above sea level; everywhere the horizon is gently rolling or flat, broken only by the occasional rocky headland or bluff. It is a horizontal landscape, its skyline unbroken by the sharp outline of high mountains, or by steep cliff faces rising up into the sky. Everywhere in the lowland Arctic there is a curious "sameness" to the landscape, brought about by three main factors: the smooth, rounded surfaces of the land as a result of scouring and/or deposition by massive glacial ice; the complete absence of trees or other vertical vegetation which would add variety in line, colour and perspective; the winter-long blanket of snow and ice that fills in the hollows of an already low, rounded landscape in a uniform white cover for most of the year. To these three factors can be added a fourth, one that affects all land areas on the Arctic coast—the absence of the works of modern man. On the Arctic coast there are no farms with their linear pattern of buildings and fences, no towns and cities with their vertical skylines, no systems of roads and railroads to pattern the land, almost no radio and television antennae, no power transmission lines to stand out against the sky.

In summer this lowland Arctic is a land of monotones with only the occasional splash of colour to relieve the generally brown or grey landscape—the white of Arctic cotton grass, the yellow of Arctic poppies, the mauve of purple saxifrage, the orange of lichens on the rocks, the yellow-green of moss in the valleys. Here and there along the edges of the sea are patches of green, lush grass to mark the sites of Eskimo camps of old where extra nitrogen has enriched the local soil. Great stretches of the lowland are bare rock, scraped clean and deeply grooved by glacial ice; other sectors are rugged hills of frost-shattered rock, generally dull brown or grey-blue in colour. Snaking across the landscape of the mainland Arctic west of Hudson Bay are the bright, bold outlines of sand and gravel eskers, materials deposited by sub-glacial streams during the waning days of the glacier lobes. Around the eskers hundreds of lakes fill every glacier-carved hollow in the rocky land; over fifty per cent of this area is under water in the summer. Everywhere the strand lines of former marine beaches rim the hills and the coasts with their low ridges of rounded stones and pebbles.

Underfoot the surface of the lowland Arctic presents one constant quality; it is almost all bad for walking. Pebbles, stones, boulders and sharp shale litter the surface of the ridges and the plateaux. The smooth, rounded stones of the raised beaches slip and roll underfoot. In the valleys the stream beds are a confused jumble of water-worn stones; the slopes dotted with close packed hummocks of frozen earth jutting up from swampy soil above the permafrost lid on the land. In many areas the tops of the rugged, rock hills are dotted with boulders of all sizes left behind by the retreat of the glacial ice. Everywhere, on swampy plain or rocky plateau, the lowland Arctic stretches out endlessly, flowing off to meet distant horizons, a vast empty land looking today much as it has looked for the past thousand years, as it will look far into the future.

In winter two new factors are added to the landscape of the lowland Arctic—snow and ice. Everywhere in the Arctic snow and ice must be considered as landforms for they will be the materials most underfoot during the greater portion of each year.

In the lowland Arctic snow and ice help to further smooth out an already horizontal landscape; the meagre snowfall sweeps clear of the hilltops and ridges to pile up in drifts in the hollows and valleys. In the rugged areas of bare rock hills the hilltops stand out against the white snow cover but in the plains country land, lake and sea blend into one surface of endless white. In the very flat lowlands of Foxe Basin or northeastern King William Island it is often necessary to dig down through the snow to find out if the surface beneath is land or sea ice. There is nothing to break the smooth curve of the distant horizon, nothing to distinguish a peninsula of land from the sea. In regions of great fluctuations in tidal flow, a rim of broken ice will mark the edge of the sea but, wherever the tide range is small, snow-covered land blends into snow-covered sea.

The snow that covers the Arctic lowland is dry and hard; only rarely does it fall free from the sky, usually it is whipped along by the winter winds, piling up into drifts, creating landscape in much the same manner as the wind-blown sand of the desert. Unlike grains of sand, snow granules pack tightly together in the extreme cold and, if allowed to come to rest in a hollow or in the lee of an obstruction, they quickly come to resist further attempts by the wind to remove them. Once formed, snowdrifts tend to remain in one place. However, the surface of the hard packed drifts can be eroded by the abrasive action of the hard snow granules of future blizzards; the upper surface of the drifts is carved into a myriad of delicately sculptured shapes and forms. In areas where the wind blows constantly from a single direction the resulting drift pattern on the snow surface will be an unending series of low, fluted ridges of hard-packed snow that run for miles across the tundra, a built-in winter compass for the overland traveller in this featureless land.

The hard-packed snow retains almost no indented footprint

The retreat of the glacial ice has exposed a mass of small stones over most of the lowland Arctic making walking difficult.

Once formed, snowdrifts tend to remain in one place, but the erosive action of hard snow granules can alter their shape.

to mark the path of man or beast. But it can retain an upraised mark of their passing. If a fox, or a bear, or a man walks over Arctic snow that has begun to pack but is not yet hard, the weight will press the snow under foot or paw more firmly in place than the snow all around. Wind blown granules of hard snow cut away the less firmly packed snow and leave a replica of the foot or paw raised in bold relief a few inches, often as much as a foot, above the level of the surrounding snow. This factor of snow compaction is used to advantage in the construction of Arctic airstrips and roads; snow is not ploughed as this would produce side hummocks and induce drifting; instead the snow is packed down by weighted rollers, if possible during the time when the wind is blowing hard. The wind then erodes the unpacked snow and leaves a road or runway of hard, compacted

snow that is raised above the level of the snow all around. The snow of future blizzards will blow right across it with a minimum of lateral drifting.

There are winter days in the lowland Arctic when the air is calm and clear, when the pale blue of the sky meets the gentle flow of the white horizon in a sharp line; when the only sound in the land is the sharp, rippling crack of the lake ice as it heaves and splits in the intense cold. Then the lowland Arctic is a vast, near-empty land of space, and peace. But there are far more days when the air is not calm and clear, when bitter winds howl down out of the northwest, carrying with them millions upon millions of tiny granules of hard Arctic snow, building into the infamous ground-drift of the Arctic tundra lands.

Ground-drift is a miles wide mass of whirling snow granules

Winds blowing at ten miles per hour or greater pick up snow from the ground and can reduce visibility to a few feet.

that can fill the air up to fifty feet above the surface of the land. Above the ground-drift the sky is often bright blue; from an aircraft flying at 5000 feet the snow-covered landscape below is clearly visible. But on the ground the whirling snow reduces visibility to as little as a few feet in every direction; the sun is merely an area of brightness in the whirling snow mass overhead. Arctic wind begins to pick up snow when it reaches a speed of about ten miles per hour, causing a light ground-drift condition. When the wind blows about twenty miles per hour the ground-drift will be moderate, horizontal visibility will be cut to a maximum of a quarter to half a mile. At thirty miles per hour the ground-drift will be severe, visibility generally less than one hundred feet; at forty miles per hour it will be difficult to see at all due to the effect of hard snow granules hitting the eyes.

Arctic ground-drift is often confused with white-out, another tundra phenomenon. Ground-drift is the result of blowing snow; white-out occurs in air free of snow particles, but under sky and surface conditions that cause a loss of depth of perception. White-out occurs most often when a low overcast of light clouds occurs above a uniformly snow-covered land surface, or sea ice surface, or glacial ice surface. Under such a condition the eye can see, but it cannot see anything; or if it can see objects, it is unable to see them in perspective. In a white-out it is not unusual for a person to walk right off a ten-foot high snowbank without ever seeing the drop, or to stumble over foot-high ridges of hard snow that cannot be seen. In a white-out there are no shadows, no relief, no perspective; sky and snow blend into one continuous, unending, all-encompassing entity. A foot diameter rock on a small mound fifty feet away can be mistaken for a huge boulder on a high hilltop a mile away, and vice versa. A white-out condition can produce snow-blindness very quickly; with a bright sun the tendency is to shutter the eye to protect it but in a white-out the eye opens wide as it strains to see.

2 THE MOUNTAIN ARCTIC

In direct contrast to the horizontal landscape of the lowland Arctic is the terrain of the mountain and ice cap Arctic. This is the classic Arctic of mountain, snowfield, glacier and iceberg. Over much of the land areas of the eastern and far north-eastern islands the landscape is vertical, and horizons are angular. Massive cliffs of red, brown and grey-blue rock rise sheer out of ice-clogged waters on the sea or loom silent and still against the blue-black, star-spangled sky of the long Arctic night. Coastlines in the mountain Arctic are indented by steep-sided fiords that twist and turn far into the land, often terminating in massive walls of glacial ice, the tips of long glacial tongues flowing down from the inland ice caps high above. Many of the Canadian Arctic coast fiords are immense; Admiralty Inlet cutting deep into north Baffin Island is the longest fiord in the world. It is very deep, just how deep is not known, but so deep that at one point about midway down the Inlet there is a huge patch of open water that remains ice free the year round, kept that way in the minus fifty below winter weather by the warm water welling up from the bottom far below.

In summer this mountain Arctic is often obscured by fog rising from the open water of the leads in the floating pack ice or drifting down from the icy slopes of the upper snowfields. Fog can cling to the mountainsides for days clamping a grey lid on the land, robbing it of most of its colour and vitality. But when the fog clears and the land and sea and ice stand out in bold relief, then the mountain Arctic coasts come to life. The white ice of the glaciers glistens and sparkles in the sun, each rock and snow cornice stands out hard against the blue of the sky. The colours of the rock—red, brown, grey-blue, sometimes yellow and orange where the lichens grow—glow with an intensity quite unusual in a land of monotones. The waters of the open sea reflect the blue of the sunny sky; on cloudy days the surface of the sea turns green. Every crevasse in every floating iceberg transmits pale blue or green as the bright sunlight shines through the ice, transforming it into opaque sheets of colour with only an upper surface of gleaming white.

In the mountain Arctic there is not usually the steady, strong wind that is so characteristic of the tundra. But cyclonic

A well-developed drumlin pattern is clearly distinguishable against the horizontal landscape of this section of southern Victoria Island.

winds from off the many ice caps can howl over the mountain valleys and far out over the sea ice with demonic fury. Such areas of high wind are very local, an important point to remember when travelling on the ground in a mountain Arctic region; no matter how bad the wind is, continue to move, for usually it will be only a short distance through to calm conditions again. But travel with caution for the extremely high winds off the glaciers and ice caps will blow dogs off their feet, if they get onto bare ice, to say nothing of the traveller himself. And if there is open water nearby be extra careful; a sudden gust of very strong wind and you could easily be blown bodily into the ice-cold sea.

In midwinter the Arctic coast region is a dim world, for long periods lighted only by the crisp white glow of moonlight reflected from millions of stars that twinkle and dance in the blue-black void above. In the far north there is no sunlight for weeks on end, in the far south it shines only for a few hours each day. Across the night skies of the Arctic coast, especially in the middle Arctic between latitudes 60° and 75° N. the ghostly light of the *aurora borealis* flickers and dances; the northern lights that have terrified and mystified peoples of the world since the earliest days of man. Today we know they are simply a neon-like glow induced in the upper air of the earth's atmosphere by streams of charged particles from eruptions on the surface of the distant sun, making the thin air glow in patterns of shifting, weaving bands of light, sometimes coloured but usually clear white. Science tells us that no sound comes from these heavenly displays. But the words of the scientist fall on deaf ears of trapper and hunter of the far north, who, standing alone on a winter night, gazing upward in awe as the brilliant bands of cold fire weave their ghostly patterns across the vast, empty universe of space above, listen to the unearthly whispering of their faint message to the earth below.

In the far north regions of the Arctic coast it is late winter before light begins to return to the land. At first it comes as only a slight lightening of the southern sky about the hour of noon each day. Gradually the light period grows longer, and longer; the rays of the invisible sun, riding low beneath the horizon, send shafts of colour lancing across the pale blue and grey of the southern sky. For days on end sunrise is sunset, but each day it lasts a little longer, each day it gets a little brighter, each day the colours grow more vivid and intense. One day there is a brilliant corona of yellowish light on the horizon to the south, but it comes to nothing, and darkness falls again. It returns the next day, and the next, growing stronger until one day, at roughly the hour of noon, the huge, fiery red rim of the distant sun peeks above the hills to the south, rests there for a few minutes, and slips below the horizon. The sun has come back to the Arctic coast again.

As this time exposure shows, in summer the sun does not sink below the horizon but seems to merely circle the top of the world.

The White Glacier is retreating (left) and, as it does so, is slowly merging with the tongue of the advancing Thompson Glacier.

Everywhere the ice cliff is studded with embedded rocks, lined with many alternating layers of dark soil and white ice.

The noise at the cliff face can be deafening as huge blocks of ice tumble down to the ground.

A glacial trip to Axel Heiberg Island

Thousands of years ago immense masses of ice ground across most of Canada. Today only shattered remnants of the ice remain in the high mountains of the western cordillera and in the Arctic coast region. Most of the glaciers are in retreat, melting back slowly to return to the sea from whence they came long, long ago; but a few glacial tongues are advancing over the land, creeping down through mountain valleys, pushing huge masses of rock and soil ahead of them and carrying moraine materials and earth boulders within their mass. One such advancing glacier is the Thompson Glacier on central Axel Heiberg Island.

right: Scientist with ice drill on back pack scrambles over the surface of the White Glacier.

3 THE NON-LAND OF THE ARCTIC COAST

The thick ice cover on sea, lake and river is the non-land of the Arctic coast region. The ice is landlike; it is a major landform during most of the year, in many areas for all of it. Yet, each year the ice cover melts away, or it drifts away, or it drifts about, carried far and wide by wind and current, always to be replaced at its point of origin by other drifting ice, or by new ice that forms with the return of cold weather each autumn.

Men who have fought to get their ships through, or around, or over sea ice have invariably come to regard it as something very special in their lives. Like the Eskimo hunters before them, they soon came to realize that the simple term "sea ice" was wholly inadequate to describe a phenomenon of such complexity and power. Gradually they evolved a special vocabulary to describe sea ice in all its many shapes, actions and moods. Ice *makes* on the surface of the sea; in the early stages of its formation it is *slush* ice and *rind* ice, *pancake* ice and *young* ice. It becomes *one year old* ice, *two year old* ice, *three year old* ice; *winter* ice, *cake* ice, *brash* ice. On the surface of the sheltered inlets the smooth *sheets* of *land-fast* ice are *bay* ice. On the land-fast *floe* there is a *floe-edge*, an *ice-foot*, and *ice tongues*. On the open sea the *free-floating* ice is *pack* ice. *Fields* of *pack* ice are often hundreds of square miles in extent, made up of thousands of ice *chunks* that are *hummocked* and *rafted* into haphazard shapes and formations.

Sea ice can be *broken, weathered, cracked, submerged, rounded, honeycombed, rotten*. Floating with the sea ice are the massive *icebergs* and *ice islands* from which are *calved* smaller *growlers* and *bergy-bits*. Among the ice are *leads* of open water; on the ice surface in summer are *streams* of fresh water; amongst the Arctic Ocean *ice fields* are *polyanas* of open water. Into the air above the sea ice rises *steam-fog, sea-smoke, frost-smoke*; reflected in the sky is the *ice-blink* or *water-sky*. Within sea ice ships are often *trapped, nipped, crushed, heaved, elevated* and sometimes *buried*. This special language of the ice has grown so complex over the years that the World Meteorological Organization recently compiled and issued a basic list of standard English terms normally used to describe sea ice.

The freezing of the sea on the Arctic coast is a magnificent process. It can take place slowly, as is usual in the more southerly areas, or it can take place with startling rapidity as is often the case in the high Arctic. On north Baffin Island it is not unusual for an Eskimo to hunt over a sheltered bay by kayak one afternoon and then hunt on foot over the new ice of the same bay the following morning.

If the sea freezes over during a long spell of calm, clear cold, its surface will be as flat as a table top for miles in every direction, criss-crossed only by tiny, rounded pressure ridges caused by the expansion of the ice sheets in the deepening cold. But, if the wind blows hard during the early days of ice formation, then the smooth ice surface will be broken up into hundreds of smaller ice floes, each of which bobs up and down as it turns round and about on the heaving sea, rotating and rubbing one against the other, each tiny floe building up rough, raised edges of crumpled ice until the sea looks as if it is covered with hundreds of small, round griddles. This is the pancake ice of the sea. When the wind dies and the sea is calm again, these "pancakes" cement together into a new ice surface that is flat but not smooth, for now it is a matrix of hundreds of small pieces each with a raised edge cemented firmly to those of its neighbours. For a few days, or a few weeks, this new ice surface will form a patchwork of intricately interwoven tiny ice hummocks, until the next snowstorm piles the loose snow into drifts and cloaks the ridges beneath a hard white crust.

Sea ice can be land-fast, or it can be free-floating, or it can be a combination of both, split into two, sometimes three, sections by the action of the tide. Rimming the coast along the contour line of the highest tide is a narrow ice-foot that remains firmly cemented to the shore, building in thickness only at the times of the high tides. Out from the ice-foot, between the contours of the highest and the lowest tide, is a jumbled mass of broken ice and lumpy hummocks that is constantly being raised up and let down by the advance and retreat of the tide. Huge ice hummocks gradually build up over the many big boulders that lie on the bottom in the tidal zone, as the ever-thickening ice is repeatedly raised up and then lowered down onto the tops of the rocks. This area of rough, land-fast ice forms a new coastline in the winter, less visible in areas of low tidal range but spectacular in areas of high tides. On the coasts of Frobisher Bay, where the tide range is great and the waters are often shallow, an area of rough, broken ice in the tidal zone extends as much as a mile out from the rocky coast. Along the shores of the tiny enclosed harbour at the settlement of Repulse Bay, sections of the outer edges of the land-fast ice-foot terminate in sheer cliffs up to fifteen feet high whenever the tide is out. But the ice cliffs vanish completely when the tide comes in and raises the floating ice of the harbour up to the level of the ice-foot.

Beyond the rough ice of the tidal zone is the smoother ice of the land-fast floe, winter highway for the Arctic traveller on dog sled or skidoo. Floe ice covers the surface of all the inlets, sounds, straits and bays of the Arctic coast region. It grows out from the open sea shores of Hudson Bay, Hudson Strait, Foxe Basin, Baffin Bay, Beaufort Sea and the Arctic Ocean, plus a few fast-water straits and sounds, to create enormous areas of new coast "land" each year. This land-fast floe ice extends out to sea for as little as five feet in areas with strong currents sweeping along deep water shores, or as much as five to ten miles in areas where the coast waters are shallow and quiet. Sometimes it is smooth and unbroken; sometimes it is rafted and hummocked. At the outer floe edge huge sheets of ice break off under the press of wind and tide to join with the main mass of the free-floating ice of the central pack.

The free-floating pack ice of the open sea is an enormous mass made up of hundreds of ice pieces ranging in size from huge, flat floes many hundreds of square yards in extent, to miles wide jungles of smashed and tumbled ice blocks that often send towers and pinnacles of tumbled blocks rearing thirty to fifty feet into the air. These huge areas of free-floating pack ice move about under the constant press of wind and current, some days separated from the land-fast floe by a wide stretch of open water, other days pressed hard against the floe edge by onshore winds so that along miles of land-fast ice edge, no open water can be seen. At times the ice of the central pack appears to be a silent, white desert stretching off to the horizon in all directions as far as the eye can see. But its mood can change in an instant; in moments it can shift, break up, thunder and charge about, ride up over itself, crush anything that lies in its path. The power of the sea ice moving under press of wind or ocean current can inspire only fear or awe; fear if you should happen to be helpless on a ship caught in its embrace, awe if you should be lucky

Arctic coast glaciers are shown in the white areas of this glacial map. Icebergs seen in the north Atlantic Ocean originate here.

When the advancing glacier reaches the sea the massive weight of the ice breaks free and floats out to sea in the form of an iceberg.

27

enough to stand on a rocky shore and watch from the safety of the land as the charging ice turns a quiet strip of coast into a scene of wild disorder and din.

The ice that forms on the bogs and swamps, and on the lakes and rivers is the second form of non-land in the Arctic coast region; each year it converts great sectors of swamp and lake-dotted tundra into a continuous "land" mass across which animals and men can travel in any direction they wish. Although almost as important within the region as is the ice on the sea, freshwater ice has never been anything but ice to the men who have lived and travelled across the length and breadth of this far north land. For freshwater ice there is no stylized vocabulary, merely a few terms to indicate certain unusual conditions of the ice. Northerners hold ice on the sea in special regard; freshwater ice is merely taken for granted.

Late each summer on the Arctic coast the fresh water in the lakes and rivers begins to turn into ice. The surface layer exposed to the lowering temperatures of the air changes first, freezing into a thin, brittle film along the shores of all the ponds and streams, gradually creeping out to form an ever-thickening cover over the entire mass. Day after day, as the cold increases and the hours of daylight grow shorter, the ice grows thicker and thicker, clamping a tight lid on all the lakes and rivers in the land. If there is no snow and little wind the surface of the largest lakes freezes over flat and smooth as a marble table top, with ice so clear that fish swimming in the water far below are clearly visible from above. So transparent is this ice that it cannot be seen when looking straight down and one gets an impression of walking-on-water when travelling over the ice surface. Often this impression can lead to a mild panic developing as thoughts of plunging through the ice cover into the deep, cold water below begin to form in your mind.

Sometimes all during the late autumn, the outflow of water from the larger lakes will continue long after the river into which it flows has frozen completely, forcing the water to run over the top of the river ice, building up layer after layer of glistening new ice until the flow from the lake is finally stemmed. In a few localities the channels of large rivers are so confined that the turbulent, rushing water continually mixes the cold surface water with warmer water from below; such places remain free of ice all year round. Steam-fog rising above the tumbling waters of the great falls on the Kazan River, south of Baker Lake, can be seen for miles as it boils up into the forty below zero temperature of the midwinter air.

Many shallow lakes freeze to the bottom, as do the smaller streams and rivers. But the larger lakes do not; the amount of heat within the deep water layers is too great for even the intense cold of the Arctic coast to overcome. Ice on the major lakes reaches a maximum thickness of about six to eight feet sometime in March, early in the month in the southerly areas, later in the far north. Then follows a short period in which no new ice is formed while temperatures remain low but the returning sun brings warmth to the land. Heat from the sun affects the snow on the land first and melt water begins to run from the hilltops down onto the ice of the streams and rivers. The ice absorbs heat from the water and it too begins to melt; first in the smaller streams, then in the larger rivers, then on the ice of the lakes at the rivers' mouths, then along the shores of the lakes where the warmer, inflowing waters congregate. By mid-June in the south, somewhat later in the north, all the large lakes are free of ice around their shores but they still have a large free-floating ice cover in the centre.

Gradually this huge mass of centre ice melts. Shifted about by the wind it breaks up into smaller and smaller individual floes until it melts completely away, or until it is blown out of the lake into a river that will carry it off to the sea. Melting of the freshwater ice is a reversal of the process that formed the ice the previous fall. The ice absorbs heat from the air above and from the warmer water flowing under and around it; the millions of tiny air spaces within the mass warm up, particularly in the upper layers where the ice becomes honeycombed and disintegrates into a porous and jagged surface. The thick ice cover of the lakes, melted from above by the sun and from below by the warming waters grows thinner and thinner until it becomes a mere foot or two thick mass of ice crystals and entrapped pockets of air. This is the "candled" ice of the northern lakes, very dangerous to walk on for it crumbles to nothing beneath a person's weight. For days huge sheets of "candled" ice float about the larger lakes. Suddenly, almost as if by magic, the ice sheets disintegrate and disappear; the non-land surface of the lakes and rivers has become water again.

All along the mountainous northeast rim of the Arctic

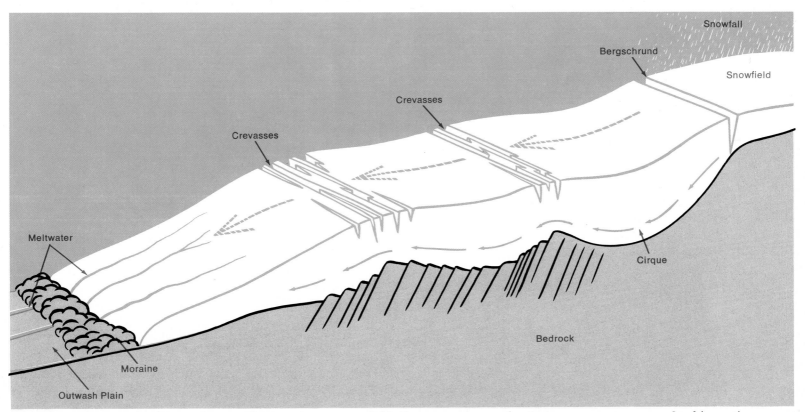

A bergschrund is formed when a glacier pulls away from a snowfield. Crevasses open as the glacier passes over uneven land formations.

coast region is found the third form of non-land—the ice caps and glaciers of the Arctic islands. From Baffin Island in the south to Ellesmere Island in the far north much of the land is covered with ice in its most dramatic form; huge snowfields cover most of the highlands, spilling out through the mountain valleys into long, winding tongues of glacial ice, or spreading out in wide lobes across the upland plains and plateaux that slope down to the shores of the Arctic seas.

In the accumulation areas of the upper *snow fields* the snow and ice mass is *firm* or *névé*. At the outer edge of the upland snowfield there is often a large crack that develops where the ice begins to flow down over the steeper ground beneath; such a crack is a *bergschrund*. Glacial ice is said to be *plastic*; where it flows over steep drops or broken ground it bends and develops *crevasses* that cut deep into its surface. As it flows it picks up

debris—stones, rocks, boulders, gravel that tumble down onto it from the slopes above—to form *lateral moraines* along the edges. Two lateral moraines that meet on a piedmont glacier become a *medial* moraine. At the *terminus* of the glacial tongue the steep cliff of ice often pushes up an immense mass of rocks and boulders into a *push* moraine. Out from the terminus of the glacial tongue extends a wide *outwash plain* into which the swift, tempestuous streams of melt water cut and re-cut their tortuous channels. Water flowing out from the glacier is never clear; it is dirty brown wherever it flows out onto an outwash plain before heading off to the sea, and when it issues from the face of the glacial tongue directly into the sea or onto the steep bare rock floors of mountain valleys, the water is milky-white, heavily saturated with rock *flour,* the pulverized materials scraped from the land over which the glacial ice has flowed.

Wherever a glacial tongue flows from the coast to float on the surface of the sea it *calves* the immense chunks of ice called *icebergs* or *bergs* that are at last free to float wherever tide and current may take them before finally melting back to join with the waters of the sea from which they had come hundreds of years before.

The alpine snowfields and glaciers of the northeast Arctic islands provide some of the most beautiful and spectacular scenery in the world today. Near the centre of Axel Heiberg Island are two alpine glaciers, the White and the Thompson; the former is the smaller, draining out from a well defined accumulation basin of modest size. The Thompson is a huge glacier, flowing out from the immense McGill Ice Cap that covers almost half of Axel Heiberg Island. The White is a re-treating glacier, its gentle, sloping snout curves back to merge into the weathered and pitted surface of the long glacial tongue. At the end of the snout is a huge pile of unsorted rocks and small boulders that towers up as a terminal moraine over a wide out-wash plain.

Along one edge of its retreating terminus the White glacier merges with the mighty tongue of the Thompson; and the Thompson is a very different kettle of ice. It is an advancing glacier, its snout a fifty foot high, half-mile long cliff of jagged ice that towers up into the sky. In front of the advancing snout is an immense push moraine, nearly one mile deep, two miles wide and fifty to seventy-five feet high, a huge landform of gravel, stones and boulders complete with small lakes on its surface, that is being relentlessly pushed ahead by the steep face of the advancing ice. Everywhere the ice cliff is studded with imbedded stones and rocks, and lined with alternating layers of dark soil and white ice that are twisted and torn into wild swirls and tor-tured patterns; an artist's nightmare done in charcoal and chalk. From beneath the glacial snout a great stream of dirty brown water rushes through a narrow channel cut through the moraine, to dash headlong down an ever-shifting shallow cut that winds across the outwash plain to the sea.

The noise at the cliff face is deafening; the ice sighs and grunts as it shifts and settles; the crash of huge blocks tumbling down from the heights to shatter on the ice mounds below echoes across the wide valley. From a dozen openings in the cliff face great jets of milky white water shoot straight out, then curve majestically through the air to fall into the waters of the muddy stream below. Behind all is the noise of the main stream itself, a continuous, heavy thunder as the roaring waters hurtle along the shallow channel, rolling along the uneven bottom boulders of every size and shape that grind and scrape together in a never-ending deluge of sound and wild motion.

About half a mile back from the glacial front, where the ice of the Thompson first meets the ice of the White at the base of a high rock hill, is an enclosed, roughly triangular pocket formed between the walls of rock on one side and the walls of ice on the other two. Into this pocket melt water drains to build up a between-glaciers lake. Such lakes are common features in mountain glacier areas; they can be big enough to contain small icebergs calved from one of the glacial snouts along their shore, or small enough to be mere puddles. Between-Glacier Lake at the junction of the Thompson and the White is about a mile long and half a mile wide, large enough to have two small islands jut up from its surface.

Usually this lake drains off excess inflow each summer through a submarine channel to the outwash plain. But, in the summer of 1961 the weather over the entire high Arctic islands area was very warm; melt water in huge quantities ran into all the glacial lakes. Between-Glacier Lake level rose until the water overflowed and started to run over the ice surface of the White glacier in a wide, shallow wall of water nowhere more than a few inches deep. Swiftly, however, the running water began to cut a winding, twisting channel down through the ice of the glacial tongue; within hours the channel was twenty-five feet deep, within a day it was fifty feet deep and the waters of Between-Glacier Lake were draining out with tremendous force. The channel deepened until it cut right through the ice to the bedrock almost a hundred feet below. Along the bottom of this twisted, steep sided canyon in the ice a great torrent of muddy water smashed its way with enormous force as it raced pell-mell for the sea. At the terminus of the glacial tongue a wild river of water mixed with mud and rocks and boulders hurtled out through a deep slit cut through the terminal moraine. Within fifty-six hours Between-Glacier Lake was almost completely drained dry, and the long glacial tongue of the White was cut lengthwise by a hundred foot deep chasm at the bottom of which wild water still dashed headlong to the sea.

THE BARREN GROUNDS

Northern Boothia Peninsula is the furthest north part of the mainland of Canada. Largely uninhabited, even by Eskimo hunters, it is a bleak, near-barren peninsula, scoured by glacial ice, deeply incised by melt-water streams. In winter bitter winds sweep across its frozen surface, piling the meagre snowfall into huge drifts. Many drifts do not melt away in the summer but remain as visible evidence of just how massive glacial ice forms on a cold, northern land.

Elasmosaurid
(long-necked Plesiosaur)

Mosasaur

A warm beginning

Many millions of years ago much of North America, including most of the Arctic coast region, was inundated by the sea. In rocks laid down in the Silurian period there are unmistakable signs of coral reefs produced by warm water species that can exist only in seas constantly above 70°F. In rocks of the Cretaceous period that are now exposed on the west coast of Greenland (which was part of the north coast of North America at that time) there are fossils of such warm weather plants as breadfruit and fig. And the creatures of the deep, as can be seen here,

Hesperornis

Herring-like fish

Belemnites

were very different from those found in the icy waters of the Arctic region today. Far below the eerie glow cast by the dancing Northern Lights, giant marine lizards, mosasaurs, battled for survival against fearsome, forty-foot long reptiles known as plesiosaurs. Both of these marine animals were carnivorous, possessing sharp teeth, and used their strong paddles or flippers to propel themselves along. Other inhabitants of the warm Cretaceous seas were the hesperornis, a wingless diving bird that ate herring-like fish, and schools of belemnites, which resembled today's squid.

Path of earth around sun

Arctic Summer

N

Arctic Circle

Equator

Antarctic Circle

S

Sun

In summer the earth is tilted with the North Pole toward the sun; north of the Arctic circle the sun does not set for varying periods.

A gradual cooling

The weather on the Arctic coast of Canada isn't quite as cold as it is often assumed to be; the extremes of low temperature in the world occur in the interior of Antartica, in the deep, mountain valleys of the Yukon, and on the vast wind-swept prairies of Russia. Nevertheless, the Arctic coast region is cold, its basic weather governed by interaction of the four elements that control all the weather of the world—the sun, source of radiant energy that heats the earth and its atmosphere; the earth, because of its position, its shape and the tilt of its axis in relation to the plane of its orbit about the sun; the topography of the earth because of the way it guides, shapes and obstructs the free flow of the air; and the atmosphere, a huge heat engine driven by energy emitted from the sun.

Inflow of water comes from the north Pacific (8%) and north Atlantic (85%). Outflow is around both sides of Greenland.

Arctic Winter

In winter the tilt of the North Pole is away from the sun, and the Arctic coast, north of the Arctic circle, gets no light for days on end.

Penetration of the Arctic by low pressure systems which cause cyclones occurs only in the far west and in Baffin Bay in the east.

Sea ice melts from within due to salt concentration, and from the surface by heat convection from the air and meltwater. Over 60% of the thermal energy of the sun is absorbed by sea ice.

The bright snow surface on the land reflects over 80% of the thermal energy from the sun. This accounts in part for the much colder temperatures found inland than those experienced on the coast.

At one time the north pole of earth was in the vicinity of present day Hawaii, with the south pole in the south Atlantic Ocean. We know also that a great ice age occurred in the Permian period when almost all of Africa, India and also parts of Australia were under ice. Today, the south pole is in Antartica which is completely covered by glacial ice, and the north pole is in the Arctic Ocean.

Carved by the cold

The most spectacular form of ground ice is the pingo, ice-cored hills found in the Mackenzie Delta that are often a thousand feet high. Pingos are formed as a result of what is called a "closed" system of unfrozen soil developing within an area of permanently frozen ground. A large lake, beneath which there is no permafrost, fills with sediment or partially drains away (1). Permafrost will form on the bottom and sides so as to trap a huge core of unfrozen, water-saturated soil above it (2). Year by year, the freezing continues (3); hydrostatic pressure forces the water upward toward the surface of the land (4) to form a huge ice "pingo." Polygon soil formations pattern great areas of the Arctic. The ground cracks during freezing in the autumn, water collects in the cracks where it freezes to form tapering wedges which continue to grow and fracture year after year, driving the soil into saucer-like depressions of polygon shape.

THE FORMATION OF A PINGO

Unfrozen water-saturated sand   Zone of permafrost in sand   Ice

Glacial Gouges

Tundra Polygons

Unfrozen Ground

Permafrost

Ice

Limit of Permafrost

Unfrozen Ground

Limit of Permafrost

Pingo

"Drunken" Forest

Stone Rings

Ice

Unfrozen Ground

Permafrost

Sphere of earth's magnetic
field with cutaway
Van Allen Belts

Solar radiation (paths
of selected particles
shown in red)

Solar flare

Aurora borealis – strange illuminations in the night

Displays of Northern Lights, *aurora borealis,* generally occur at the southern sector of the Arctic coast sky. High above the earth are the Van Allen Belts, two great bands of radiation materials trapped in the earth's magnetic field, which trap, in turn, most of the deadly radiation material emitted by the sun, thus protecting all life on earth from this lethal solar rain. But the Van Allen Belts are shaped like a doughnut, with the hole over both north and south polar regions. Thus protection from solar radiation is very slim on the Arctic coast of Canada, so slim that airliners flying the polar routes during times of maximum emissions from the sun must fly at substantially lower altitudes in order to minimize possible hazard to passengers on the planes.

Electrically-charged particles from a solar disturbance (left) bombard the outer Van Allen Belt, causing a magnetic storm which can black out high-frequency radio communications. The most spectacular visible results of this upper atmosphere impact are auroras, and in the north the display is known as the aurora borealis.

The airplane (right) is flying within the troposhere, the lowest level of a complex, many-layered atmosphere, and the one in which man exists. This level ends at 5 to 10 miles above the earth and contains the air currents which shape most of our weather. Glimmering displays of light hang like curtains at the upper levels.

MILES

600

500

400

300

200

100

The mountains of Baffin Island.

PART TWO / GEOLOGY

4 IN THE BEGINNING

5,000 million years ago there was no Arctic coast region of Canada; there was only the proto-earth, gradually cooling, gradually shrinking, gradually forming a thin crust over its mantle of warm, viscous rock.

About 4,000 million years ago rock flows from within began to build what are now the shield areas of the earth. The shields were formed originally by the deposition near the surface of masses of light, granitic rocks carried up from deep within the mantle by convection currents in the viscous rock. These masses of lighter rock gathered together in the eddies formed between the huge, slow-moving currents, at the point where the currents met near the surface and deflected downward as they cooled and sank. As the lighter rock gathered in the eddies it began to build up; the masses grew thicker and wider through the constant addition of new materials on the bottom and the sides. Eventually they broke through the surface crust to rise as mountains, high above the shallow seas. The bases of these shield mountains floated deep in the heavier basaltic rock of the mantle similar to the way in which the base of an iceberg floats deep in the supporting sea. Like the iceberg, the bulk of the shield mountain mass lay beneath the surface of the earth. Today, with the tops of the mountains worn away, the deep roots remain, and the crust of the earth is much thicker under the continents than it is under the surrounding seas.

The shields are the ancient nuclei of the present continents. There are nine such areas in the world and the largest single mass is that of the great Canadian shield which forms the geologic base for over half of Canada, and for over three-quarters of the Arctic coast region. This Canadian shield represents the most stable area of our land surface, but this was not always so. During the long Percambrian era, the Canadian shield was the centre for a number of great revolutions of the earth's surface, each involving the building of high mountains. But, from the moment the rocks of the shield mountain rose into the atmosphere they were subject to all the forces of erosion. They began to wear down and the material of which they were built was carried as sediment to be deposited on the edges of the shield.

Over long periods of geologic time these sediments were compressed into sedimentary rocks and many areas of such rocks were themselves raised up into new mountains by forces acting from within the earth. Sedimentary rocks were often changed into metamorphic rocks through intense pressure and heat when they were buried deep in the earth because of subsidence of the land and then brought to the surface again when the land of which they were a part rose again into the sky. The same forces behind these movements brought to the surface new rock materials, magma, and forced it through the earth's crust with extreme violence, in the case of volcanoes, or with slow, majestic movements in the case of immense lava flows issuing from fissures. On the surface this magma cooled to become igneous rock, to form new mountains which the forces of erosion began to attack immediately and slowly wear down.

This complex, slow process of change and mixture in the rocks of the Canadian shield went on through millions of years of time – more than five-sixths of the total time span since the earth was formed. The older rocks are in the shield core, the younger toward the outer edges, showing that the continent has grown laterally through geologic time, spreading out to form the land area now known as North America. Millions of years of erosion and deposition of materials transformed the original shield mountains into a great plenaplain, much larger in area than the original shield but nowhere very far above sea level. The profile of this great plain was that of a large dome, sloping gradually down from the centre to lower outer edges on which rings of deposited materials had built up, prior to being raised high into new mountain ranges. In the far north, most of the present Arctic archipelago formed the outer edge of this great continental plain and the north coast extended much farther east, north and west than it does today. The present site of Hudson Bay was land. There was, in effect, no Arctic coast region as we know it today; throughout most of the four and a half billion years of earth history the changing geology of what is now the Arctic coast was similar to that of the remainder of the Canadian shield. The sequence of geologic events in the northern sector produced results that were similar to those in the rest of the shield to the south.

The relief outline of Canada today is that of a great trough having a general northwest-southeast axis. On the west side of

The basic elements of the earth's surface can be combined into many forms. Hard igneous rock exposed to erosion disintegrates into sediment, is later compressed by pressure within the earth into solid sedimentary rock and the process starts again.

Ellesmere Island

Baffin Island

Hudson Bay

Rock structure of the
Arctic coast region

Sedimentary Rocks

Flat-lying Sedimentary Rocks

Sedimentary and Igneous Rocks

Metamorphosed Igneous and Sedimentary Rocks

Igneous and Metamorphic Rocks

the trough the land rises up into a continuous series of mountain ranges that run the length of the Yukon and British Columbia; on the east side are the mountains of the northeast Arctic islands, Baffin Island and Labrador. In between the east and west mountains is the main land mass of Canada; a region of lowlands and uplands, plains and plateaux. The Arctic coast region consists of the northeastern third of this huge trough; along the east side are the high mountain ranges of Ellesmere, Axel Heiberg, Devon and north Baffin Island, and the lower mountains of south Baffin Island and the northern tip of Labrador. From this mountainous region the land slopes down to the southwest through uplands and plateaux to plains and lowlands in the central areas. In the west it rises again to plateaux that are 3,500 feet above sea level, but dropped off again to a low coastal plain in the extreme northwest. Down the centre line of the

trough, the low area is not continuous but is made up of a number of basins separated by higher ground, or divided one from the other by tongues of upland. In general, the physiography of each basin is related to that of all the other basins, an indication that the entire Arctic archipelago was, at one time, a continuous land mass, parts of which are now submerged beneath the sea.

The basic structure of the Arctic coast region consists of two types of rock. By far the greater part is underlain by Precambrian rocks of the shield that lie like a huge, irregularly-shaped doughnut under the central and eastern portions of Canada, with the water mass of Hudson Bay as the hole in the centre of the doughnut. In the Arctic coast area all of Ungava, all of Baffin Island except for the northwest corner and a small piece of the west coast, all of the Keewatin District on the west coast of Hudson Bay, most of the Arctic sector of the District of Mackenzie, and small segments of the western islands are underlain by the rocks of the shield.

Upon these ancient rocks, worn down by erosion through the tremendously long passage of most of geologic time, have been deposited sedimentary rocks ranging in age from Palaeozoic to Tertiary. These sedimentary rocks form a wide belt through the central and western Arctic islands from the north coast of the Mackenzie and Yukon Districts through Victoria, Banks, King William, Prince of Wales and Somerset Islands, and on into Devon and southern Ellesmere Island in the high Arctic. Portions of the outer edges of the western islands of the high Arctic are also of sedimentary rock, as are sections of the many northern peninsulas of the mainland west of Hudson Bay, parts of all the islands in Hudson Bay and Foxe Basin, and the northwestern corner of Baffin Island. Most of the high Arctic islands area is underlain by moderately folded rocks ranging in age from Precambrian to Cretaceous. At one time there must have been a fairly deep and uniform cover of these sedimentary rocks over the Precambrian rocks of the shield in all sectors of the Arctic coast region. But most of this cover was removed by the scouring action of the glacial ice during the successive flows of ice across northern North America during the million years of the Pleistocene period, leaving great areas of the Arctic coast almost denuded of its sedimentary rock cover and obliterating the record of much of its early history. It is interesting to speculate that much of the fertile soil now covering various parts of southern Canada was originally sedimentary rock in the Arctic, transported to present localities by the movement of glacial ice.

There is a lack of detailed information on the early geological history of the Arctic coast region, partly due to removal of the record of the rocks by the glacial ice and partly due to a lack of study brought about by problems of travel to and within the region that were not solved until very recent times. Geologically the region can be broken down into areas that are closely related to other regions of Canada: the Arctic coasts of Hudson Bay form part of the northern half of the Canadian shield; the central Arctic and the western Arctic islands area is an extension of the Plains region to the south; the high mountains of Baffin, Devon and southern Ellesmere Islands are edge-of-shield mountains, similar in formation to the mountains of the Cordillera region of the west; the low mountains of southern Baffin Island and Labrador are similar to the Appalachians.

Because of this wide variety of topography the Arctic coast region cannot be said to be a cohesive unit by virtue of its geology; rather it is a region due solely to its uniformly severe, cold climate. However, there is a good deal of evidence to show that the area now occupied by the Arctic coasts of Canada has not always had a cold "Arctic" climate, that it has been related to other parts of Canada not only geologically but in climate, flora and fauna as well. Until the late Tertiary period the entire Arctic coast region was the northern extension of a continental land mass, with a climate to match that of southern Canada, varying from temperate to sub-tropical most of the time. The sequence of events that produced the surface contours and present climate, flora and fauna of the Arctic coast, in effect creating the Arctic coast region, did not begin until well into the Tertiary period, most likely about twenty million years ago, when there occurred the uplift of the eastern and northeastern mountains from Labrador to Ellesmere Island and the concurrent depressing of the land to form the deep basin of Davis Strait and Baffin Bay. At about the same time a new period of mountain-building broke out in western Canada along the length of the Cordillera, and the entire Arctic coast region, along with almost all of northern North America, rose until it stood about three to four thousand feet higher above sea level than it does today.

The combined factors of the great uplift of mountains in the northeast and west, and of the higher general elevation of all the land of northern North America, were to be of tremendous significance in the next stage of the natural history of the earth, and for the Arctic coast region in particular. For it was following this period of mountain-building and general uplift of the land that the world's most recent ice age settled in over the northern lands of the world. Until this time there had been no "Arctic" coast region. It wasn't until the beginning of the Pleistocene period, about one million years ago, that the natural history of the cold "Arctic" coast region of Canada really began.

In the tidal zone ice lying over boulders on the sea floor is cracked and forced upward with each falling tide. By late winter jumbled ice hummocks over this boulder may be fifteen feet high.

5 THE BIRTH OF THE "ARCTIC" COAST

Accounts of the glacial age in North America during the Pleistocene period usually begin "About a million years ago the climate over the northern hemisphere grew colder. . . ." While this statement is true, it is somewhat misleading, for there is no way of knowing at present if the temperature fell and the climate grew colder so as to initiate conditions that led to the formation of glacial ice. Certainly the climate over the northern hemisphere grew colder once the basic element or elements required to set in motion an ice age came about. But the actual condition or conditions required to start an ice age are speculative, and a lowering of the earth's temperature may or may not have been one of them, as is shown by the theory of a warming climate precipitating the ice age of the Pleistocene.

It is known that about one million years ago, for reasons not yet clearly understood, the universal warmth which had bathed the earth for the 200 million odd years of the Mesozoic and Cenozoic eras gave way to a time of fluctuating temperatures in the northern hemisphere. Gradually, over many thousands of years, the seasonal fluctuations increased and the period of cold grew longer each year. The cold winter rain changed to snow which melted away each summer. As the years flowed on, as the centuries passed one into the other, the time of melting was delayed a little later each year, the time of the first snowfall arrived a little earlier. There came a summer when a few patches of winter snow did not melt but remained on the ground to be buried by the new snow of the following winter. On the Arctic coast this most likely occurred first in the high mountain areas of the far northeast, and only a little later in the lower mountains of the southwest.

Winter followed winter, each a little longer, each piling up new drifts of unmelted snow throughout the Arctic coast region until the mountains of the east and west and all the far north land areas were buried year round under unmelted snowdrifts with only the steep faces of the mountain peaks clear of snow.

"Candled" freshwater ice in the final stage of summer melt – the thawing ice settles into hexagon pencil-shaped crystals as it melts.

The snow didn't fall evenly, some areas received more than others, areas that were in the proper geographic location for heavy snow to fall almost continuously and build up many times faster than elsewhere. As the centuries passed the snow in these areas of extreme accumulation became thicker and thicker—tens of feet, then hundreds of feet. Weight compacted the snow into ice, as a ball of snow is compacted into ice by squeezing it in the hand. Deep down in the ever-thickening ice masses the pressures were enormous, so great that the seemingly solid ice began to act in a strange way—it began to flow out in all directions, guided only by the contour of the land beneath or about. Slowly but relentlessly the ice pushed out from its source areas, propelled by the continuing pressure of the new layers forming at the centre of the mass.

In the mountains of the northeast the ice flowed along the valleys, or it carved out new valleys in the softer rock, or it built up to over-ride the mountain ridges. On the plateaux and plains it oozed over the land in all directions, pushing out immense, bulging lobes of glistening white. The fronts of the lobes, and of the glacial tongues in the valleys, were huge cliffs of jagged ice that ground across the land surface like the blades of enormous bulldozers, scraping up the loose soil, grinding the sedimentary rock cover of the land into a mixture of silt, sand, pebbles and boulders, pushing it ahead with irresistible force or plastering it onto the land in layers of sticky clay. This grinding and stripping of the softer rock was aided by a matrix of rock particles in the bottom of the ice mass; the bottom of the glaciers were rock-studded grinding tools with undersurfaces not unlike pieces of giant emery paper. The embedded rocks did not stay in one place but were constantly being rolled about in the bottom of the ice as it ground over the land, presenting fresh edges to gouge the land beneath.

Over thousands of years the ice kept accumulating and spreading out over the land. By the time it stopped, a huge mass of glacial ice buried all of Canada, except for mountain peaks in the Cordillera and northeast Arctic islands, some pockets in the Yukon Territory and the outer fringe of western Arctic islands. The ice was thousands of feet thick, about three miles deep over the present site of Hudson Bay. The vast amount of water locked up in the ice caps of the northern hemisphere lowered the level of the earth's oceans between 300 and 400

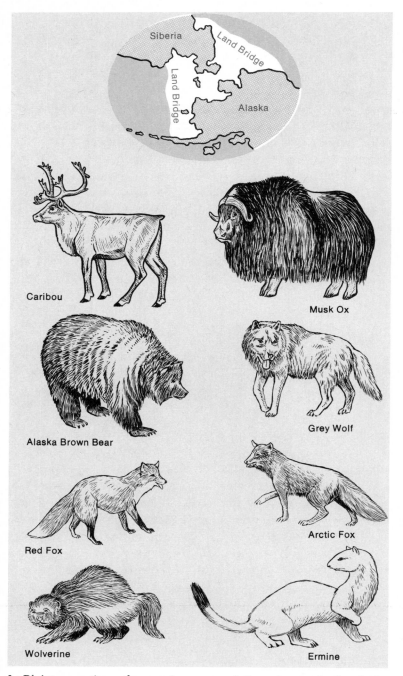

In Pleistocene times the massive accumulation of water in the glacier ice caused a lowering of the sea level, permitting a few hardy animals to cross the Bering Strait from Asia to America.

feet, exposing nearly two and a half million square miles of new coastal land. Because of this North America was connected to Asia by a land bridge across what is now Bering Strait.

Then, either the temperature grew too warm for the snows of winter to remain on the ice divides the year round, or the source of the water supply vanished, or a combination of both occurred. Without new ice to push out from the source areas, the glacial lobes and tongues began to thin down and to melt back from their leading edges. Once started, the ice melted back quite rapidly, much faster than it had crept down across the land. It didn't melt evenly, or at a uniform rate; sometimes the melt was rapid, then it would slow down for a while. It might even make small local advances. But, over a few thousand years, all the great mass of the ice sheets melted away.

For many thousands of years Canada, its far north included, remained largely free of ice with a climate not unlike the one it has today. Then, the ice began to form again in the accumulation areas, and to flow out over the land. Before it stopped all of Canada and much of the northern United States lay buried beneath glacial ice once more. This time the ice advanced even farther south, reaching to within 650 miles of the Gulf of Mexico in the central U.S.A. It remained for a longer period before melting almost completely away. Four times, some say five, the glacial ice crept out of the north and west this way and retreated back again; each time the ice advance lasted for about 100,000 years while the intervening warmer periods when the land was ice free were much longer, the longest about 300,000 years. Today we are living in the last stage of the latest retreat of the ice and no one is sure that it will not start south again.

One of the most intriguing questions about the ice ages of the Pleistocene, and about ice ages in general, is what caused the ice to fluctuate, to flow out and then pull back so many times, and possibly will cause it to flow out again in the future. An interesting, and quite plausible explanation, that seems to fit the facts of the glacial advances and retreats as they are known to have happened in Canada, and one that has some direct evidence found in bottom deposits laid down in the north Atlantic Ocean during the Pleistocene to support it, hinges around a rather startling possibility—that of an open polar sea.

It must be remembered that two main elements are vitally necessary before snow can fall and accumulate on the ground in sufficient quantities to produce masses of glacial ice—very cold temperatures over large areas for a major portion of the year, and a huge source of water nearby, lying in the direction from which the prevailing winds blow. Without sufficient water cold alone cannot produce glacial ice, which is why much of Alaska in the far northwest escaped being covered with ice during the Pleistocene ice age even though it must have had a very cold climate.

There is evidence to suggest that the Arctic Ocean was free of ice at times during the Pleistocene period. If so, the normal flow of air in the northern hemisphere would have brought polar winds down across a long stretch of ice-free Arctic Ocean, picking up moisture as they flowed south and warmed up. These moisture-laden winds would have blown across the north coast and up the slope of the northern mainland, which at the time of the late Tertiary and early Pleistocene was an upland about 3,000 to 4,000 feet higher than it is today. The winds would have dropped their moisture as they rose over the land, and in the deep interior of the continent this moisture would have fallen as snow at the higher altitudes. The winds would have caused tremendous blizzards in the interior of northern Canada.

A similar situation would have applied to winds blowing off the north Atlantic Ocean onto the high land of Labrador and northern Quebec; winds from off the north Atlantic Ocean, the Greenland Sea, Baffin Bay and Davis Strait would have dropped snow on the mountain areas of Greenland, Baffin Island and the eastern high Arctic islands. And it is quite probable that, long before this happened, there were already permanent snowfields in the very high mountains of the western Cordillera region of British Columbia and the Yukon.

Once the ice caps had developed and risen to heights of thousands of feet in the accumulation areas and had flowed out to merge together, the massive ice mass would have become a major landform that would further reinforce the intensive accumulations of snow and its conversion into glacial ice. The blizzards produced over the accumulation areas must have been of an intensity and degree of violence as is found only in the Antarctic continent today. In the area of what is now Hudson Bay they must have been especially fierce, with winds from the north Atlantic storms meeting and battling with the winds from off the Arctic Ocean. Small wonder that this area is thought to

During the Pleistocene cold winds blowing over the open sea picked up moisture, which later fell in the form of snow when the air masses rose to traverse the uplands. The area around Hudson Bay, became the centre of major snow accumulation.

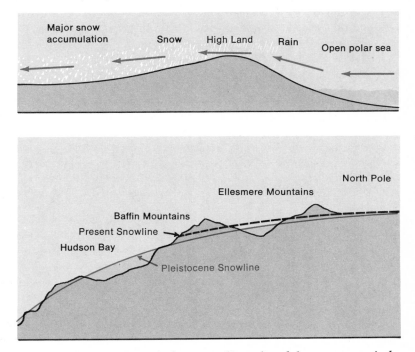

A moderate lowering of the snow line placed large areas of the plateau in the zone of snow accumulation and initiated the growth of the continental ice-cap during the Pleistocene period.

have been the region of the deepest accumulation of glacial ice; small wonder that the crust of the earth was depressed so much that it resulted in the formation of the depression now filled by the waters of Hudson Bay.

On the lowlands and plateaux of the Arctic coast erosion by massive glacial ice flow removed all of the unconsolidated soil and a good deal of the sedimentary rock cover, in places all of it. Great stretches of the Arctic coast consist of bare, polished rock surfaces which still bear the deep striations gouged into them by the boulders in the bottom of the flowing ice. In the island groups along the southeast coast of Hudson Bay, entire island surfaces are polished and grooved, with the grooves often a foot deep in the surface of the perfectly smooth rock. West of Hudson Bay and on Victoria Island the land is patterned into long ridges and alternating valleys that run for miles over the landscape making the land appear, when viewed from the air, like an immense ploughed field. Some of this ridge and valley pattern is due to the actual gouging out of the land, some of it to the fact that the glacial ice deposited the materials it scraped up into long rows of small drumlin hills, all oriented in the direction of the main glacial flow. One of the most spectacular forms of glacial deposition west of Hudson Bay is the esker. Eskers are formed from materials deposited in the beds of subglacial streams as the glacier melts away. Throughout the plains country west of Hudson Bay there are dozens of these miles long sand and gravel ridges that snake across the flat land in a variety of patterns.

Much of the Arctic surface is covered with glacial till, masses of unsorted rock, sand and gravel that have been deposited on the land in a haphazard fashion as the ice melted away. A till surface forms the typical tundra landscape, low in relief with very little systematic drainage, often patterned with hundreds of small, shallow lakes. In the early years after the retreat of the ice, glacial till was probably scattered in a more defined hill and valley arrangement, but long years of water and frost erosion has tended to flatten out the ridges and fill in the valleys helping to produce the level landscape of the tundra areas. Erratic boulders are everywhere on the land, often up to house-size boulders that have been carried to their present locations on the glacial ice and then left as the ice melted.

A major feature of the Arctic landscape is the raised beach-lines along the shores of the shallow seas and, inland west of Hudson Bay, around the tops of the high hills. The latter beaches, many of which are at heights of from six to nine hundred feet above present sea level, are thought to mark the successive levels of a large glacial lake that once formed in the interior country along the axis of the Thelon River-Baker Lake water system. From the air the hills appear to be ringed with concentric circles of water-washed reddish stones, splotched black with lichen and moss. The raised beaches along the seashores are the result of a gradual uplift of the land that occurred, and is still occurring, following the removal of the tremendous weight of the glacial ice. Geologists believe that the weight of the ice depressed the crust rocks downward into the viscous rock of the mantle of the earth. With the pressure removed the mantle is returning to its original shape, pushing the crust up with it.

The actual rate of the uplift has been accurately measured on the east coast of Pelly Bay in the central Arctic coast region. Radiocarbon dating of the remains of marine animals found buried beneath the beach sand of three uplifted terraces reveal that the first terrace, 175 feet above sea level, was cut about 7,160 years ago; the second terrace, now at 290 feet above sea level, was cut about 7,880 years ago; and the third terrace, now at 540 feet above sea level, was cut 8,370 years ago. These figures show that the uplift of the land immediately following the melting of the ice cover was quite rapid, about five inches per year. The rate slowed down to about two inches per year as the crust returned closer to the original equilibrium.

Geologists have calculated that the bottom of Hudson Bay, over which the ice accumulation was the deepest, will continue to rise in the future by as much as another 825 feet. This would mean the disappearance of Hudson and James Bays from the maps of Canada; the area would become a broad plain, drained by a major river system flowing north to the Arctic sea. The future benefits to the Arctic coast region from a continuing retreat of the glacial ice are many, not the least of which will be a second major river flowing from south to north, to an open polar sea!

Soft rock on the west coast of Hudson Bay, sculptured and polished by water and shifting ice, is gradually rising out of the sea.

6 THE TUNDRA BIOME—THE SOIL

In early spring of the year 1838 Thomas Simpson, accompanied by a small band of Indians of the northern bush, set off to the north from Great Bear Lake by sled. As the group made its way along the frozen river valleys the forests grew gradually sparser; the trees on which they depended for fuel became more stunted. Soon they reached areas where no trees grew at all; they moved out onto the open, treeless tundra across which bitter winds howled to bite into their bodies no longer protected by the wall of the northern bush. Moving through this edge-of-tree country about fifty miles northeast of Great Bear Lake they topped a rise and came down a long slope onto the ice surface of a narrow lake that stretched for miles off to the northwest where it joined another equally long and narrow lake, both rimmed on either side by low, snow-covered rock hills.

The land about them seemed absolutely devoid of life; only in a few sheltered hollows along the southern shore could they find small stands of stunted trees to use as wood for their fires and as supports for their tents. "Never have I seen a land so desolate and dismal as that which stretched before me," Simpson wrote later. He named the bodies of water the Dismal Lakes.

In later years another Arctic traveller reached the shores of the Dismal Lakes but he came from the north, travelling south after spending many months beyond the tree line on the ice surface of the sea along the north-west Arctic coast. "As I came over the hill and started down the slope toward the edge of the snow-covered lake I began to encounter small groups of trees standing upright in the shelter of tiny valleys. To my eyes, accustomed for many months to seeing only open, windswept north coast, this place seemed like a little bit of heaven, and I wondered how anyone could possibly have described these as—the Dismal Lakes."

This duality of appearance is characteristic of Arctic coast lands; eyes accustomed to the seemingly endless expanse of the northern bush, or to the lush growth of southern Canada, often see the treeless Arctic as a vast, empty and desolate wasteland in which grow only dwarf birch and willow bushes, a few acres of stunted grass, scattered patches of alpine flowers, and thousands of acres of nothing but moss and lichen-covered rock and gravel ridges. But others see the Arctic tundra as a high north wonderland—a land where flowers and plants thrive in the short but sunlit summer; where valley floors are carpeted with acres of cotton grass and sedges, alive with the buzz of insects and the flickering flights of bees and butterflies, supporting vast herds of caribou and smaller groups of musk ox, to say nothing of the lemmings and hares, and the thousands upon thousands of migratory birds that come north to nest and raise their young.

Whether the Arctic coast region is wasteland or wonderland is a subjective judgment, based entirely on human emotion and individual human experience. Within the more objective world of science the Arctic coast is neither wasteland nor wonderland; it is simply another area of the earth's surface within which distinctive life forms, especially adapted to the extreme seasonal variations in temperature, moisture and sunlight, have evolved and multiplied to fill many of the niches in the ecological structure that separates and unites all elements of the natural world. As the geologist divides the earth into regions, each a unit by virtue of its physical structure, so the ecologist divides the earth into realms, each a separate entity by virtue of its life forms.

North America, from Cape Columbia on northern Ellesmere Island south to the Tropic of Cancer, lies within the Nearctic Realm of nature, a huge land area that is further subdivided into a number of smaller and more cohesive regions called Biomes, each having its own volume of rain and snowfall, its own pattern of the seasons, its own relationship of day to night hours, all of which have combined to produce a unique selection of life forms that are found nowhere else in the world. The invisible barrier of climate defines the boundaries of a biome and, because it is climate that defines the main southern boundary of the Canadian Arctic triangle, the Arctic coast of Canada lies within a single natural unit—the tundra biome.

Range of temperature, hours of sunlight, amount of moisture, the cycle of the seasons determine the type of flora, and therefore the type of fauna, the tundra biome will support. Of basic importance to the flora is the type of soil within the region in which it can grow. Only lichens and some mosses are able to exist on bare rock; all other plants and shrubs must have soil in which to sink their root systems and from which to draw their sustenance. Some areas of the Arctic coast are completely without soil, such as the bare, ice-scraped rock islands in eastern Hudson Bay, and the stony beaches of some of the northern islands; but over most of the tundra biome the land has a surface covering made up of a mixture of soil and coarse rock particles, or of finer silt materials laid down by the rivers.

Most of the tundra soil is of glacial origin, a matrix of rock flour and rock particles stripped from the land by the scouring action of the flowing ice and then plastered onto the land wherever the ice flowed. The farther away from the glacial source, the finer the grind of the rock flour and the deeper the deposits of glacial soils become. Being within or close to the source areas for glacial ice the rock particles and soil of the Arctic coast received little grinding and, following the retreat of the ice, were deposited on the land surface in comparatively thin masses of completely unsorted materials—clay, gravel, sand, broken rock pieces, boulders of all sizes. Some of this material was later sorted and stratified by the water from the post-glacial lakes and by subsequent rain and frost action which combined to further disintegrate the rock particles and to carry the finer soil from the hilltops down onto the valley floors.

On the Arctic coast in summer the running water tends to wash the soil from the hilltops and ridges down into the valleys. But this process of erosion and deposition is very slow compared to such action in the temperate zone; for one thing the summer rainfall on the Arctic coast is light, consequently it cannot be a great agent of erosion. More important is the fact that the late spring and early summer melt period, the only time that a large volume of water runs down over the hillsides, occurs while much of the ground is still frozen solid and thus is resistant to active erosion by the running water. This has resulted in a surprisingly uniform distribution of the soil—on the hills it is coarse and thin, in the valleys it is finer and thicker. The coarse soil of the hills and ridges rapidly absorbs the moisture, the fine soils of the valleys retain it and hold it on or near the surface. Such conditions of soil and moisture have produced predictable results in the pattern of vegetative growth; on the hills plants and brush are sparse, restricted to the hardier types used to growing in dry soils, while in the valleys the vegetation is heavier and more varied, often made up of water-loving species.

Arctic soils are relatively infertile, especially deficient in nitrogen mainly as a result of low bacterial action; the bacteria being inhibited in their activity by the low temperatures in the soil. Experiments with Arctic plants have shown that the nitrogen levels of plants grown in cold soils are often equal to those of plants grown in warmer soils, but the low temperature reduces the assimilation of the nitrogen into organic compounds. Whenever nitrogen is introduced into Arctic soil, the resulting increase in the growth and quantity of the vegetation is quite startling. The carcass of a caribou or a musk ox, left on the ground to rot, will often be enough to initiate a luxuriant bed of local flora; the ancient campsites of Eskimo hunters of long ago are easily visible from the air, or from a boat coasting the shore,

After the spring and summer melt period, valley soil is fine-grained and retains moisture near the surface; vegetation is heavy and varied.

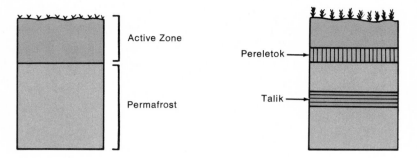

Much of the subsoil in the Arctic is permanently frozen the year round. Only the top few feet has a chance to thaw in summer.

The waters of Hudson Bay, or any large river or lake, serve as insulation and prevent formation of permafrost in ground below surface.

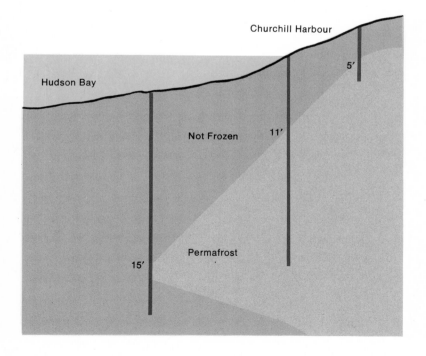

by the bright green of the local grasses and the dots of colour of the Arctic flowers that have grown up in the nitrogen-enriched soil. The slopes of the rocky hilltops on which the effluent pipelines of stations of the Distant Early Warning Line regularly discharge their waste materials, support growths of grass of a density and height quite unlike that found anywhere else in the area. The steep, rock faces of the many bird-nesting cliffs of the Arctic coast always support a lush and vivid growth of yellow, red and orange lichens; the tops of every small knoll in the tundra, favourite resting places of the larger birds, and denning places for foxes and ground squirrels, support luxuriant growths of grasses and Arctic flowers. And, however deficient the Arctic plants may be in nitrogen, they have an exceptionally high level of sugar thus making them highly nutritious food for the caribou and musk ox that roam the valleys, plains and plateaux.

The action of frost in the soil is a primary environmental factor in the growth and development of individual plants and of plant species. Not only have the Arctic plants had to adapt to a land of very low air temperatures and hard driving winter winds, they have had to contend with having their root systems encased in frozen materials for most of the year, subject to the break-up action of alternate thawing and freezing. During the autumn period the roots are often heaved up, torn and split by the tremendous power of the frost. Wherever the soil is unprotected by a cover of snow, which means on most of the hilltops and ridges of the Arctic coast, sudden, sharp drops in temperature in the autumn often split the ground wide open, tearing apart the root systems of the plants growing in the area of the crack. This results in the formation of greatly deformed root systems, if the plant is not killed outright, and it also causes the deformation of the stems of the upright perennials whenever the root is tipped, for the shoots will always grow vertically from the tilted stem.

The most widespread of the adverse ground conditions due to frost that must be met and conquered by Arctic plants is that of permafrost—the permanently frozen ground that extends down for varying distances beneath all the Arctic coast land surface. Permafrost underlies as much as one-fifth of all land areas of the world, principally in the northern hemisphere; in Canada between forty and fifty per cent of the land is underlain by permafrost. In the southern sectors of the Arctic coast region permafrost extends down for as little as a few dozen feet, while in the high Arctic islands it is known to penetrate more than twelve hundred feet below the surface.

The origin of permafrost is still not well understood. Most scientists agree that it probably made its appearance in northern North America during the cold periods of the Pleistocene period, although not necessarily beneath the land when it was actually under glacial ice; the thick cover of ice and snow would provide an insulating blanket superimposed on any frost that may have existed already in the ground. During the periods of fluctuating warmth and cold of the Pleistocene there must have been corresponding fluctuations in the depth and extent of the areas of permafrost; it may have disappeared altogether during the warmer periods.

Today permafrost in both Canada and Russia is forming in some areas, retreating in others; it is not present beneath the floors of the large Arctic lakes and rivers, even in the high Arctic. There is no permafrost under the bed of the Mackenzie River nor under the floor of Lake Hazen on northern Ellesmere Island, and it is thought to be absent beneath the waters of Hudson Bay for it is known to thin out very quickly seaward from the thickness of about 140 feet it attains in the vicinity of Churchill, Manitoba. But, whenever an island forms in a lake or a sandbar builds up in a river, permafrost begins to form in the soil immediately. Permafrost is known to form in southern Canada; not long ago it was discovered within the city limits of Edmonton, Alberta, when a large icehouse, in use over a long period of time, was dismantled and the ground beneath found to be frozen down to a depth of several feet with every indication that it had been permanently frozen during all the period that the ice-house stood above.

The formation of permafrost in soil is governed by a number of inter-related factors—air temperature, amount of precipitation, degree of cloud cover of the sky, direction of prevailing winds, the texture and water content of the vegetation above the ground all play important roles. Theoretically it can form whenever the mean annual temperature at the earth's surface falls below 32 degrees Fahrenheit, but in fact it does not begin to form until the temperature falls several degrees lower than this, due mainly to differing local soil and weather conditions. The actual rate of growth of permafrost has been observed in the

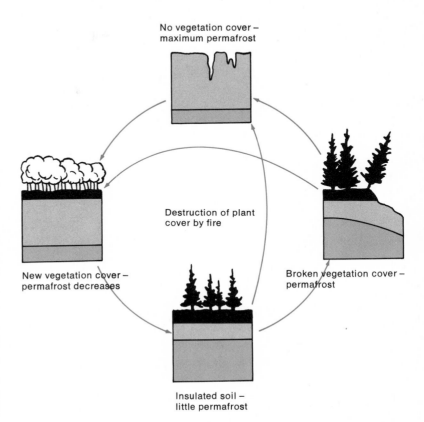

Surface vegetation provides another source of insulation, preventing the ground from freezing into a state of permafrost.

Arctic buildings are constructed on a cover of insulating material, to prevent the building sinking due to heat melting the permafrost.

area of the mouth of the Nelson River on the lower west coast of Hudson Bay. During the construction of the Hudson Bay Railway, which originally was to have had its northern terminus at Port Nelson and not at Churchill, a swamp with an unfrozen bed was drained. During the following winter frost penetrated the ground beneath the drained area to a depth of eight feet and did not melt the following summer. The second winter it deepened its penetration to twenty feet and in the third winter extended down to thirty feet which was the lowest depth of the permafrost for this area. At thirty feet it stopped forming, having reached the level at which the local seasonal changes in temperature had diminished with depth to the point where no new frost would form.

Near the surface the permafrost is divided into two layers, a deep layer that never melts (in contemporary terms), and a thin surface layer that thaws each year during the summer. The thawed layer of the permafrost is the "active" layer, and it is in this thin film of thawed soil that most Arctic vegetation grows. The active layer can be as thin as a few inches or as thick as a few feet; on an average within the Arctic coast region its base in summer would be about twelve to eighteen inches below the surface. Wherever the active layer is shallow the frozen ground near the surface represses all deep-rooted plants for their roots cannot penetrate the permafrost, although they can exist quite close to its upper surface. Plant roots growing near the permafrost often have an ovoid cross-section because of the greater amount of annual growth on the upper side of the root away from the frost surface.

Permafrost also affects vegetation through its influence on the drainage patterns of the Arctic coast; its upper surface provides a water-impervious base close to the surface of the land confining drainage to the surface layer, making the low lying regions of the tundra wet and bog-like, eliminating from such areas all but the water-oriented species. Were it not for the permafrost base beneath such land all surface moisture would drain away and great stretches of the Arctic coast would revert back to barren desert. It is paradoxical that the icy lid of permafrost keeps much of the Arctic tundra in bloom during the short summer.

One result of the trapping of large volumes of water in the thin layer of soil above the lid of the permafrost is soil creep or soilfluction. Soil creep occurs in southern Canada, the most readily visible example of this earth phenomenon is the slippage of the surface layers of earth on the newly graded embankments of the highways, where large masses of sod and soil often slide downhill before the roots of the grasses have a chance to take firm hold and keep the soil in place. On the Arctic coast soil creep occurs when the thin layer of soil in the active layer becomes heavily saturated with water in the summer and then slides gently downhill, coasting on the frozen top of the underlying permafrost. On gentle slopes this results in the development of a step pattern on the hillside; soil creep can occur on hills with a gradient as little as two percent and the resulting step configuration has a decided effect on the plant growth; the drier swells of soil support a different type of vegetation than the wet troughs between. In the high Arctic Islands soil creep often results in minor, sometimes major, earth movements.

Not only do Arctic plants have to contend with the violent freezing action of the surface soil each year and with the permanently frozen ground close to their roots, they have to adapt to a number of freeze-thaw phenomena that result in the formation of the surface soil into distinctive ground patterns. Throughout the Arctic coast region much of the land is clearly marked off in series of more or less symmetrical forms—circles, stripes, steps, polygons—that are the result of intensive frost action, the most common of which is the polygon. Best seen from above, polygon soil formations pattern great areas of the plateaux and the gentle slopes of the valleys. Rarely do they appear singly; usually they form an interconnected grid often covering wide stretches of ground dozens of square miles in extent.

Permafrost is both a negative and a positive factor on the Arctic coast—negative because of its deleterious effect on plant growth; positive because if it wasn't for the permafrost floor supporting the mixture of thawed soil and water on the surface of the land in summer there would be no vegetation at all over large stretches of the Arctic coast. In turn, the Arctic vegetation helps the permafrost near the surface by acting as an insulator from the heat of the sun's rays, preserving the permafrost table. Thus, the killing cold of the permafrost and the gentle heat mat created by the Arctic flora exist in symbiotic harmony, enemies yet friends, each playing a part in the preservation of natural life in a land dominated by cold and ice.

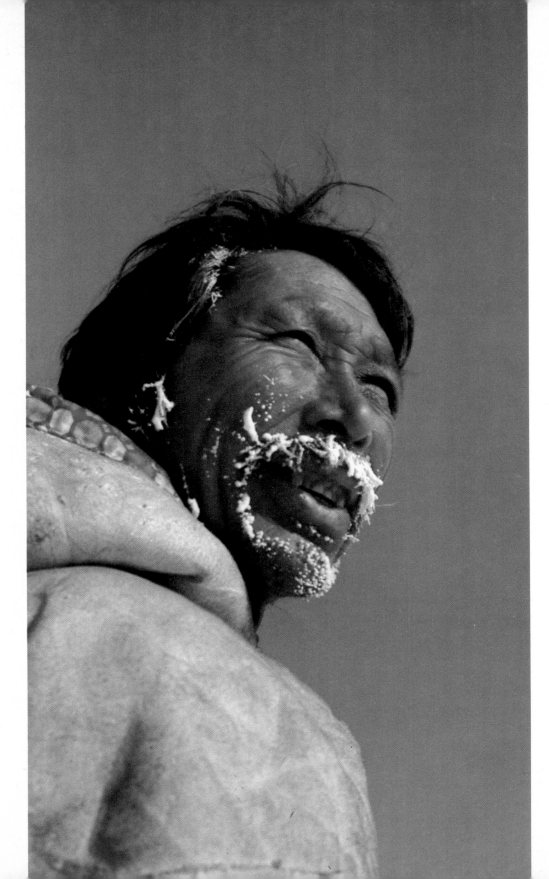

NATIVE MAN

Centuries ago, just how many centuries no one is quite sure, the mammal, man, moved into his ecological niche in the tundra biome of North America. He came from the east, out of the great Oriental branch of humankind, to migrate first over the dry land that connected Asia to North America about 10,000 years ago, and later across the narrow channel of Bering Strait, formed when the rising waters of the world's oceans, replenished by the melting of the glacial ice, encroached upon the lowland. Man came to northern North America as a hunter, already well adapted to life in the cold; a tundra nomad who gradually drifted along the coast on the top of the world until he occupied almost every corner of the emerging Arctic coast from Alaska to Greenland and as far south as Hudson Bay and the Gulf of the St. Lawrence River.

Note: Eskimo groups in black type
Indian tribes in red type
Areas of Eskimo settlement shaded purple

A collision of cultures

Eskimo hunters killed other Eskimo hunters
but, on the Arctic coasts of Canada, Eskimo
groups never engaged in inter-tribal war.
The ethic of the true Arctic coast hunter was
one of peace and understanding, a balanced
quiet broken only by the occasional family
feud and murder. However, all Eskimo groups
lived permanently in a state of war with the
neighbouring Indian tribes, from the mouth
of the St. Lawrence to the far off Beaufort
Sea. This warfare was so intense that the
Eskimo people were unable to colonize the
more hospitable lands to the south. Only
the barren Arctic was left to these early
colonizers from Asia.

*Naskapi Indians attack an Eskimo encampment
on the southeast coast of Ungava Bay.*

Narwhal. "Unicorn" of the Arctic Seas; outer skin, muktuk, contains Vitamin C; ivory tusk made into harpoon shafts.

Right Whale. Almost completely exterminated today, right whales once provided Eskimos with meat, fat and building materials.

Snow Goggles. Piece of antler or bone with two narrow slits.

Caribou Sinew. From the back of the caribou came the sinew for use as thread.

Caribou. "Supermarket" of the tundra – meat for food, skins for clothing, bones and antlers for knives, sinew for thread.

Arctic Char. "The" fish of the Arctic coast – so important to Eskimo hunter that many fishing places were "holy ground."

Sled. Made of wood obtained in trade with groups near tree line or from driftwood; basic mode of winter transport.

Water Bucket. Made from skins of mammals.

Kayak. The classic hunting craft; sealskin or caribou skin over lashed driftwood frame.

Walrus. Tough hide used as cover for umiak and for making harpoon lines, harness, lashings for sled.

Umiak. The huge "woman's" boat, walrus hide over a driftwood frame used on whale hunts or for general transportation.

Husky. Harness fashioned from walrus hide.

Ringed Seal. Without seals there could have been no modern Eskimo hunter on the coast. Basic food and fat source.

Living off the land

The resources available to the Eskimo hunter were few, but he exploited them to the utmost possibility of their use. Mammals of land and sea provided him with meat and fat for himself and his dogs, and with fuel for his lamps. They gave him skins for winter and summer clothing, materials for his tents and his boats. From their bone and ivory he fashioned harpoons, bows and arrows, knives and needles. From soapstone he made items such as pots, lamps and his pipe.

Sealskin Float and Harpoon. Harpoon head was of ivory, with handle attached to float.

Iron Pyrite. The classic fire starter of all primitive peoples.

Cotton grass. Tufts were mixed with fat for lamp wick.

Soapstone. Lamp and cooking pot.

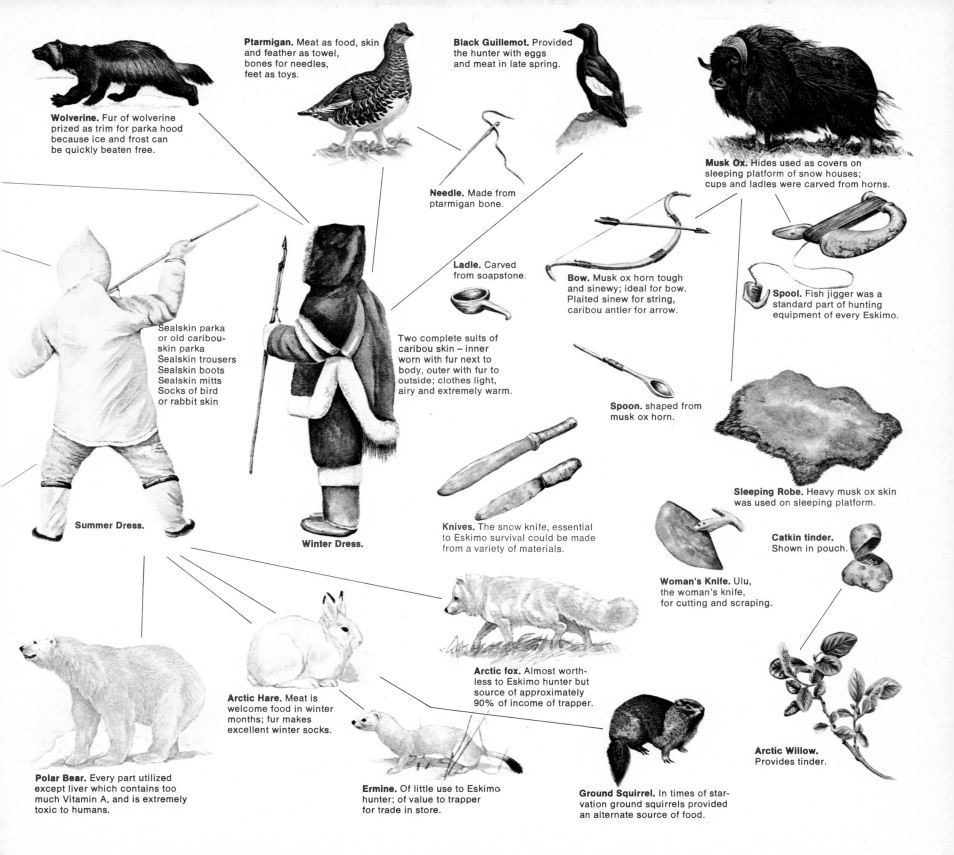

Wolverine. Fur of wolverine prized as trim for parka hood because ice and frost can be quickly beaten free.

Ptarmigan. Meat as food, skin and feather as towel, bones for needles, feet as toys.

Black Guillemot. Provided the hunter with eggs and meat in late spring.

Needle. Made from ptarmigan bone.

Musk Ox. Hides used as covers on sleeping platform of snow houses; cups and ladles were carved from horns.

Ladle. Carved from soapstone.

Bow. Musk ox horn tough and sinewy; ideal for bow. Plaited sinew for string, caribou antler for arrow.

Spool. Fish jigger was a standard part of hunting equipment of every Eskimo.

Sealskin parka
or old caribou-
skin parka
Sealskin trousers
Sealskin boots
Sealskin mitts
Socks of bird
or rabbit skin

Two complete suits of caribou skin – inner worn with fur next to body, outer with fur to outside; clothes light, airy and extremely warm.

Spoon. shaped from musk ox horn.

Summer Dress.

Winter Dress.

Knives. The snow knife, essential to Eskimo survival could be made from a variety of materials.

Sleeping Robe. Heavy musk ox skin was used on sleeping platform.

Woman's Knife. Ulu, the woman's knife, for cutting and scraping.

Catkin tinder. Shown in pouch.

Arctic Hare. Meat is welcome food in winter months; fur makes excellent winter socks.

Arctic fox. Almost worth-less to Eskimo hunter but source of approximately 90% of income of trapper.

Arctic Willow. Provides tinder.

Polar Bear. Every part utilized except liver which contains too much Vitamin A, and is extremely toxic to humans.

Ermine. Of little use to Eskimo hunter; of value to trapper for trade in store.

Ground Squirrel. In times of star-vation ground squirrels provided an alternate source of food.

Eskimo architecture

The Eskimo snowhouse, although found only in the central Canadian Arctic, has come to symbolize Arctic architecture. In order to conserve heat the interior of the dwelling was at different levels—the floor was below ground level, allowing little cold air to enter, while the top of the sleeping bench was at a height greater than entrance level to take advantage of warmer air. The snowhouse tended to be warmer if built on sea ice since the water was not as cold as permafrost on land. The sleeping bench was covered with willow branches and musk ox skins. Body warmth and heat from the lamps kept the inside of the house warm enough to allow a minimum of clothing to be worn.

In summer the hunters made tents of sealskin or caribou skin held upright by driftwood or whalebone poles. Some Eskimos made winter homes from blocks of peat-like turf, or dug semi-caves in hillsides and roofed them over by stretching sealskins over a whalebone frame.

The Eskimo's most ingenious dwelling was the winter snowhouse. First he found a snowdrift of just the right hardness, from which he cut blocks of snow, laying them in a circle. By back-cutting some of these first blocks he was able to start an unending upward and inward-leaning spiral, building his home around him as he went, not cutting his way out until the final "key" block was inserted and the house was complete.

Eskimo hunter scans the sea-ice surface looking for sleeping seals.

Sled dogs wait patiently at floe edge of ice as hunter retrieves seal.

Hunters of the Arctic coast

The earliest known migrants to come to the Arctic coast of Canada were proto-Eskimos, called by scientists the Pre-Dorset people. Seasonal nomads, the Pre-Dorsets hunted seals and walrus on and in the sea. First appearing in Alaska about 3500 B.C., by 2000 B.C. they had spread all the way east to Greenland where further expansion was halted by the wide expanse of the Greenland Sea. For 3000 years, until roughly 800 B.C., the Pre-Dorsets hunted and travelled throughout the Arctic coast region of Canada, gradually evolving into the Dorset culture people, originators of the snow-house or igloo. Dorset hunters reigned supreme on the north coast until about 900 A.D. at which time a thin wave of immigrants of a different Arctic culture, Thule, began to drift slowly along the coast from Alaska to completely replace the Dorsets as the dominant group. The Eskimo hunter of today is a direct descendant of the Thule people still wedded largely to life on the edge of the sea.

Hunter removes seal skin with a "snow" knife; the skin is used for clothing, boots, tents or kayak cover.

Bent in position with a harpoon, this hunter waits for a seal to rise up in the breathing hole hidden beneath the snow.

Using a white canvass screen to camouflage his dark figure, this hunter stalks and kills a seal sleeping on the ice.

Lichens grow well on the smooth surface of glacial-scoured rock.

PART THREE / **PLANT LIFE**

7 THE TUNDRA BIOME–THE FLORA

The myth of the year-round frozen north dies hard, for cold is our enemy and a cold climate the sign of a disordered land; only gradually are we coming to recognize that, despite its long background of development in a world of warmth, life on earth has adapted to the condition of cold in the same way that it has adapted to the condition of aridity that produced the deserts, to the condition of excessive wetness that produced the bog and swamps. Hunting man developed clothing and shelter that enabled him to live in the coldest of Arctic coast lands, providing at least a part of the land was free of permanent ice and he could find food; mammals of land and sea developed special physiological features that enabled them to resist the debilitating effect of extreme cold on their warm bodies. But all such adaptations among the fauna pale in comparison with the special traits developed by the flora that enabled certain plant species to live and propagate their kind under the severest conditions found anywhere on the face of the earth. On planet earth, where the factor of continual change is the one constant element, adaptability is the key to ultimate survival and nowhere is this quality better illustrated than by the flora of the Arctic world.

On display at the Plant Research Institute of the Experimental Farm in Ottawa are a number of tiny plants that are probably the oldest growing flora in the world today–Arctic Lupines grown from seeds found embedded in the permanently frozen soil of the northwest Arctic coast where they had lain undisturbed since they were placed in an ancient burrow by Arctic lemmings more than 10,000 years ago. For all of this immensely long period of time the seeds had been frozen, surrounded by frozen soil. Yet, brought forth into the light, supplied with heat and moisture, they were still capable of reproducing their kind. For 10,000 years the seeds had remained in a state of suspended animation, dormant yet viable, awaiting only the right set of conditions to spring to life again. "And," states Dr. A. E. Porsild, the recently retired chief of the National Museum's Herbarium and a long time researcher and collector of Arctic flora, "there is no reason to believe that there aren't seeds in even older deposits in the north. They could go back 1,000,000 years, to the beginning of the ice age."

How it is possible for life to withstand freezing for 10,000 years and then grow again as though nothing had happened, we do not know as yet. But it happens, and it is significant that it happens in the world of the flora, the plants that stand at the beginning of the food chains that link all living creatures together in a state of complete inter-dependency; without plants

EDIBLE PLANTS

No true Arctic plant is poisonous and all are possible sources of vitamins, yet the short growing season and the nomadic life of most Arctic peoples have kept their dependance on plants as a source of food to a minimum. These plants, however, are all eaten when available and are especially valuable to non-native peoples who do not eat the internal organs of animals and miss the prime source of vitamins that is available to the Eskimos.

Fernweed Sweet Coltsfoot Mountain Sorrel Arctic Sourdock

there would be no mammals, no man. Freezing will kill all fauna, permanent ice and perpetual cold will drive them from a region; but such conditions cannot completely kill or drive out all the flora. Most Arctic plants can be frozen stiff and then continue growing without any ill effect the moment they are thawed out; certain seeds have the remarkable ability to hibernate, to lie dormant through thousands, perhaps millions of years of freezing. Surely this must be the ultimate in adaptation for survival of species in a cold land.

To the gardener in southern Canada, often struggling to grow flowers and plants under next to ideal conditions, with varying degrees of success, the idea that plants and bushes thrive on the Arctic coast of Canada, a land under the control of ice, might seem a little strange. However, soil needed for plant life exists in many areas of the north coast, all the way up to the farthest north land areas on Ellesmere Island. Almost everywhere on the Arctic coast temperatures in the short summer climb high enough to provide a short growing period that is immeasurably assisted by the fact that the sun shines on the land for twenty-four hours of the day in many localities, helping plant life survive and thrive. But, in order to live and propagate, plants have had to develop species with characteristics of growth adapted to the rigorous conditions, plants with life cycles geared to a land where for the greater portion of the year they must lie dormant in or on the frozen ground while surface temperatures drop to fifty and sixty below zero and icy winds from off icy seas sweep over them; plants that can put down short roots into the thin layer of cold, thawed ground above the permanently frozen soil; plants capable of absorbing moisture mainly during the brief period of spring and early summer thaw.

On the Arctic coast of Canada there are five types of flora—lichens, mosses, grasses, plants and shrubs—that grow in three distinct community groupings, the tundra community, the rock and gravel hill community, the seashore community. On the seashore are the salt-tolerant grasses and sedges of the tidal flats, sandwort and sea pink; on the rock and gravel hills are lichens, mosses and cushion-type plants such as the saxifrages, plus the hardiest of the colonizing plants, the Arctic poppy. The tundra supports the lushest growth and the most varied Arctic vegetation; valleys carpeted in thick grasses, banks of rivers and streams lined with dwarf shrubs such as creeping birch and dwarf willow, slopes of the hills cloaked with the berry-bearing bushes interspersed with clumps of Arctic heather and vast areas carpeted with caribou moss.

With its great variety of plants and shrubs the tundra goes through a seasonal colour cycle that is a counterpart of the cycle in the deciduous forests of central and southern Canada. In spring the land is white with snow. Very quickly it turns to

Seabeach – Sandwort   Liquorice Root   Alpine Bistort   Baked Apple   Bilberry

brown as the snow melts away; then the brown coloration is relieved by splotches of green as the grasses renew their growth. Tiny splashes of bright colours appear wherever the flowers bloom; fields of white Arctic cotton grass flutter in the breeze.

There are almost no animal species of Arctic plants, the growing season so short that the normal life processes of the annual plants cannot be completed in one season. Almost all plants are perennials, able to spring into life quickly following a long period—nine to ten months of the year—of winter hibernation. Many of the plants lie dormant through the winter with seed in an advanced state of germination; many have seed pods covered with fluffy down for insulation against the heavy frost of the winter. In early summer, often before the snow has left the land, the plant will come to flower under the warming effect of the twenty-four hour daylight period. All plants spring to life, bloom quickly, turn colour and then go into hibernation again. This factor of very quick, yet very low, annual growth rate dominates all development of flora in the Arctic coast region.

The ubiquitous lichen is the humble plant of a not-so-humble land, a flat, rootless growth that flourishes where no other plant could possibly grow. Lichens grow almost anywhere on earth, their advance halted only by perpetual snow and ice, but they are especially well suited to life on the Arctic coast because of their capacity to withstand cold and lack of moisture, and because of their fondness for subsisting on naked rock. Lichens are among the first plants to move into barren ground and often they enable higher forms of vegetation to obtain a foothold on the new land.

Lichens are actually a composite of two separate entities linked together in a strange partnership; one part of the lichen is a fungus which produces acids that disintegrate the rock on which it grows, thus supplying minerals to its other part which is an algae. The algae, in turn, supplies the fungus with organic materials without which it would not be able to live. Lichens can be black or green, yellow or brown, bright red or bright orange; growing on the rocks of the Arctic coast they provide the land with much of its colour, both summer and winter. Many lichens are edible; the most important is the reindeer moss, *Cladonia*, which is sometimes mistaken for a moss but is actually a lichen, the main winter food for the great herds of caribou that roam the tundra valleys.

Although the plant life of the Arctic coast is far too sparse and too dwarfed to be considered as a food supply to man, all Arctic plants are edible and contain varying amounts of vitamins, proteins, sugars and starches. It is possible to eat any Arctic plant that looks at all appetizing without fear of being poisoned—there are no poisonous plants, no poisonous mushrooms, roots or berries. The easiest to pick and eat, and certainly the most wholesome to man, are the small fruits of the various bushes found everywhere in the sheltered valleys of the mainland and Baffin Island. Most of these berries are very hardy; they are not damaged by freezing on the branch, in fact freezing often improves the flavour. They can be collected from under the snow in the winter and even the next spring after the snow has melted away.

The leaves and stems of a number of flowering Arctic plants can be eaten like a salad, or used to make soups or flavour stews. Roots of other plants serve the same purpose. Leaves of certain plants can be boiled to produce a drink; even the lowly lichen can be boiled in water to jell into a nutritious and readily digestible food. Many different kinds of edible puff balls and mushrooms grow throughout the Arctic, especially in the grasslands of the tundra. Along the sea coast there are edible species of seaweed and marine algae.

A favourite of the Eskimo hunter is Arctic sorrel grass, a plant that looks like a miniature rhubarb and grows everywhere in the country north of the tree line, from the tundra of the mainland interior to the mountain valleys of northern Ellesmere Island. Sorrel grass stems and flowers can grow to a height of almost a foot, but four to six inches is closer to normal and the leaves are often as big as twenty-five cent pieces. Leaves and stems are succulent and juicy, with the strong acid taste of "green" apples. Cooked, the leaves resemble spinach and taste not unlike that vegetable; the liquid from the boiling can be sweetened with a little sugar, cooled and drunk as a refreshing summer beverage. Sorrel grass is the only plant of the Arctic that I have ever seen Eskimo adults actually collect and eat as a part of the summer food supply. When hunting on the sea in summer with my Eskimo "father," Idlouk, a small sugar sack was always stuffed into the bow of the kayak and often we would go ashore at certain locations near good sealing and whaling waters to collect the sorrel grass that grew in abundance.

THE ARCTIC IN BLOOM

A few inches, at best a foot or two, beneath these flowering Arctic white heather and Lapland rhododendron, lies the icy mantle of the permafrost, permanently frozen ground extending down as much as 1200 feet below the surface of the land. Each summer in the thin, thawed layer of soil above the permafrost, the Arctic plants burst into bloom to dot the treeless tundra with patches of brilliant colour. Battered by icy winds and often dusted with summer snow, their root systems branching out horizontally, Arctic plants, mosses and shrubs flourish wherever there is soil and water to support growth.

Much of the Arctic coast is rock, but lichens grow almost everywhere.

A miniature "forest" of tiny Arctic plants flourishes here.

The broad leaves of Salix reticulata *soak up the 24-hour sun.*

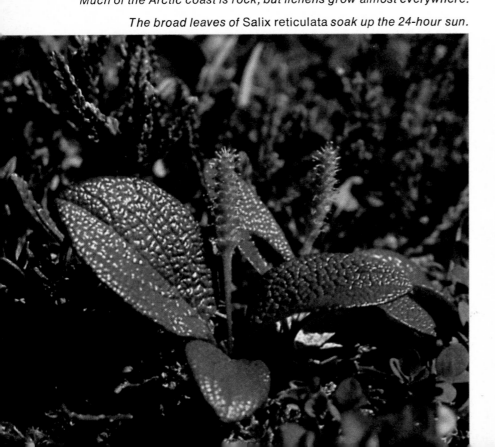

Summer splendour

In the short Arctic coast summer the treeless land comes alive. On cloudy days the land is a monotone of gray or brown, but when the sun shines throughout the 24-hour long day, rock and earth is patterned with vibrant colour—the yellow and green and orange of lichens growing on the rocks, the yellow of the Arctic poppy, the purple of the saxifrage. Sections of tundra are not unlike parts of southern Alberta—foot high grass bends under the wind; scrub bush grows in the sheltered waterways; bees and butterflies flit from flower to flower; spiders dart across the springy turf. Each year the tundra goes through a seasonal colour cycle—from late winter white, to brown, to green and then to the brilliant reds, yellows and golds of autumn. Then, as the sun slips lower on the southern horizon, cold re-establishes control over the land. Lakes and rivers freeze; snow covers the tiny tundra "forest." It will be nine months before the plants are seen again.

The caribou could not exist without the lichen, or caribou "moss."

Huge patches of purple saxifrage splash brilliant colour in the area.

Arctic willow pods are protected from the cold by fluffy down.

Arctic cotton grass is used as wick material for seal oil lamps.

The bright yellow marsh fleabane (above) is a common and beautiful edible herb.

Most Arctic flowers, like the delicate-looking Stellaria ciliatosepala (above) and the brightly-hued rhododendron (below) hug the ground to escape the bitter winds.

A burst of colour

Summer in the Arctic does not get as hot as the winter gets cold, but the region does have 24-hours of sunshine, and earth and water. Nourished by these elements, plant life grows and has developed many special features to overcome the relatively low summer temperatures and chilling winds. Temperatures within the brightly-coloured flower petals are several degrees warmer than those in the few white flowers which have survived. Many plants have hair covered leaves and stalks, to help along an earlier flowering, while others can freeze stiff and then thaw out to resume growth without suffering any ill effects.

The hardy Arctic poppy (right) sends its flowers 6 to 12 inches above the soil.

8 FLORAL ADAPTATION TO THE COLD

Of the various factors affecting the growth and development of plants in the Arctic the most important is temperature during the critical weeks of late spring and early summer. In vegetation the onset of photosynthesis takes place at a temperature of about 43° Fahrenheit. Because of the generally low Arctic air temperatures in summer and because of the further effect of chilling due to the cold winds that blow over the treeless land, Arctic flora has a hard time keeping warm enough for photosynthesis to take place. To overcome this difficulty plants have developed a number of special features.

Arctic plants and shrubs grow close to the ground where they are able to escape some of the effect of wind-chill but, more important, they create for themselves a tiny "forest" of vegetation about four or five inches high which may cover acres, as in the tundra valleys, or mere inches, as in the single, cushion-type plant. Within this "forest" temperatures are considerably higher than those found generally in the area. This permits the metabolic processes of the plants to proceed at a much faster pace than would be possible otherwise. In effect, the Arctic flora has adapted to the condition of summer cold by creating its own micro-environment within which the range of summer temperatures will differ from those of the open air only a few inches above.

In a recorded instance, with the air at minus 12 degrees Centigrade, the temperature within the mass of dead leaves of a saxifrage plant was plus 3.5 degrees Centigrade and within a dark clump of heavy cluster moss it stood at plus 10 degrees Centigrade. While these actual temperature differences may not be great compared to those created in the temperate or tropic zones, within the Arctic tundra biome a relatively minor increase in temperature within and around the plants is highly significant to processes accustomed to operating at close to borderline conditions most of the time.

There is a specialization on the part of some plant species that has seen the development of another micro-environment, one that exists beneath the many snowbanks that remain on the ground long after the general snow cover has disappeared. Certain plants are able to begin growth while still buried beneath as much as three to four feet of snow. This may not be quite the hardship it seems; plants buried under the snow have a great deal of extra protection from cold during the critical stages of spring and early summer growth, when unseasonably low air temperatures accompanied by high winds can arrest growth and even destroy the plant. Some Arctic species can remain in a state of arrested development while buried under snow banks for two years or more. Under such conditions, many physiological processes do not occur but the large carbohydrate reserves in the plant roots enable them to survive until the ground above becomes free of snow again.

It is known that the acceleration of the physiological processes in plants through temperature changes, such as occur during diurnal cycles and through the variations of cloud cover in the sky, is much greater within the lower range of temperatures than in the higher values. Although temperatures are relatively low on the Arctic coast they do show significant gradients within the day-night time cycle and Arctic plants are able to carry out growth and development patterns much faster than do their cousins in the temperate and tropic zones of the world. As well, temperature gradients on a south-facing slope in the Arctic will have an even greater variation within the lower range and will tend to produce and support a greater variety and quantity of plants. Almost all Arctic flowers are brightly coloured and the temperatures within the coloured petals are between five and six degrees warmer than the temperatures within the petals of the few flowers that are white; white flowers have failed in their adaptation to an extremely cold climate while brightly coloured flowers have succeeded in keeping warm enough to propagate and spread. As well, most Arctic flowers have quite large blooms in relation to the size of the vegetative shoots. This factor of large size is important to all life in a cold land, flora and fauna, for large size generally assists any organism in its flight to counter the effect of cold.

A good proportion of Arctic plants have a thick cuticle and an abundance of hair on the leaves and stalks both of which raise temperatures about the plant by trapping long-wave radiation, allowing much earlier flowering than would otherwise be

THE PRESERVATION OF HEAT BY ARCTIC PLANTS

Labrador Tea

Dwarf Willow

All Arctic plants must retain enough heat to enable photo-synthesis to take place. The chilling Arctic winds and the short periods of warm sunlight have made many special adaptations necessary. The Labrador tea is a low-growing plant, with its leaves covered beneath by a dense rust-coloured felt. The small leathery leaves serve as storage for winter food and are resistent to the drying effects of the wind. The mountain avens form a clump for warmth but this plant endures exposed winter sites where it does not have the insulation of snow cover, so that it can begin growth before the snow has melted. The dwarf willow hugs the ground to escape the deadly wind chill. The hardy leaves are hairy on both surfaces to retain all available warmth. The purple saxifrage is extremely adaptable, can make optimum use of the environment and is the most common flower of the northern region.

Mountain Avens

Purple Saxifrage

possible. Many have a cushion-growth that enables them to conserve heat and take full advantage of the higher surface temperatures and reduced wind speeds within the cushion. Still others disdain to adopt any special configuration, they merely freeze stiff during cold snaps and then thaw out to resume growth without seeming to suffer any ill effects. It is not at all unusual for Arctic plants to be frozen in air temperatures of minus three degrees centigrade and be covered with rime ice, then to thaw without sign of frost damage. Some species are able to arrest development and over-winter in any stage, ready to continue the growing process the following summer. Flowers of such plants take two years to develop, with the initiation of the flower in the first year and the expansion into the full flower the next. Such species are poised and ready for instant flowering in the second spring, often bursting forth before the snow cover has disappeared from the land.

All Arctic flora has a very low annual rate of growth; this is particularly true of the shrubs such as the willow and birch and juniper. Part of the reason for this is the generally low temperatures on the Arctic coast, but another important factor is the wind. Wind-chill is as hard on plants as it is on man; as a result Arctic brush hugs the ground where the velocity of the wind is less and the effect of the wind isn't as great. In sheltered valleys along the well-watered river courses willow will grow upright, reaching heights of three to four feet in such valleys along the north shore of Baker Lake; but on the bare, windswept ridges willow and birch creep along the ground, nowhere rising up more than an inch or two, often ten to fifteen feet long, and very old. Counts of annual growth rings, which can be seen only under a microscope, have revealed such bushes to be as much as four hundred years old.

From present knowledge it appears that not every year on the Arctic coast is suitable for seed production and germination. The pattern seems to be one of considerable production of seedlings over a few years followed by several years during which few, if any, seedlings take root. As yet not a great deal is known about pollination among Arctic plants although it is known that self-pollination is an important method, as would be expected in such a severe environment where little time is to be lost if the plant is to propagate and grow. There are bees, flies, moths and butterflies on the Arctic coast and indications are that plants depend on them for cross-pollination which helps to ensure a much greater genetic diversity within the plant communities than would be possible otherwise. Some Arctic plants do not conform to the general hug-the-ground pattern but extend flowers and seed pods upright on straight stems in order to take advantage of the Arctic summer winds in carrying the seeds far and wide across the land. In addition a number of species do not drop seeds until after the first falls of snow in the autumn; the seeds are transported by the later shifting and melting of the snow cover.

The high frequency of plants with asexual seed production ensures the continued propagation of new and vigorous types and also permits a rapid (for the Arctic) build-up of well adapted, genetically similar plants. Such plants are no doubt the first to colonize newly available land areas such as those laid bare by the retreat of glacial ice. Often they will move into a new area before the lichens and mosses have taken hold, and they will continue to grow on land surfaces that are under the shadow of massive walls of ice. The outwash plain of the Thompson and White glaciers is a scene of cold, hard beauty, a section of land about to be engulfed by a huge mass of glacial ice that is bearing down over it relentlessly, year after year. Across the front of the ice cliff of the Thompson glacier a wild stream runs rampant throughout the short summer, tearing at the rocks and gravel of the plain, ripping off great chunks of its banks that vanish into the swift waters and are carried off to the sea. Down from off the glacial tongue icy winds pour their never-ending streams of cold air across the plain, keeping the temperature at the base of the ice cliff near the freezing point all summer long, helping to make this place a most unlikely spot to find anything growing, except the wall of glacial ice.

Yet, about ten yards from the eroding bank of the glacial stream, a mere fifty yards from the face of the fifty foot high wall of ice, an infinitesimal patch of colour breaks the fierce monotony of brown and white; a tiny, yellow Arctic poppy bobs gently in the icy wind, completely contemptuous of the coarse rock and gravel soil at its base, equally contemptuous of the wall of ice rearing high overhead. Surely this little flower must share with the hardy seed of the Arctic lupine the honour of the near-ultimate in adaptability for survival in a land controlled by ice and cold.

THE LIVING ARCTIC

The wolf (above) is a predator, feeding mainly on caribou meat, but he can live well on ground squirrels, lemmings and birds' eggs. Seals must have air to breathe yet they live all winter in the sea under six feet of ice. The polar bear is a land animal but spends most of his life in the sea. Musk ox resemble, but are not related to, buffalo or ox, nor do they smell of musk; they are relics of a bygone age, descended in unbroken line from species first evolved one million years ago.

The sea in summer

Beneath the floating ice-pan of the Arctic sea in summer swims an occasional Greenland right whale, hunted almost to extinction by the rapacious whalers fifty years ago. More numerous are the Belugas—white whales—ten to fifteen feet long, toothed, slate-blue in colour when born but turning milk-white by the time they are four years old. In the open water near the floating pack swims the narwhal, unicorn of the Arctic seas. About the same size as the white whale, the narwhal is mottled black and white on the back and sides, whitish underneath. The male narwhal develops from its left upper jaw a spirally-grooved tusk of ivory that is often eight to nine feet long and can weigh as much as thirty pounds. The odd male has two tusks, one much shorter than the other. Even rarer is a female narwhal with a developed tusk. Swimming in the sea or sunning themselves on the floating ice are ringed seals, the layer of fat about their rotund bodies so thin in summer that they will not float when killed. Cleaving the dark green water of the open sea is the head of a polar bear as it swims strongly towards the distant shore. The polar bear paddles with front feet only when swimming; hind feet simply trail out behind. Above the water surface, and at the steep rock cliffs along the shore, fly the sea birds—gulls, kittiwakes, terns, fulmars, and murres. Diving beneath the sea for its food is a king eider duck, sharing the underwater domain with Arctic char and Arctic cod. In the shallows the huge walrus grubs on the bottom for clams and molluscs, somewhat prosaic fare for such a mighty mammal of the sea.

Arctic Terns

Polar Bear

Beluga Whales

Polar Cod

Crustacean

Herring

Fox Den Arctic Fox Cubs Willow Ptarmigan Ground Squirrel Arctic Poppies Lesser Fritillary Arctic Bee

Summer visitors and winter residents — an ever-changing panorama

In winter the Arctic coast is a near-empty land of ice and snow. In their dens the barren ground grizzlies sleep quietly, and ground squirrels barely breathe in hibernation. Many of the great herds of caribou have retreated into the sub-Arctic northern forest, leaving behind only scattered bands to winter on the tundra. Beneath the snow cover lemmings

Barren Ground Grizzly Bear Ground Squirrel Barren Ground Caribou Rock Ptarmigan

Barren Ground Caribou   Arctic Hare   Wolf   Male Pintail   Female Pintail   Barren Ground Caribou

scamper about in their tunnels; beneath the thick ice cover on the larger lakes, Arctic char swim and feed. Near the edge-of-trees the wily wolverine hunts Arctic hares; ptarmigan feed in flocks, preyed upon by the falcon in its white phase. In summer all this changes; the snow disappears, the ice on the lakes melts, flowers bloom and insects buzz, pintails swim gracefully in ponds, and herds of caribou invade the tundra once more to feed and drop their calves. Everywhere there is life and movement and sound as bears and ground squirrels awake, hares flee for their lives from the Arctic wolf, and thousands of migrating birds fill the air with their cries. *Panorama continued overleaf.*

Wolverine   Arctic Hare   Arctic Char   Wolf   Falcon   Rock Ptarmigan

Arctic Crocus   Arctic Wolf   Lemming   Musk Oxen   Lichen   Lemming   Arctic Cotton Grass

Under the stimulus of twenty-four hour sunlight, flora buds, blooms and withers with startling rapidity. Arctic crocus and white tufts of cotton grass bob in the breeze. Among the grasses and flowers, lemmings and ground squirrels search for food, and become food, for prowling wolves and foxes. Herds of musk ox prowl placidly across their home valleys while the young grow big and fat on the combination of fresh fodder and mother's milk. Great flocks of snow geese feed in the marshes and lay their eggs in down-lined nests on the gravel ridges. Through the long day of the short summer, the mean daily temperature on the Arctic coast remains uniform at about forty degrees (compared to sixty-eight degrees at Winnipeg and seventy-one degrees at Montreal) but the mid-day temperature can climb as high as sixty-five to seventy

Lemming   Arctic Fox   Female Polar Bear and Cub   Snowy Owl

Snow Geese

degrees at some locations, and has been known to reach a high of eighty. All this is in violent contrast to the winter months when great stretches of the Arctic coast appear to be snow and ice-covered wasteland. Most of the birds have gone; insects have disappeared; flora is almost all buried under hard-packed snow. But life goes on through the long, dark winter; lemmings scuttle about in tunnels under the snow, polar bears prowl inland looking for food, followed in turn by hungry foxes and ravens which share the find. The snowy owl wings his silent way over the snow, and the long, eerie howl of the wolf echoes across the snow-covered valleys as he and his family group hunt caribou, and, when driven by a need to fill their hungry bellies, will attack the powerfully-built musk ox. In winter, the Arctic coast is a land of feast or famine.

Wolf Pack

Musk Oxen

Raven

Polar Bears

Arctic Fox

Snow

Ringed Seal Pup in Den

Snow

Breathing Holes

Ringed Seals

Ice

Ringed Seals

Mother Seal

Ice

The ringed seal – a mammal of the northern sea

Without seals there could never have arisen the coastal Eskimo hunting culture. Seals provided the Arctic hunter with almost everything he needed – skins for clothing and summer shelter, fat as food and as oil for the lamps, flesh for food. Four main types of seals are to be found – the rare bladder-nose seal; the harp seal of the southern waters; the solitary square-flipper, or bearded seal, and the ringed

Sabine's Gulls

Glaucous Gulls

Stranded Ice Floe

Eskimo in Kayak

Ringed Seals

Phalaropes

Ringed Seals

Arctic Char

seal, or jar. The seal must have air to breathe and comes to the surface often in order to get air. In the fall, the seal pushes up the rubbery sea ice with its head to form a number of shallow domes filled with air. Through winter the seal returns to these domes to breathe, keeping each opening clear of new-forming ice. In the spring the females enlarge one or more of the holes, usually one beneath a large snowdrift in the lee of rafted ice. The seal pups are born in a cave cleared under the snow. Young seals are the favourite food of prowling foxes and bears who break in the cave tops to get at them before they can escape down the breathing hole to the safety of the sea. By mid-April the seals scramble onto the ice surface through the breathing holes, to bask in the warm spring sun.

Sun

Raven

Wolf Pack

Man with Bow
and Arrow

1900
Before the
introduction of
the rifle, immense
herds of caribou
brought life to
a desolate
land.

Nature's balance and
the onslaught of technology

Before the introduction of the rifle, immense herds of caribou roamed the land,
feeding on sun-nourished moss and lichen. Eskimo hunters, using their primitive
weapons, could not kill many, and the superbly-built wolves perhaps helped the
caribou by weeding out the weakest of the species. Scavenging on leftover kills
came the raven, the Arctic fox, the gull and the aloof barren-ground grizzly.
Modern-day enemies of the caribou include track vehicles, which disturb the tundra, fire and aircraft which terrify and cause stampedes, and although there are
fewer of the fearsome wolves, man now wields a deadly accurate rifle.

Arctic Fox

Raven

Aircraft

Fire

Tracked Vehicles

Man with Rifle

Wolves

1965
The handsome caribou, an important
link in the food chain of the Arctic,
has been depleted over a sixty-five year
period to one-tenth its former population.
Range-destroying fire, and poor calf
crops due to bad weather have been
contributing factors, but the
excessive kills caused by the
rifle have been most to blame.

Gulls

Grizzly

A scavenging raven feeds hungrily on caribou meat.

PART FOUR / ANIMAL LIFE

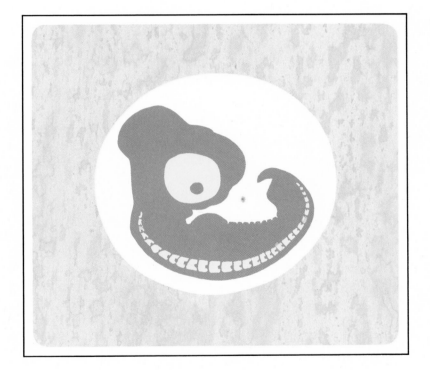

9 THE AIR ABOVE

All winter the land and frozen water surface of the Arctic is a white wilderness; mile after mile it stretches away endlessly to the distant horizon, thousands upon thousands of acres of treeless, snow-covered soil and rock and ice, a vista of white broken only by the dark rock hilltops or the shiny blue-green of the wind-blasted ice along the northern shores of the lakes. Across the face of this bare, and often bitter, land the winter wind shrieks in wild abandon, whipping up the snow to blot out the sun and the sky until the Arctic world is shrunk to a few square feet within the swirling walls of formless white. On quiet days the wind rustles gently over the snow; the land lies still and serene, the air filled with millions of dancing, twinkling diamonds of ice that reflect the red, red rays of the three suns hanging low on the horizon to the south.

In mid-winter the tundra seems devoid of life; rarely is there any movement other than that of snow granules snaking their sinuous, shifting lines across the hard packed snow. The winter tundra has its herds of caribou, sometimes hundreds of them together; it has its groups of musk ox, grazing in their sheltered valleys; it has its wolves and foxes and hares, but so vast is this far north land that it swallows them all; it engulfs them, singly or in their hundreds so that the tundra is like an immense white desert, a harsh and often cruel land, merciless to the unwary, granting life only grudgingly, quick to drive out or destroy any who fail to adhere to its terms for survival.

Empty the land seems, and especially does it seem empty of birds—no cheeps or song, no graceful forms flitting across the blue of the sky. And why should this not be so? This Arctic land has destroyed or driven out far mightier forms of life than the fragile birds; it destroyed the mighty mammoth, it forced the huge barren ground grizzly to endure a life pattern of winter sleep each year, it imposed upon the great herds of mainland caribou a life of constant movement in which most must head south for the shelter of the trees each autumn. Indeed, it would seem strange if the delicate birds did not go south for the winter, as most of them do. Most of them, but not all; for so adaptable is life on planet earth that it has developed within a few species of

birds special qualities that enable them to live year round, to reproduce and multiply in a land completely dominated by cold. And in one bird it has developed a body and a spirit so tough and unyielding that it makes no visible concession to cold; winter and summer the coal-black, bare-footed raven sneers contemptuously at its Arctic environment as if by strength of will alone it has met and mastered the worst conditions that can come its way.

The raven is a bird of the north, big, tough, strong, afraid of nothing, and in possession of an uncanny ability to "home" on any form of food from extremely long distances away. Even in mid-winter, when deep cold renders any odour almost negligible, the raven can sense a meal from afar. To see three or four ravens winging their way above the frozen tundra with a definite sense of purpose and direction to their flight, is to know that a herd of caribou with its attendant wolves can be found in that direction, that before long the ravens will be picking at a carcass lying bloody and still on the snow. To travel on the sea ice off the high, rocky cliffs of east Baffin Island and encounter ravens heading toward the edge of the land-fast floe some three to four miles out from shore is to know that a polar bear has killed a seal, and is now enjoying a meal of fresh fat and meat that it will soon have to share with the croaking birds winging their way unerringly toward the food that is far out of their sight.

Just how the raven senses meat over distant horizons is not known; nor is it known how the raven is able to exist on the Arctic coast year round without seeming to make any concessions to the cold and bitter winter weather. But live on the Arctic coast it does, coal-black the year round, feet and legs bare of any protecting feathers, seemingly completely indifferent to wind and cold, and equally indifferent to the threat of death or injury under the claws and jaws of the mammals upon whose fresh kills it so often feeds. I do not know if ravens tease polar bears or wolves, but I suspect they do. I do know they tease dogs unmercifully, often acting in concert in order to get at desired food. At an Eskimo camp on north Baffin Island I watched as three ravens sat on the snow-covered sea ice about ten feet from a big sled dog who was gnawing on a piece of frozen seal meat. The dog was untethered but the ravens, positioned in a circle about him, were not the least bit afraid. After a few moments one of the ravens hopped in toward the dog and immediately the dog stopped gnawing and growled deep in his throat. A second raven hopped in closer; with a rush the dog came to his feet and dashed at the first raven which merely hopped back, with considerable dignity, barely keeping clear of the dog's jaws. The second and third ravens dashed for the piece of meat lying unguarded on the snow but before they could reach it the dog had turned on them to send them into squawking flight.

The dog settled down to eat; in a few minutes the ravens again took up their positions on the snow; again one of them hopped in close. The dog's head came up and a low growl rumbled in his throat. Once again the second raven hopped in close; the dog leaped up, charged first at one raven and then turned to charge back at the other. But the second charge led him too far from the piece of meat; the first raven hopped in with almost contemptuous slowness to pick up the meat and rise majestically into the air. All three ravens flew along the beach, enticing the baffled dog to follow them, before sweeping into the sky to disappear around a distant point where they could enjoy their stolen meal in squabbling peace.

Of the many birds found in the Arctic there are only eight that spend their lives in the country north of the tree line—the raven, the snowy owl, the gyrfalcon, the willow and the rock ptarmigan, and three members of the auk family, the black guillemot, the thick-billed murre, and the dovekie. All other birds are migratory, coming to the Arctic each spring and summer to nest and raise their young, but flying south as soon as the first touch of winter sweeps over the land. Even the snow bunting, which is a northern bird and often re-appears on the tundra late in winter long before any sign of spring melt, abandons the Arctic in mid-winter for the somewhat less rigorous climate of southern Canada where it can be seen feeding in large flocks along the roadsides and in the farm fields.

The true Arctic birds have made adaptations to the cold, and to the fluctuating temperatures, of their far north homeland in much the same way as the Arctic mammals. For the birds, feathers perform their basic flight function but they also serve as excellent insulation, corresponding to the fur of the mammal. Feathers of Arctic birds are generally a little longer than those of related birds to the south and, in most species, plumage changes in density with the season—more feathers in winter than in summer for extra warmth. Snowy owls and ptarmigan grow

The red-throated loon builds his nest in a heap of moss or other vegetation, very close to the water's edge in marshy areas.

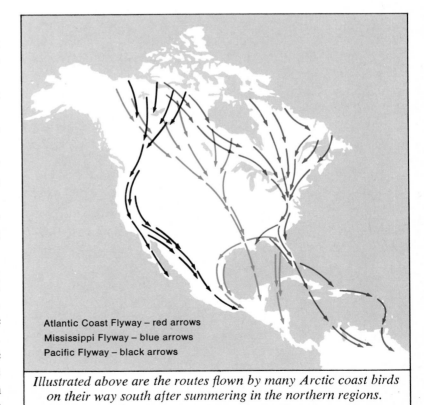

Atlantic Coast Flyway – red arrows
Mississippi Flyway – blue arrows
Pacific Flyway – black arrows

Illustrated above are the routes flown by many Arctic coast birds on their way south after summering in the northern regions.

Sparrow (northern)

Sparrow (southern)

Willow Ptarmigan (winter)

Willow Ptarmigan (summer)

Willow Ptarmigan Hiding in snow bank

Larger than his southern counterparts, the sparrow is better able to withstand the cold; willow ptarmigan change colour with the seasons.

feathers on their legs as well as on their bodies; in winter ptarmigan even grow a thick covering of feathers on both feet right up to the claws, giving them a somewhat comical appearance as they strut over the hard-packed snow. At the start of an Arctic storm ptarmigan will plunge into the nearest bank of softer snow where they will remain snug and safe from the violent winds above.

Although the raven is the most unusual, the ptarmigan is the most truly Arctic bird. Two species are found north of the tree line—the willow ptarmigan and the rock. The willow ptarmigan is the larger; its habitat is the tundra and upland valleys of the mainland Arctic coast and the lower Arctic islands. The rock ptarmigan has a more extensive range over the tundra biome; it is found everywhere from lower Hudson Bay in the south to northern Ellesmere Island in the far north, both summer and winter, although many of the far north flocks migrate to the southern edges of the tundra during the winter, occasionally travelling as far south as James Bay.

The ptarmigan belongs in the *Tetraonidae* family, fowl-like birds widely represented all across the northern hemisphere. It is a relative of the grouse but a little larger than its cousin to the south, thus taking advantage of the general, but not infallible rule, that larger size enables a bird, or a mammal, to better withstand cold—the larger the body surface is in proportion to the bulk, the less is the amount of heat that will be lost through the body surface. The matter of large size is also an advantage

to birds during the Arctic winter when food is in much shorter supply. A small bird has more surface per volume of heat producing tissue than a large bird and therefore it needs more food per unit of body weight. Of all species of birds that live in the Arctic for at least a portion of each year about sixty per cent are pigeon size or larger, compared to only thirty per cent of all birds in southern Ontario.

In summer the rock ptarmigan has a brownish-grey speckled plumage (male) or a barred, black and white plumage (female), except for the wings which are white. In winter both sexes have an all-white plumage except for an eye bar of black, and black tail feathers with white tips, of which only the white tips show unless the bird is in flight. The all-white covering is an excellent camouflage; ptarmigan will freeze if danger threatens so as to be practically invisible against the white snow. The black, or white, or black and white pattern of coloration is standard among Arctic birds; the tundra is a hard land, not prone to encourage the development of non-essential frills of any kind. Arctic birds have few colours and when they do such colour is confined to the naked areas of the head and feet.

Arctic birds share with Arctic mammals the ability to maintain a double standard of internal body temperature, especially the sea birds that spend the greater part of their time, winter and summer, swimming on or in the icy water of the sea, or standing for long periods on the ice itself. Extra body fat, an undercoat of down plus fluffy, oily feathers keep the body and the wings of

The golden plover is a migratory bird, while the snowy owl and the raven have adapted well to a year-round life in the cold regions.

Snowy Owl
Feathered legs
Luxurious coat

Raven
Intelligent
No visible adaptations

Golden Plover
Summers in Arctic region

Golden Plover
Migratory Route

the guillemot warm and dry as it explores for food far down in the water beneath the sea ice cover. But its legs and feet have no such protection. Similarly the gull that stands for hours on a pinnacle of ice waiting and watching for food, has bare feet in direct contact with the ice. Experiments in Alaska have shown that the temperature within the feet of a gull can be near 32 degrees Fahrenheit, just above the freezing point and about 70 degrees cooler than the rest of the body. Along with this colder temperature in the legs, the gulls seem able to increase the circulation of the blood to the legs and feet without any rise in temperature taking place. Such birds, extremely tolerant of cold, are able to move about and function well at low temperatures that would completely immobilize a bird accustomed only to the temperatures of the temperate zone.

Despite the phenomenal ability of the gull to stand for long periods on bare ice, it, like most of the birds that come to the Arctic, is a great coward, or it is blessed with an extraordinary amount of common sense, or it reacts to stimuli implanted within its being many thousands of years ago. Most birds found on the Arctic coast in summer don't wait around for the winter weather; long before the cold turns the Arctic into a land of ice and snow, they head off south, flying fast and far, over and around almost all barriers of mountains, seas and deserts. For most Arctic birds their adaptation to cold has been to flee, to head west, east and south away from the Arctic coast in a great mass movement that we call migration.

In summer the tundra is home to hawks, falcons, jaegers, owls, all of which prey upon the smaller birds, ptarmigan, plovers, turnstones, curlews, sandpipers, phalaropes, larks, sparrows, longspur, and the ubiquitous snow bunting. In certain areas sandhill cranes nest and feed; in the marshy regions loons, swans and ducks fight for territory, nest and raise their young before gathering in huge flocks to fly south again. Year after year the birds return to the same nesting grounds, usually arriving within a few days of a certain time in the late spring. Despite their tremendous ability to navigate, the birds are poor weather prophets, regardless of the climatic conditions at the nesting site. the birds always arrive at their allotted time to begin the nesting. In 1953 summer on north Baffin Island was very late in arriving, June was a month of extreme cold and violent storms. At the snow geese nesting grounds on Bylot Island geese sat on eggs in nests on the ground, buried up to their necks in new snow, with long drifts extending downwind from their bodies.

On the tundra the small birds feed on the millions of insects that fill the air during the summer months. Others feed on the seeds of the grasses, on the berries of the bushes. The predators feed on eggs, on the smaller birds, and on the lemmings and mice that scamper about the tundra biome "forest." All through the twenty-four hours of daylight each summer day the birds are on the nests or on the move, full of energy and vitality, as if conscious of the fact that their time on the Arctic coast is short − urgency is the order of the day, there is no time to lose. So well developed is this sense of limited time that some species go through the annual courtship stage on the long flight north, arriving at the breeding ground ready to nest immediately. Nesting must be a success the first time; failure means a wait until next year to try again. The eggs are laid, the young are born and grow to youth in a non-stop cycle of activity, allowing no time for any post-breeding loaf period; often the birds moult gradually while on the move or they postpone this process until after their arrival on the southern wintering grounds.

On the treeless tundra all species of birds nest on the ground, either on the gravel ridges as do the snow geese; within the hummocks of patterned ground as do most of the small birds; on the grassy hummocks of the swamps as do the loons. Often species of birds, or certain birds and mammals, will establish a symbiotic relationship at the nesting grounds to help ensure their survival. On the wide gravel hills of southern Bylot Island colonies of snow geese nest each year, building their foot-diameter, down-lined nests in slight hollows in the gravel. A single colony will extend over some three or four acres, the flat, stony ground covered with nesting hollows in which the female lays anywhere from half a dozen to a dozen and more, chicken-size eggs. Sometimes the colony will have one or more brood nests in which surplus eggs are laid and abandoned; it is not unusual to find such nests full to overflowing with two or three dozen unattended eggs, often so many that the ground around is covered as well. Many of the snow geese colony sites will have a small hill within the area, on which a snowy owl will nest. The owls do not harm the geese or their eggs; they serve as sentinels, warning of the approach of foxes, driving away foxes by their swooping attacks and thus helping both themselves and the geese.

Without the advantage of nesting in trees away from ground predators, Arctic birds have had to develop other means of ensuring their continued survival. Many species have exceptionally well-developed distraction techniques by which either male or female flutters along the ground dragging a wing as if injured, thereby distracting the fox or the wolf away from the nest and the young. The generally dun-coloured ground birds fit well into the background of grass and moss among which they build their nests; the ptarmigan in its summer coat is almost as invisible as it is in its winter white. Jaegers and terns use a dive

bomb technique to drive away foxes and wolves, and humans as well, swooping down from heights of fifty to seventy-five feet in near vertical dives at the bottom of which they often hit the mammals a blow with a wing before streaking back up into the sky for another swoop. The birds also use such dives as a hunting technique; often they will follow foxes, wolves, bears, even caribou walking over the tundra, watching for the small birds startled by the passage of the animal.

Although the tundra is home for thousands of summer land birds, the biggest groups contain the sea birds that nest on the bird cliffs found all through the eastern Arctic coast region. Gulls, fulmars, kittiwakes, murres all nest in huge colonies at specific locations to which they return year after year. Every Eskimo hunter knows the locations of the bird nesting cliffs in his area and, in the days of old, would travel there with his family in the early summer to eat the eggs and the young birds as a welcome change to his winter diet of meat and fish. Digges Island, at the western entrance to Hudson Strait, is the site of huge murre nesting colonies, fulmars nest at cliffs all along the east coast fiords of Baffin, Devon and Ellesmere Islands; the rugged cliffs of Pelly and Committee Bays on the north coasts have famous gull cliffs, both on the sea coast and on the steep cliffs of the inland hills.

One of the oddities of the Arctic is a little bird, a summer dweller which comes to the Arctic each year to nest and raise its young before heading south for the winter. The bird is the phalarope, a small water species related to the sandpiper. The phalarope looks much like any other shore bird but the superficial resemblance is deceiving. In the bird world it is almost always the male that is the bright-coloured member of the family. Not the phalarope—the female is bright-coloured while the male is dull. In the bird world the male is always the first to arrive at the breeding ground, to select the nest site and then remain with the female while she lays the eggs and raises the young. Not so the phalarope—the female arrives first at the nesting area and picks out the site. She lays the eggs but it is the male bird that sits and hatches them while the female defends the home. In the phalarope, at some time in the distant past, chance mutation seems to have caused certain sexual characteristics to become reversed and, as a result, the phalarope ended up as a freak in the bird world.

BIRDS OF THE NORTHERN SKIES

In summer the Arctic coast plays host to thousands upon thousands of birds, most of which, like the long-tailed jaeger in the picture above, have flown hundreds of miles along ancient migration routes. Some birds arrive from the south, like the Arctic tern which has come all the way from Antarctica. Other birds come from southeast and southwest—the yellow-billed loon winters on the Pacific coast; Canadian fulmars winter in the North Atlantic. Wheeling and crying over land and sea the birds bring visible and audible life to every nook and cranny of our far northland.

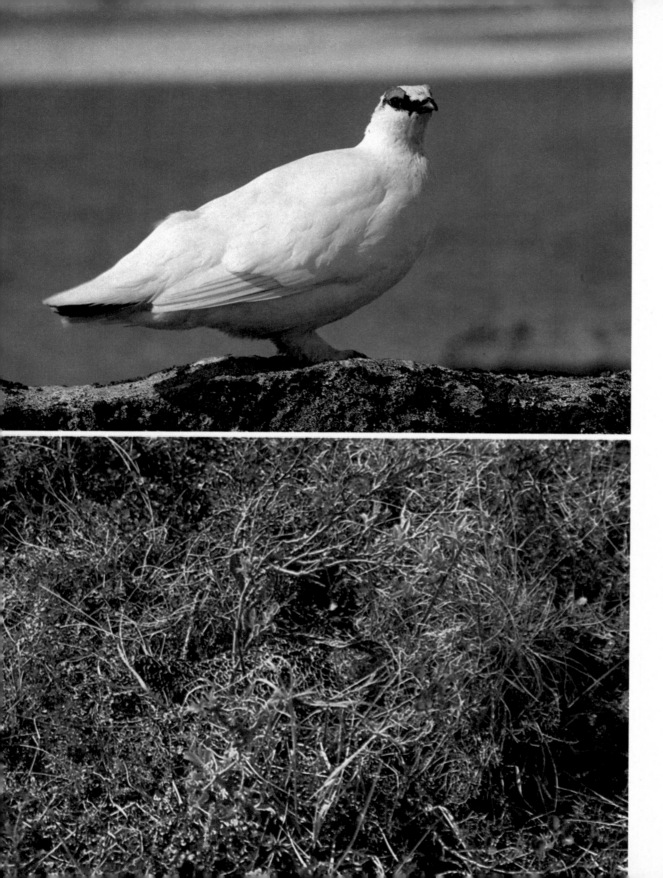

Techniques for survival

Having to nest on the ground robs most birds of the protection from predators afforded by nests in trees. Different protection techniques are used by different species of birds. Ptarmigan depend on camouflage in winter and summer. Almost invisible in winter white or summer brown, ptarmigan will freeze when danger threatens, exploding into violent flight only if directly threatened. Small birds build their tiny nests under low bushes, or beneath overhanging clumps of hummocky, frozen ground. Geese and swans remain white all summer and nest in plain sight, relying on size, fighting ability and distraction techniques to ensure their continued survival. Loons nest on dry hummocks in the middle of swampy areas; hawks build their nests on ledges of the rocky cliffs. At the bird cliffs or the steep rock shores of many Arctic islands, sea birds such as gulls, kittiwakes, terns, fulmars, nest high on the rocky ledges safe from all but predatory birds, and hunting man. For three months the birds are everywhere on the land; then, almost overnight, they are gone on the long migration routes to their summer homes.

The male rock ptarmigan is shown at upper left, complete with protective feathers covering his legs and feet. Crouching immobile in her summer nest, the female willow ptarmigan, left, is well camouflaged.

The four eggs shown below belong to
the tiny tree sparrow, a summer
visitor to the Arctic. The nest is
almost invisible in the dense under-
brush, and the young are guarded and
fed (right) by an adult sparrow who
depends on her summer camouflage
for protection against predators.

The newly-hatched cygnet sitting in a
nest safely hidden by the long grass,
(above) will mature in a few years into
a beautiful whistling swan. Skins of
these summer visitors were once traded
as furs, but are now protected by law.

A wary young gyrfalcon (pictured overleaf) sits safely in his nest on the
cliffside high above the Kazan River.

10 FAUNAL ADAPTATION TO THE COLD

The Arctic coast region is a land area under the influence of ice, within which all life must adapt to the fact of extreme cold. But the basic adjustment of the life forms is not so much to the cold itself as it is to the very wide fluctuations in temperature through the yearly cycle of heat and cold. As a minimum requirement all tundra fauna, as well as flora, must be able to exist at a temperature of 60° above zero as well as at a temperature of 60° below, a range of 120 degrees.

Insects have had no difficulty in adjusting to the variations of climate within the Arctic, a fact that can be verified by anyone who has suffered under the clouds of millions upon millions of mosquitoes that swarm over the tundra during the summer months. In 1743, the Chief Factor of the recently completed Fort Prince of Wales on the west coast of Hudson Bay, observed that "Mosquitoes bite with their sharp bill in such a manner that shall have our heads swelled as big as a tilterkin (a large cask); as to a man's not seeing a mark he fires at for them is nothing, . . . you may very well sweep a bushel off one man's head; they have been so thick we have been obliged to shovel them away before we could get in at the doors!" In the years since that time mosquitoes haven't lessened in numbers at all.

But why should insects be bothered by the minor inconvenience of cold? Insects have existed on earth in approximately the same numbers as they are today for the past 300 million years during which time they have had plenty of time to work out adjustments that enable them to live under almost any conditions known on planet earth. Certain insects live in hot springs where the temperature of the water reaches 120 degrees Fahrenheit; others have been frozen solid and lived to breed and multiply; some species survive in laboratories in an almost total vacuum. Insects live in deep, underground caves; others can exist in the air at altitudes of 20,000 feet. The young of the brine fly live in almost pure salt; petroleum flies spend their immature stages in pools of crude oil; a grain weevil can live for hours in an atmosphere of pure carbon dioxide. On the bleak Antarctic continent, although there are no truly land mammals or birds, over forty kinds of insects live and thrive.

To the insects the cold and fluctuating temperature of the Arctic coast region must have seemed a rather minor problem to which they adjusted with ease. Bees, beetles, moths and butterflies live as far north as flowering plants grow, decreasing only in variety of species and in numbers of certain species. Mosquitoes live wherever there are warm-blooded animals like the caribou and musk ox, the Arctic hare and the ground squirrel, from which they can draw blood. Blowfly larvae breed wherever there are carcasses of lemmings and mice to serve as their hosts; earthworms, spiders, mites, midges, flies find food and protection in the burrows and nests of these Arctic rodents. No Arctic land surface seems too poor or too cold to support some insect life; tiny Meighen Island in the high Arctic, described by Stefansson as "the most nearly barren land that I have ever seen," supports at least two arthropods that find sustenance from seventeen types of plant life, and from the scattered droppings of a few visiting birds and the odd, wandering caribou.

The land mammals and birds of the tundra biome have not been able to duplicate the extremes of adaptation of the flora and the insects; they found other means to protect their warm bodies in order to ensure continued survival and reproduction of their own kind. Most birds take advantage of their flight facility to leave the Arctic coast altogether during the cold period, returning only when the weather has warmed up again. Some mammals enter a state of dormancy or hibernation, a pale imitation of the hibernation of the flora, in which they exist for at least a part of the long, cold winter period. Other mammals, and a few of the birds, have insulated covers for their bodies, either as fur or feathers, that change density with the season allowing them to exist in reasonable comfort at sixty below or sixty above and it is becoming increasingly evident that all Arctic mammals and birds have developed controls that regulate metabolism and circulation so as to cope with excess heat as well as excess cold.

All birds and mammals of the tundra are warm blooded, deriving their body heat from energy produced from the foods they eat. The colder the outside air temperature, the more food they require to maintain body heat. The temperature at which man, a warm-blooded mammal without fur covering of any kind, starts to lose heat is quite high, about 80 degrees Fahrenheit. In order to halt this loss, or slow it down, some form of

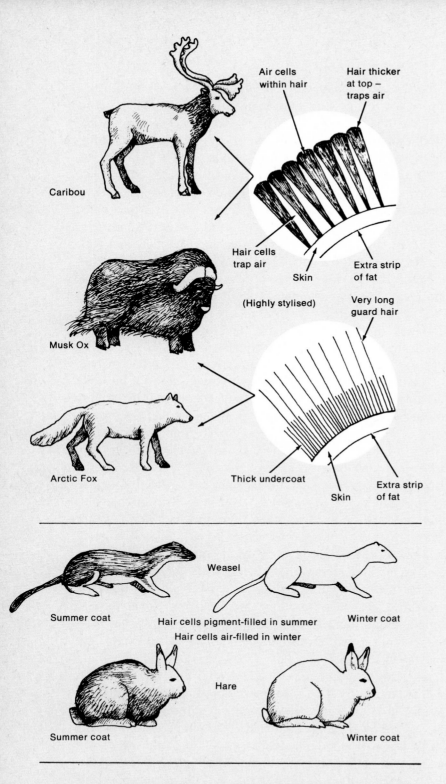

Caribou

Air cells within hair

Hair thicker at top – traps air

Hair cells trap air

Skin

Extra strip of fat

(Highly stylised)

Musk Ox

Very long guard hair

Arctic Fox

Thick undercoat

Skin

Extra strip of fat

Weasel

Summer coat

Hair cells pigment-filled in summer
Hair cells air-filled in winter

Winter coat

Hare

Summer coat

Winter coat

Survival of animal life in a generally harsh Arctic environment necessitates several adaptive techniques, such as seasonal changes in the extent, type and coloration of the Arctic mammal's fur coat.

outer covering becomes a necessity and the greater the degree of cold the heavier the covering that will be required. Thus, all warm-blooded mammals of the Arctic coast have developed thick coats of fur to trap the heat produced by eating large quantities of food. Most mammals reinforce this fur insulation by taking shelter for at least part of the time, in burrows in the ground, in burrows under the snow, or in snow caves dug into the deep drifts that form in the lee of the hills and ice hummocks.

The type, extent and coloration of the fur on the Arctic mammals varies considerably. Probably the best protected is the Arctic fox which has a fur coat consisting of long guard hairs over a short underwool. So efficient is the protection of his luxuriant winter coat, the fox has no need to move about to create warmth until the outside temperature falls below minus forty degrees. The huge musk ox is another example of this double type of coat; it has a thick undercoat of wool up through which grows a mat of very long guard hairs, so long they trail on the ground by the late winter, providing extra protection to the legs and feet. The pelage of the caribou is of a different type; it is a single fur covering of hair that grows anew each season, getting progressively longer all through the cold months of fall and winter before being shed in the early summer. Each hair of the caribou fur is full of tiny air cells within the hair stem, and each is thicker at the tip than it is at the base, thus trapping dead air within the fur coat, increasing greatly the insulation value without any increase in the weight.

Many Arctic mammals change the colour of their fur to white, or off-white, in the winter months; the fox, the weasel, the hare of the mainland and lower islands, all change from a generally brownish summer colour to a winter coat of almost solid white. This serves as a protective device against their predators, but it also serves an insulation function as well, for the cells within the hair that are filled with pigment in the summer are filled with air in the winter. The polar bear remains white, or off-white, the year round; the musk ox retains its brown colour. Caribou of the mainland seem to have more white hair in winter than they do in summer, although this may be a result of the hair being longer; the polar caribou of the high Arctic islands have considerably more white hair in their fur than do their cousins on the islands and mainland to the south.

Insulation about the body of the mammals also takes the form of an invisible layer of fat immediately beneath the skin. This is less well developed in the land mammals than in the sea mammals and probably serves more as storage of tissue to produce extra heat during the winter months. The fat is produced from the carbohydrates in the food eaten during the relatively warm days of summer and fall. The long, thick strips of fat that form along the back of the caribou are a favourite delicacy of the Arctic coast Eskimo hunters.

Although it is not an all-encompassing principle, Arctic mammals are often larger than their counterparts to the south; the larger an object, the more slowly it tends to lose heat which is a definite advantage in the tundra biome. Along with larger size, Arctic mammals have much smaller appendages; ears, noses, tails are almost always stubby with less surface to radiate away body heat. Mammals like the fox, the wolf and the husky dog can fluff out the fur around their bodies to entrap more air and add, at least temporarily, to their warmth. They can also modify their basic shape so as to make it more compact and reduce the amount of surface radiating heat to the outer air. Anyone who has seen an Eskimo dog curled up into a tight ball with nose tucked under curled-up tail, feet and legs hinged beneath the ball of the body, tiny ears pressed flat into the heavy fur of the head and all fur fluffed up while he sleeps soundly in the open, oblivious to the thirty below temperature and the howling wind, will have seen the near ultimate of inter-acting forces designed for the conservation of body heat in the cold.

The least understood of all the factors that enable Arctic mammals to withstand great cold and extreme fluctuations of temperature are the internal processes which act so as to conserve or dissipate heat. Dissipation of excess heat is almost as important as the retention of heat, especially to animals like the caribou which may be grazing peacefully one minute and in full flight over the tundra the next. Thinner fur on the belly area, ears, legs and tail serve, along with the standard panting tongue, as means of getting rid of excess heat. In addition, many Arctic mammals can withstand temperatures as much as fifty degrees higher than those tolerated by some desert mammals, their metabolic processes geared to respond to excess of heat through the same set of controls that acts to cope with excess cold. Caribou, dogs and wolves, as well as birds, have a double standard

Bison

Musk Ox
Shorter legs and longer hair

Arctic Fox
Smaller appendages with less surface
to radiate away body heat

Eastern Fox

Husky
Thinner fur on legs and belly

Husky curled up for warmth with
hair fluffed up to trap air

Temperature much lower in caribou's legs
than in the body; cuts down heat loss

The Ground Squirrel is the only
Arctic mammal who hibernates

The metabolic processes of Arctic mammals are geared to respond to excesses of heat or cold, in order to be able to withstand an extreme temperature fluctuation from sixty below to sixty above.

of body temperature; in their legs temperature is kept as much as fifty degrees lower than in their bodies, cutting down on the heat loss through these extremities. This temperature differential is accomplished by means of a simple heat-exchange mechanism in the body; arteries carrying warm blood toward the legs are closely bunched and twined with veins carrying the cold blood from the legs back to the heart; in this way the warm blood is cooled and the cold blood is warmed in a never-ending exchange of heat and cold.

Strangely enough, although it would seem that hibernation would be the simplest method by which the smaller mammals could avoid the excess cold and the restricted food supply of the long winter period in the Arctic, only one mammal actually hibernates—the little Arctic ground squirrel. True hibernation, as opposed to long periods of otherwise normal sleep accompanied by periods of wakening and movement, is a rare thing among all mammals of the earth. What physiological process triggers hibernation is not yet known, except that the onset coincides with the advent of cold weather in the autumn and the resulting disappearance of the food supply. It is possible that the shortening of the daylight hours may be what triggers hibernation. Many northern mammals can be induced to vary normal reproduction cycles when subjected to periods of artificial light that do not correspond to the actual length of the day; normal spring activity of the pituitary and sex glands can be slowed down by artificially keeping the "day" short as if it were still mid-winter or the mammals can be induced to reproduce in winter under the stimulus of an artificial, very long day.

When the ground squirrel hibernates for the winter its body temperature drops to only a few degrees above the freezing mark and its normally rapid breathing slows down until it is difficult to tell if the animal is breathing or not. Its heart beats at the very slow rate of five to ten beats per minute as opposed to a normal two to four hundred. Curled up in a tight ball in its snug burrow under the sod and snow, a hibernating ground squirrel is almost dead; it can be picked up and put down again without a stir.

Mice, lemmings, shrews, all small mammals of the tundra, are content to spend only a small part of the winter in a state of dormancy; most of the time they scamper about within their interlocking tunnels under the frozen ground and under the snow, foraging for frozen green vegetation or feeding on stored seeds and roots, or in the case of the shrew, on stored insects. The weasel, the hare, the fox and the wolf roam the tundra all winter. The barren ground grizzly enters a period of long winter sleep in its tundra den but this is not considered to be true hibernation. The polar bear does not hibernate, although the female bear will den up in a huge snow cave to await the birth of her cubs early in the spring. The male bear roams the ice of the Arctic seas so long as he is able to find food for his stomach; when food is scarce in mid-winter he digs a den in a snowbank and goes to sleep for a few days, or a few weeks, existing on body fat and stored energy in his tissues. Eskimo hunters fear few Arctic mammals but they have a healthy respect for the polar bear, and they are especially cautious when approaching a hungry male just out from a long sleep.

Although research is not yet sufficiently well developed to provide a complete picture of exactly how each Arctic mammal has adapted to the cold and fluctuating temperature regime of the tundra biome, present studies indicate that a close inter-relationship between various physiological, morphological and behavioral factors exists within each mammal. These can be best illustrated in a study of the musk ox, the largest of the Arctic coast strictly land mammals, and the one best adjusted to a year round existence on the open tundra.

The musk ox stands up to five feet in height at the shoulder and can weigh as much as seven to eight hundred pounds. Being so large it requires large quantities of food, both summer and winter, for it roams a restricted range at all seasons of the year. The musk ox is herbivorous, preferring certain foods like willow and grasses, but it will eat anything that grows on the tundra, an important survival factor for such a large animal in a cold land where food is often sparse and annual production of all vegetation is low. Because the musk ox must move about and find food through the very long dark period of winter as well as the correspondingly bright period of spring and early summer when glare from the snow cover is extreme, it has eyes that adapt well to either condition. From the plants it finds and eats it derives energy for growth and, in addition, it seems able to store energy within certain organs of its body. During the summer months, when the vegetation is plentiful, the weight of its liver increases quite considerably, suggesting that food stored in this organ

Circle formation
Attacking wolves represented by arrows

Straight formation

Musk Oxen butting

Defence positions taken by musk oxen are in the shape of a circle or a straight line, protecting the females and the young. When aroused by sensed danger, two huge bulls will often charge each other, and after the tremendous crash, back off to resume grazing.

during the summer and early fall may be an important source of energy during the lean months of winter. The musk ox produces within its rumen the various B vitamins, therefore these need not be a part of the food it eats. Biologists believe that the musk ox is able to synthesize protein from the nitrogen contained in the food it eats, which is especially helpful when the protein levels in the food are low as they must be in the dry grasses eaten during the winter months. They believe also that the musk ox is able to recycle nitrogen within its body instead of discharging it in the urine. Musk ox dung changes form from winter to summer—in summer it is soft, loose material while in winter it is hard, dry pellets. While this change may be partly due to the low water content of the dry winter foods and to the restricted winter water intake of the animals, it also serves to conserve energy which the musk ox must use in winter to convert the snow it eats into water, and any conservation of energy in winter helps it to resist extreme cold.

The reproductive cycle of the musk ox is well adapted to the climatic extremes of its far north land. The breeding season begins in late June or early July and by the end of July the fighting between the bulls for a stable of cows is in full swing. The height of the rut occurs between the first and the third weeks in August, at a time when food is plentiful, the weather is reasonable, and the musk ox can put its energy to matters other than the gathering of food. Although there is no firm evidence to in-

dicate the actual period of gestation in wild musk ox it is believed to be eight to nine months long, with the calves being born over an extended period from the latter part of April to the first week in June, most calves appearing in May. At first glance this would seem to be a most inopportune time for a newborn calf to arrive on the tundra; at that time of year temperatures may be as low as minus 20 degrees Fahrenheit, especially on the far north ranges. But the musk ox calf is born with a thick coat of fur and, once dry, is well able to stand quite cold temperatures. What would be vastly more difficult would be to be born a few weeks later, when temperatures were higher, but when its chances of being exposed to freezing rain and wet snow along with high winds, would be quite high. Any such combination would mean certain death for even the hardy, newborn musk ox calf. Thus its early arrival is actually an adaptive feature to the realities of this cold land.

By being born at the very beginning of the summer period, the musk ox is able to take maximum advantage of the complete cycle of summer growth of the plants. Arctic plants spring to life very quickly in the early summer, often before the snow has left the ground; as the musk ox calf is able to browse on vegetation within a week after birth, it is able to start immediately to feed its growing body and to store up the energy it will need for the long winter ahead. The calf will suckle from the mother within a few minutes of birth and continue to take part of its food this way until it is as much as a year and a half old. This period of prolonged lactation provides the calf with extra food during its first long winter, when it might have difficulty obtaining enough to meet its needs for energy and growth.

Although the musk ox is a big animal it has very short appendages; its tail is only about four inches long and its legs are quite short and stocky, allowing quick circulation of blood from the body to these extremities and back, thus reducing heat loss in the limbs. Heat is further imprisoned within the musk ox by its almost complete covering of fur, the dense, fine inner hair and the much longer outer guard hairs. The combination of both provides excellent insulation and the guard hair, which is often so long it trails on the ground hiding the feet, provides shelter for the calf. The only bare skin the musk ox exposes to the elements is at the tip of its nose. In summer the fine, inner hair is shed (it is an excellent wool) allowing the animal to better cope with the higher temperatures.

The musk ox is a slow-moving animal, rarely given to flight over the tundra. When alarmed it usually goes into a type of stockade defence, either a circle like the famous circle of carts on the western plains, or a straight line, with the young and females taking up positions slightly behind the male defenders. The circle formation is an excellent defence against groups of wolves; the straight line is better for a single wolf. As the musk ox moves about feeding, it proceeds slowly, with great dignity, and this slowness of movement, plus the lack of a flight characteristic for defence, helps it to conserve energy and heat; a behavioral adaptation to the cold climate of the tundra biome.

One of the more comical (to the observer) traits of the adult musk ox bull is the form of displacement activity it adopts whenever threatened by sensed, but somewhat remote danger. Most birds and animals adopt some form of what science calls displacement activity, whenever they are stimulated to attack or to flee and can do neither. Under such conditions a male human will kick his dog, or slam his fist on the table, perhaps even beat his wife instead of his boss. A gull will freeze immobile in an attack attitude; a blackbird will peck at a leaf instead of the other bird. Whenever the adult bull musk ox is confronted by such a situation, as when a human observer sits in full view on a nearby hilltop not threatening but not going away, the bull, or bulls, will first pace out in front of the group where they paw at the earth and wipe their foreheads on their forefeet, which is the usual signal for a quick charge. And charge they do but, instead of charging the observer, the bull suddenly wheels and charges the nearest bull. Heads held low, the two seven-hundred pound bulls come together with a tremendous crash, which seems to bother neither of them for they back off, sometimes charge again, sometimes not, stand for a few moments and then resume feeding as though nothing had happened.

Adult musk ox, because of the combination of adaptations they have made, seem able to withstand the coldest and most severe weather that can come their way. Curiously enough for such a well-adapted animal, the one winter condition that can cause them great hardship, and sometimes even death, is very deep snow, particularly if the snow has been interspersed with periods of freezing rain. Musk ox have a great deal of difficulty digging down through deep snow and a hard snow crust to get at their food. Although no records exist of such conditions causing excessive loss of life on the Arctic coast of Canada, it happened in Greenland during the winter of 1953-54 when hundreds, possibly thousands, of musk ox perished, unable to dig down through deep snow and an ice crust to get at their food.

Although most of the large Arctic mammals have the ability and the opportunity to move south during the winter, only certain of the mainland herds of caribou turn to migration as a means of escaping the bitter cold of the tundra biome; these herds move south into the sub-Arctic bush late in the autumn and do not return until the warmer weather of the following spring. Other herds remain on the open tundra, as do the groups of musk ox which tend to remain close to a home valley or set of hills all their lives. The polar bear roams freely over the ice of the Arctic seas but so firmly is it wedded to its Arctic environment that, although it may be carried far to the south in Hudson and James Bay on the drifting ice in the summer and often swims ashore to a beach beyond which lies the shelter of the sub-Arctic bush, it heads north again, not south, back to the ice and cold and food of its Arctic coast homeland. This is why there are no polar bears in the Antarctic, an area in which a polar bear could live a life of plenty; the polar bear developed in the north polar zone and is now unable to migrate the long distance south through the iceless and, to it, foodless, temperate and tropic zones between.

ANIMALS OF THE NORTHERN RANGE

Life is not easy in this ice-cold region, and a combination of morphological, physiological and behavioural adaptations have been made by animals to ensure survival. Sea mammals develop a thick layer of fat beneath the skin, as an insulation against the colder winter temperatures, as well as a source of energy when the food supply lessens. A few land animals enter a state of dormancy or complete hibernation, and there is a seasonal change in the density of the insulated body-coverings of some animals. Musk oxen (above) have roamed the interior in a nearly-perfect cold-adapted state for centuries.

The weasel lives in tunnels in the broken rock or shale.

The tundra wolf, master predator of the Arctic coast region, follows the caribou herds in their ceaseless movement over the land in search of food.

The Arctic ground squirrel, "Shik-Shik," tunnels in the ground.

The polar bear, king of the Arctic coast mammals, spends most of its life on or in the sea and, in summer, often swims in the open sea, many miles from the nearest land.

The harp seal, named for the harp design on its coat, inhabits only Hudson Strait and Frobisher Bay.

The huge Arctic hare changes from winter white to summer brown except in the northern islands where it remains white.

Caribou roam endlessly over the land, sometimes in small herds and sometimes in hundreds and thousands, as shown on the next page.

Arctic coast mammals of land and sea

Prior to the massive flow of glacial ice over northern North America mammals had intermingled freely across the top of the continent. However the advancing ice drove small groups of each species into refugia, each separated from the other by the ice. Each group, in its isolation, developed along slightly different lines; caribou were divided into a woodland species, a mountain species, a tundra species and a far northern species. Shrews of the Mackenzie and Yukon District developed differently from their relatives in the southeast. Walrus were divided into two species—the Atlantic and the Pacific— and they have remained divided to this day, although it is possible for walrus to pass across the top of North America into each other's range.

In summer, walrus "heave-out" onto certain rocky islands all through the Arctic. On land they are very vulnerable and easy prey for hunting man.

11 INVISIBLE WORLD OF THE ARCTIC COAST

Four hundred million years ago, during the time when much of North America was under water and thick accumulations of sediments were building up around the core of the great Canadian Shield, when plants were slowly spreading out over the virgin face of the exposed land and life in the seas was dominated by the primitive fishes, there lived in the coastal waters off the Arctic coast region of Canada species of the first of the true vertebrates to leave behind a fossil record of their existence —the Ostracoderms, aquatic, fish-like creatures up to several feet long. Ostracoderms were bottom dwellers, without jaws of any kind, most likely scooping or sucking up their food through a round opening in their heads. Their bodies were covered with bony scales, and, when they died, the scales resisted the efforts of the chemicals in the water to disintegrate them; they remained to be buried in the bottom sediments where they survive today, fossil evidence of the dominant form of life on the Arctic coast of 400 million years ago.

In the unimaginably long span of time that has passed since the Ostracoderms fed and bred in the waters off the Arctic coast, the outline and contour of North America has changed and re-changed many times; the climate, warm for so long, has gone from warm to cold, back to warm, back to cold, countless times. Flora of land and sea have come and gone, including the Ostracoderms. But one thing has not changed from those days of so long ago—on the Arctic coast creatures of the sea remain the dominant form of life.

Draw a map of your homeland and, almost without exception, you will trace an outline of the peninsulas and capes of the land; land upon which you were born, upon which you now live and travel; land from which you draw your sustenance and in which you will be buried when you die. But ask an Arctic coast Eskimo hunter to draw a map of his homeland and he will trace an outline of the bays and inlets of the sea; the sea which gives him the meat he needs for his food, the skins he needs for his boots and his clothing, the fat he uses for his heat and light; the sea, on the surface of which he will spend the greater part of his life. On paper his map will look the same as yours; in fact they represent two entirely different worlds.

A newcomer to the Arctic coast in winter could be pardoned for feeling that the attachment of the Eskimo hunter for his sea was badly misplaced; mile after mile the snow-covered ice stretches out to the distant horizon, a desert of white on which there is rarely any movement to indicate the presence of mammalian or other aquatic life. But this surface appearance is deceiving; invisible beneath the miles of land-fast ice along the Arctic coast swim hundreds of seals; almost as invisible out among the broken ice and open water of the central pack live some of the largest mammals in the world—the Greenland right whale, the white whale and the narwhal, along with the huge walrus and the mighty polar bear. Back of the coasts, beneath the six and eight foot thick ice of the larger Arctic lakes live the cold water adapted fishes, relatives of species to the south —schools of succulent Arctic char feed throughout the long winter; lake trout and whitefish prowl the waters beneath the ice for their food; graylings, even a few northern pike, swim in the rivers of the western Arctic that flow north to the Arctic sea.

Life is not easy in the cold waters beneath the non-land of the Arctic coast region, particularly in the waters of the Arctic seas. Fish are not found in great numbers anywhere off Arctic coasts; the great fisheries of the northern hemisphere occur in sub-Arctic waters, at the places where the cold Arctic currents meet and mingle with the warmer flows from the Atlantic and Pacific Oceans. In far north water the Arctic cod inhabits Hudson Bay and the seas off the lower Arctic islands; tom cod feed in the coastal waters off the northwest mainland coast as far east as Coronation Gulf; jackfish are abundant in the MacKenzie Delta. Arctic halibut seem to be moving into the waters of the Hudson Strait region; Atlantic cod increased off the west coast of Greenland all through the 1930's but began to decline in size and numbers late in the 1950's. This movement north and south of the Atlantic cod is an excellent indicator of changing water temperatures in the Arctic seas off the northeast coast of Canada. Atlantic cod feed in the shallows of the continental shelf, preferring water between two and four degrees centigrade. Warming of the coastal water off the Arctic coast brings them north; cooling sends them south again.

The Arctic sea is home to several members of the sculpin family, and that ugly little fish, the stickleback. The only large fish of the Arctic coast is the Greenland shark, which has been appearing in ever-increasing numbers in the waters of the north-eastern Arctic all through the past decade. They seem to be especially abundant off north Baffin Island and in the Lancaster-Jones Sound region. This shark loves the cold waters of the far north; it grows to be some ten to twelve feet long but has a very small brain and is quite sluggish in the water. Its meat is toxic to humans when fresh; its main asset seems to be its huge liver, up to seven feet long in an adult fish, from which can be extracted an oil rich in Vitamin A.

In the tidal zone of the Arctic, sea life has difficulty maintaining itself; every spring, when the sea ice breaks up, huge chunks grind back and forth over the rocks and across the sandy bottom. No sessile animal is safe from being crushed off the rocks by this ice movement. A few limpets may exist in the deep clefts, along with a few amphipods and a stray fish species or two, but there are few hiding places for them in the tidal zone although worms, copepods and ostrapods are found in shallow bays that are protected from ice scour by sandbars across the entrances.

It is the lakes of the Arctic that harbour the greatest variety and numbers of fish. Whitefish and huge lake trout occur in all the larger lakes; Arctic grayling inhabit the swift flowing streams of the western Arctic; northern pike have been taken from the estuary of the Coppermine River and in certain lakes on Boothia Peninsula. An unusual fish is found in a lake a short distance inland from the south shore of Frobisher Bay—a school of Arctic cod, fish of the sea, that have become trapped in the lake. The lake has a layer of fresh water on top of a layer of salt water in which the cod live, feeding on themselves. In the past the very high tides in Frobisher Bay brought sea-water flooding into the lake and presumably brought in the cod as well. With the continued, slow rise of the land in this area, the flooding occurred less and less often; the fish have now become trapped in the lake.

The dominant fish of the Arctic coast region is the Arctic char, a member of the salmon family, not unlike the Atlantic salmon in appearance. Red fleshed, with lots of fat on the body, the average size adult char weighs from four to six pounds, although it can grow to eighteen pounds. The char spends most of its life in the fresh water of the inland lakes; in certain lakes along the west coast of Hudson Bay, where access to the sea has been cut off by the rising of the land, the char is a completely freshwater fish. But most char go down to the sea for a few weeks in summer soon after the fifth year of their life. On these moves from the lakes to the sea and return, they move in large schools, down the rivers in June, back up the same rivers about mid-August. Not all lake and river systems have runs of Arctic char but those that do are well known to the Eskimo hunters of the area.

In the cold waters of the Arctic coast region it is the sea mammals that have evolved as the dominant life forms. Seals, walrus, whales are all mammals—warm-blooded, air breathing animals which suckle their young. All have developed special methods of breathing while living their entire lives in the Arctic seas. All have limbs that are adapted to serve as paddles and rudders to propel them through the water; some are able to use them in a limited way to provide locomotion on land or on ice. The adaptations to cold they have made are somewhat different from those made by their fellow mammals on land. Land mammals have had to exist in a region where temperatures ranged from sixty degrees above to sixty below, where vicious winds robbed their bodies of vital heat and energy. The mammals of the sea had no such problems to face. The temperature of the Arctic sea-water is cold, but not very cold, all year round with only slight variations in seasonal norms. Thus the sea mammals were able to adapt to a much simpler set of Arctic conditions within their watery environment.

Nevertheless, the adaptations they made were surprisingly similar to those of the land mammals. They have no fur; some have no hair at all on their bodies, others have short, bristly hair. But all do have great layers of fat beneath the skin to serve as insulation in place of fur, and also to serve as a source of energy if food supplies get low. This layer of fat thickens and thins with the season, very thick by the end of the winter, thinner during the late summer, so thin in the ringed seals that they lose much of their usual buoyancy in the water and sink quickly when killed; during autumn and spring they float like corks. The sea

The Arctic char, favourite food of Eskimo hunters, has migrated up and down the same well-known Arctic coast rivers for generations.

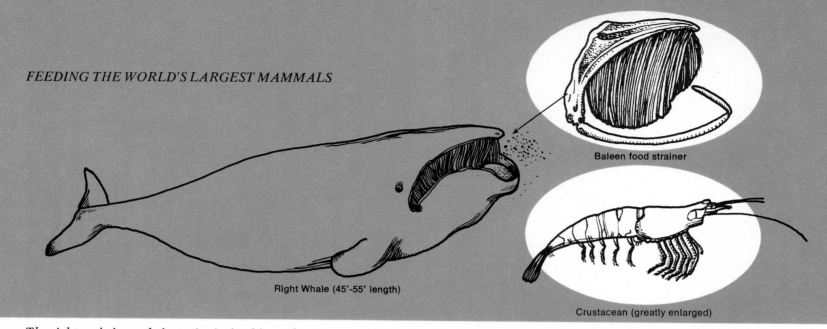

Baleen food strainer

Right Whale (45'-55' length)

Crustacean (greatly enlarged)

The right, or baleen whale strains its food from the sea water by using a unique sieve-like structure of baleen, found within its jaws.

mammals are squat and torpedo-shaped, with short extremities; like the land mammals, the temperature within the extremities is different from that of the rest of the body.

One special adaptation of the ringed seal is a birth cycle phenomenon known as delayed implantation, which plays an important role in the life cycle of this seal. Ringed seals are born live, with the mother in a cave under the snow on top of the ice. Usually only one pup is born at a time and the mother suckles it for several months after birth, first in the cave and later in the water. The seal's milk is very rich in fat, containing up to ten times as much as cow's milk; on such a rich diet the young seal grows very quickly. Within a very short time after birth of her young the female mates again, but the growth of the new embryo does not begin immediately; the embryo remains in a rudimentary condition for several weeks with very little sign of any growth occurring in the uterus during this time. The length of the delay in the beginning of development is timed so that the entire birth cycle takes almost exactly one year, with the baby being born in the spring to the mother in her snow cave on the sea ice and ready for almost instant mating again. The larger bearded seal and the walrus have a birth cycle that takes a little over one year to complete; the female cannot mate until the year following birth and young bearded seals and walrus are born only in alternate years to the same mother.

The largest of the Arctic coast sea mammals are the huge whales, but these are no longer plentiful in the north polar region. The last great herds were hunted almost to extinction in the Beaufort Sea, Baffin Bay and Hudson Bay late in the nineteenth and early in the twentieth centuries. Occasional sightings are reported by Eskimos on north Baffin Island but, after almost two centuries of relentless pursuit and killing in all the seas of the northern hemisphere, the large whales may be so reduced in numbers that they are gone forever, too few in numbers to do anything but eventually vanish completely from our northern coasts.

These large whales were all toothless, generally called baleen whales, because of the special, sieve-like structures within their mouths that allowed them to gulp in great quantities of sea-water as they swam along, straining from the water the small invertebrates they ate for food. The smaller whales left in the Arctic are all toothed; they have rows of teeth in their jaws that allow them to catch fish and other marine creatures. The largest is the most ferocious—the killer whale, an aptly-named monster that will attack almost anything moving in the water. Black above and white below, with a large black fin that cuts through the water in front of a white wake when the whale is moving at speed near the surface, the killer whale of the Arctic coast eats seals and other small whales. But it can kill the larger whales by

White Whale (10'-15' length)

Jaw with rows of teeth

Arctic Cod (9"-15" length)

The white whale, or beluga, has rows of teeth within its jaws, enabling it to catch and eat fish and other small marine creatures.

forcing open their mouths and tearing out the tongues. It will also stalk man if he is in a kayak on the water, or if he is walking on the sea ice near open water in which the whale can surface. Killer whales have been known to stalk beneath the thinner ice near the floe edge and then come up under the ice to try to break it and dump the man into the water.

The most common whale of the Arctic coast is the white whale, or Beluga, milk-white in colour, usually about ten to fifteen feet long. The white whale has no back fin; it propels itself through the water by means of a large, horizontal fluked tail and steers by means of short fins on either side of its body near the head. Breathing is accomplished through a blow hole on the top of the head while the whale is lying on the surface or cruising along in a series of shallow dives. White whales, like all Cetaceans, are highly intelligent and lead complex social lives. Sight is not well developed in these mammals but hearing is; their ears are basically similar to ours but far keener and they use a system of radar, like the bats, to locate undersea objects. White whales communicate constantly—British tars called them "sea canaries"—sound issuing through the puckered-up breathing hole in the top of the head from a sound chamber within the great bulge of the forehead.

White whales leave the Arctic coast waters in the winter and are seen off the east coast of North America as far south as Cape

Cod. As soon as the bays and inlets are free of ice on the north coast they return to spend the summer feeding along the coasts and in the estuaries of large rivers, occasionally penetrating the larger lakes that have a direct connection with the sea. Every so often white whales will be trapped in such a lake, or at the bottom end of a long fiord, by new ice forming early in the fall across the mouth of the inlet or across the outlet of the lake. As they must come up to breathe at an absolute maximum of every twenty minutes, and as they seem unwilling to navigate long distances under solid ice, they cannot escape. Inexorably the ice closes in over the open water of the lake or the fiord, up into which they must rise to breathe. Unless found and killed by hunters the trapped whales will all die, as did a group of whales caught in the Eskimo Lakes of the Mackenzie Delta district in the winter of 1966-67.

The strangest of the Arctic whales is the narwhal—the unicorn of the Arctic seas. Narwhal have been known to western man for centuries but science is still not sure about the tusk of the narwhal. Although both sexes have two rudimentary tusks, only in the male does the left one develop beyond the jaw to protrude as a long, spirally grooved, and often twisted, tusk of ivory that can be up to ten feet long. About one male in fifty or sixty will develop the right tusk in addition to the left but it will only be about a third of the length of the left. The tusk is an overgrown canine tooth and is hollow with the dental canal reaching almost to the tip. The ivory is quite brittle and it is common to find narwhal with a portion of the end of the tusk broken off. Eskimos of north Baffin Island claim that narwhal have toothache in the tusk and often break them off near the tip while scraping them on the rocks to relieve the pain. They also claim that the narwhal uses the tusk to stir up tom cod, sculpin and other food from the sea bottom and to spear big fish when feeding far from shore. Certainly the tusk must be used in some way for it is always well polished near the tip. Some scientists believe that it serves no practical purpose at all, that it is a secondary sexual ornament adorning the male.

I've hunted and photographed narwhals from my kayak many times on the waters of Eclipse Sound but my most thrilling involvement with a narwhal occurred while I was sitting on a rocky hilltop on the east coast of the sound scanning the broken ice surface in late June watching and listening for the first narwhal movement into the bays. As my telescope panned slowly across what seemed to be an unbroken stretch of flat ice, but which I knew would be laced with cracks of open water I could not see from afar, I was startled to see rising up through the ice the thrashing form of a huge narwhal. Higher and higher it rose in the air until the big head, with its ten foot long tusk, shook and danced in weird rhythm a dozen feet above the ice surface. Suddenly the whale slid rapidly back down into the water and was gone, and I knew that a killer whale hunted below the ice, driving the narwhal into such a state of terror that it had tried to climb out of the water onto the surface of the ice above.

The killer whale also preys on the huge walrus, but it prefers to eat the young animals rather than the old. With its twin tusks of ivory a large walrus is a formidable foe; there is nothing else that will tackle an adult male walrus in the water except the killer whale, although the polar bear will attack walrus on land where they are more vulnerable. Eskimos tell stories of walrus attacks on hunters in kayaks; they will attack canoes and whale-boats, even forty foot Peterhead boats. The walrus attempts to hook its tusks over the gunwale of the boat and tip the occupants into the water. An enraged walrus will attack with tusks, and by bunting with its big head, charges in repeatedly with all the skill and agility of a sea "goat."

Large walrus can be ten to twelve feet in length and weigh up to two and a half tons. The outer hide of the adult is so tough that it quickly blunts the edge of the big knife used to cut up an animal after killing. The walrus is a highly gregarious mammal; the sexes are usually segregated with the older males keeping together in herds and the adult females with young of both sexes forming a separate group. While sleeping on the ice pans, or hauled out on the rocky islands, walrus huddle together in tightly-packed "pods," although lone bulls are common. The walrus pup is born in the late spring; it swims immediately but it spends a good deal of the time during the first weeks riding about on its mother's back. When she dives deep to feed, the pup clings to the front flippers. The mother, indeed the entire herd, treats the young with a great deal of care and lavishes much affection on them. The pup nurses from the mother for up to two years as it must await the development of its tusks before it can begin to root around on the sea bottom for its food—clams and other mollusks. The life expectancy of a healthy walrus can be as much as twenty years.

An unusual feature of the walrus is that certain individuals, for reasons not yet clearly understood, deviate from their usual diet to become predators of the sea, feeding on the meat and fat of ringed seals, bearded seals, even small whales. The act of predation has never been witnessed by a biologist but tales of walrus killing seals abound in Eskimo folklore and contemporary stories, and remains of sea mammals have been found in the stomachs of dead walrus. Such walrus are almost always males, solitary bulls that are lean and slender in build with exceptionally well developed shoulders and forelimbs. Their tusks are long, slender and very sharp, often covered with scratches. Eskimos say that these walrus become carnivores when they are orphaned during the first year or two of their lives and, being without tusks, they turn to scavenging and preying on whatever they can kill. In effect, they adapt to a condition of "no-tusks," and continue as predators for the rest of their lives.

A number of different types of seals inhabit the coastal waters of the Arctic but only two can be considered as true Arctic species—the huge bearded seal and the much smaller ringed seal. Harp seals, the hunting of which caused such an uproar over killing methods alleged to be employed by the sealers, are not commonly seen in the Arctic coast region except in the Frobisher Bay—Hudson Strait area in summer. The hooded seal is seen even less; it is usually found in the heavy pack ice far out in Baffin Bay, Davis Strait and the north Atlantic. The hooded seal gets its name from a bag-like swelling on the end of the male seal's nose, which is inflated whenever it becomes angry. With bladder inflated the hooded seal is almost as fierce an antagonist as an enraged walrus.

The bearded seal, or square flipper, is a huge animal up to ten feet long, weighing as much as eight hundred pounds. Although as long as a walrus it is much slimmer and lacks the tusks. It is a seal of the open water and ice, but it will live under the land-fast ice in winter, keeping open its own breathing holes or using those of the smaller ringed seal. It is a solitary animal, usually seen swimming alone in the dark green waters or asleep,

on solitary ice pans. Only at breeding time does it gather into groups. The pups are born late in March, covered with dark grey, mottled hair.

If the dominant life form of the Arctic seas of four hundred million years ago was the Ostracoderm, today that honour must go to the ringed seal, the most widely distributed sea mammal of the north polar region, found in the sea all along the Arctic coasts wherever there is land-fast ice on which it can breed. The ringed seal, or jar as it is often called, is one link in a food chain of the sea.

In the sea the microscopic diatoms correspond to the vegetation of the land, converting sunlight that filters down through the upper layers of the water into energy through photosynthesis,

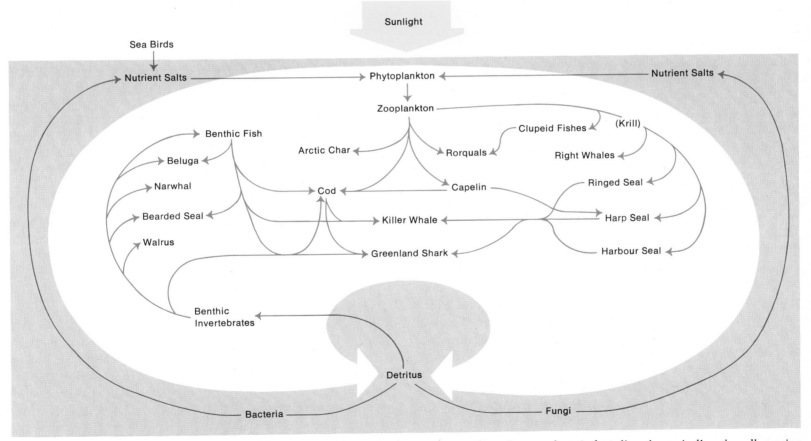

This simplified, biological cycle of life in northern seas shows (see white crescent-shaped area above) that directly or indirectly, all marine creatures, algae and the bottom-dwelling Benthic invertebrates eventually become organic detritus.

creating rich "pastures" in which certain sea life grazes. Although the Arctic seas receive no sunlight in winter the long day of summer makes up for this deficit, and everywhere the sea is not covered over by heavy ice, there is a great multiplying of the diatoms during the month of August; often the water is stained brown with their mass. Their growth is helped by the fact that cold water contains a high concentration of polymerized water molecules, which has a beneficial effect on the division and growth of plant cells.

Feeding directly on the diatoms are the plankton—larval stages of mollusks, worms and crustaceans, the copepods of the sea, and certain young fish. The cold water plankton of the Arctic seas is remarkable for the large size of the individual, compared with the same or related species inhabiting waters farther south; even in the sea there seems to be a general adherence to the rule that large size benefits all fauna in a cold region. The most common food of the ringed seal are two small, shrimp-like crustaceans; mysis, inhabiting the bottom layers of the deeper waters, and misto, a free-swimming crustacean. By utilizing both types, and supplementing its diet with small fish like polar cod, the ringed seal is able to live almost everywhere in Arctic coast waters.

In summer ringed seals swim about in the ice free waters, sometimes hauling out on shore if there are no convenient ice floes about. In winter many move out to the open sea beyond the edge of the land-fast ice where they swim and feed along the floe edge. But others remain in the sounds, bays and inlets that are completely covered over by six to seven foot thick ice. In order to breathe, each seal keeps open a series of holes in the thick ice. Starting in the autumn, when the new ice is forming on the surface of the sea, the seal rises up beneath the thin, pliable sea ice cover and pushes up a small mound of ice which cracks sufficiently for a small hole to form in the top. The seal lies vertical beneath the ice with its nose in the small air space between the ice and the water surface. It repeats this procedure at a number of places and, over the period of days while the new forming ice is thickening and losing its pliability, the seal visits each hole regularly, to breathe and to keep it from freezing over. All winter long it keeps up this constant movement from hole to hole while the ice about grows thicker and thicker. By spring each hole will be a vertical tunnel through the ice; on the sur-

face the initial tiny hole, now buried beneath a hard packed drift, has been enlarged so that the seal is able to put its head above the water surface but still be invisible to anyone above.

Early in March the female seal enlarges one of the breathing holes with her teeth and the sharp claws of her front flippers, usually a hole that lies beneath a patch of broken ice over which the winter snow will have piled in deep drifts. The seal comes out onto the ice surface under the snow and hollows out a cave, in which the young seal is born, usually at any time through the period late March to mid-April. At birth the seal pup weighs about ten pounds and is covered with a thick coat of curly, white fur which it begins to shed after two weeks. A baby seal is not unlike a human infant with tiny, almost human face, and its large, shoe-button eyes; its cries are similar to those of a new-born human infant. By the time it is six weeks old it has shed its baby hair completely and is covered with finely textured hair, silvery on the belly, dark grey on the back on which the first traces of the adult pattern of circles can be seen—the "silver jar" of the trader.

As soon as the hot sun has begun to melt the snow cover, the seal enlarges the openings over its breathing holes so that it can pull itself out of the water onto the ice surface. Here it sleeps in the sun on warm, windless days, raising its head every few seconds to look about for danger. Although exceptionally alert for anything that could cause them harm, ringed seals are inquisitive creatures; they can be kept on the ice surface, while a dog team and sled rush madly at them over the ice, by a long sustained cry which seems to arouse their curiosity as to what on earth it could be coming at them over the ice. While swimming on the open sea they are easily lured in close by soft noises, a whistle, or a sharp knock on the side of a boat.

Ringed seals mature when they are seven years of age, although females sometimes become pregnant at five to six years old. Only rarely are they found among the floating pack ice of the open ocean; their range is the sheltered waters along the coasts. Their main predators are few but, unfortunately for the seal, they are all very proficient. The killer whale hunts the seal beneath the sea and, on the surface of water and ice alike, they are hunted by two of their most implacable enemies—the huge, white ghost of the Arctic coast, the mighty polar bear, and by that most proficient of all predators—hunting man.

INVASION FROM THE SOUTH

Nearly a thousand years ago, a small band of Viking voyagers left their settlement on the west coast of Greenland to sail across the expanse of Baffin Bay. European explorers followed the Norse; whalers followed explorers; traders and developers, like this snowmobiler on Frobisher Bay, all arrived in turn, each a disrupting influence on the basic ecological pattern of the land. Technological advances have made it possible to exist in relative comfort in a land dominated by cold.

Bulldozer "rolling" an airstrip on frozen lake during blizzard.

A portable heater warms the inside of the airplane in sub-zero weather.

The changing Arctic

Western man's bulldozers build roads, airfields, townsites, but they also rip up the tundra and disturb the permafrost, setting in motion forces that could destroy the delicately balanced Arctic communities of flora and fauna. Settlements dump pollutants into air and water and his competitive and acquisitive social system leaves little room for understanding the way of life of the Arctic hunter, and so his culture heads down the road to oblivion.

right: This young Eskimo girl cashier in a supermarket at Frobisher Bay, Southern Baffin Island, is better housed, better fed, better "educated" than her hunter forebears; what does her future hold on the Arctic coast of Canada?

Bulldozer tracks scar the ground at a Melville Island oil well.

A utilidor system for water and sewage lines in the town of Inuvik.

Winter fuel oil supply, part of man's life-line from the south, covers a beach on north Baffin Island.

PART FIVE/ CONSERVATION

12 A LAND OF FEAST OR FAMINE

The month was February, the year 1954, the place—north Baffin Island, out on the snow and ice-covered surface of Tay Sound to be exact. With my Eskimo "father," Idlouk, I was travelling by sled through the darkness of a midwinter "day" checking fox traps set on the headlands and tiny estuaries jutting from the high walls of rock that flank the upper reaches of the fiord. For nine months I had been living with Idlouk and his family at their camp near the bottom of Eclipse Sound, trying to find out what it was like to exist on the Arctic coast as an Eskimo hunter with only the natural resources of a high north land to provide clothing, transportation, shelter and food. On this particular trip I was learning a lot; it was four days since we had left camp and in that time the temperature had stayed steady at about 45° below zero. For three of the four days we had taken no foxes from the traps; for the past two days we had eaten nothing at all, having been unsuccessful in our attempts to shoot hares on the moonlit slopes or seals at their breathing holes in the thick ice of the sound. I was near numb with cold, and hungry enough to eat my caribou skin boots, bearskin bottoms and all.

Late that night as I lay sleepless, cold and hungry in my caribou skin sleeping robe inside our tiny overnight snowhouse, it dawned on me that I was an active participant in one of the famous, or infamous, feast and famine cycles which are a characteristic phenomenon in the natural life of the fauna of the Arctic coast. The significance of what was happening began to filter through a fog of misunderstanding built up over thirty-odd years of growing up as an urbanite, part of a technological society which had gained a large measure of control over its natural environment; enough control that, as an individual within that society, I felt I could ignore the complex relationships that exist between all living elements of the natural world. In southern Canada my relationships with the flora and fauna were casual and often long range; neither seemed important to my continued existence. But, living the life of an Eskimo hunter on north Baffin Island, I was brought face to face with a basic reality—as a human mammal I was only one element in a struc-

ture of elements, bound by invisible threads into an interdependent relationship with the natural world around me. On this trip I couldn't connect one of the threads; I couldn't shoot a rabbit or a seal that I needed for my food and because of this I was cold and hungry; if I didn't get meat soon I would die.

That night on north Baffin Island my relationship with the natural world around me underwent a subtle change. Physically and emotionally, as well as intellectually, I joined the world of the mammals on earth, no longer simply a human, but a human mammal, subject to certain basic laws of supply and demand that govern all life in the mammalian world. For the first time it was being brought home to me very forcefully that, as an individual separate from the natural world around me, I could not exist; I lived only because of the transmission of energy through the invisible, pyramidal systems that scientists call food chains. And with this realization came new understanding; no longer did I feel myself set over against my Arctic environment, with Idlouk and the other Eskimo hunters of the area, I became as one with the seals and the walrus and the caribou, and the life forms of land and sea on which they fed; I became as one with the huge mass of the invisible sun, source of all life and energy on the planet earth.

The next day we still couldn't get food but, late in the afternoon, our sled rounded a rock point of land beyond which we could see a tiny pinpoint of yellow light. Immediately the dogs howled and broke into a run pulling the sled, bumping and crashing, through the rough ice of the tidal zone onto a gently sloping beach. From a mound of snow that almost completely concealed their sod and sealskin house, Eskimo neighbours poured forth to help us unload the sled and release the dogs. Within a matter of minutes Idlouk and I were squatting inside the low, dimly lit house thawing our near frozen faces and feet, wolfing down raw caribou and seal meat from a food box in the corner. Three cups of hot tea later I lay on the caribou-skin-covered sleeping platform jammed in among eight other tired souls. Body recharged with vital energy, I drifted off to happy sleep.

Our natural world thrives on energy; energy that originates in the sun and flows out to pervade all living matter. But different forms of life can use the energy from the sun only when it is available to them in a form they can assimilate within their

Our natural world thrives on energy, which originates in the sun and flows out to pervade all living matter.

structures. I can't exist on raw energy from the sun but plants can, and certain plants can convert this energy into a form that my body can assimilate and use. So I eat these plants, or I eat the meat of other mammals that eat the plants, and I am really eating energy from the sun; I am part of a simple food chain. The term, chain, is a little misleading, for a chain is usually a set of orderly links fastened securely one to the other. In nature a "chain" is often a very complex structure in which links are fastened to other links in a bewildering array of patterns and designs. Particularly is this true in the temperate and tropic zones of earth, where the diversity of life forms seems almost endless. On the Arctic coast life forms are few in number and often simple in form; thus they have a clear "chain" structure that ties them inextricably one to the other and binds them all to their Arctic home environment.

In the Arctic coast region, as over all the world, the beginning link in the food chain is the sun. Although the Arctic is without the sun for a part of the year in most localities, it recoups much of this loss by having sunlight for extra long periods during the summer months, when for twenty-four hours a day light pours onto the Arctic vegetation—the lowly lichens, the mosses, the grasses, the plants, the bushes—which gathers in the energy and transforms it into green growth through a process known as photosynthesis. Much of the energy is used up by the plants themselves in their own processes of growth and development; the plants are the primary consumers. But they also condense a portion of the energy and store it within their cells and this stored energy becomes available to a host of secondary consumers—certain insects, birds and mammals. The insects extract the energy from the nectar; the birds obtain it from the seeds and

125

shoots; the herbivorous mammals eat the leaves, stalks and roots of the plants. Meagre as it may be by southern standards, Arctic vegetation brings life to the tundra community.

The herbivorous animals are the big secondary consumers of the energy; caribou eat mosses and lichens during the winter months, willows, birch, grass and sedges in addition to the moss and lichen in the summer. Musk ox eat almost anything that grows on the tundra although their food preferences will vary with the season. The Arctic hare feeds on a wide variety of plants—saxifrage, crowberry, grass and sedges; the ground squirrel eats mostly leaves, roots and seeds of the plants, as do the lemmings; meadow mice prefer green vegetation with roots and bark. The secondary consumers also use up much of the energy they get from the plants in their own processes of growth and development, but they, too, store an excess in the tissues of their bodies where it becomes available to a third level of consumer— the predator, insect, bird or mammal which has developed the specialization of obtaining its energy from the stored energy in the fat and flesh of its fellow insects, birds and animals.

The huge wolf of the tundra lives mainly on caribou, although it will turn to eating ground squirrels, mice and birds' eggs if it cannot get enough caribou meat to fill its belly. The fox feeds on eggs, young birds, mice and lemmings, often digging down through the winter snow with great speed to get the lemmings it hears running about in their tunnels underneath. The weasel darts among the rocks and shale of the tundra hills eating mice and lemmings it is able to trap and catch in the burrows. The shrew is the insectivore of the Arctic coast, its numerous, sharp-pointed teeth enable it to crush the hard-bodied beetles, the spiders and centipedes and, on occasion, a mouse or a lemming that has been caught in a trap. The snowy owl eats mice and lemmings; the gyrfalcon hunts ptarmigan on the slopes; jaegers eat eggs and young birds; the tern takes small fish from the lakes and the sea. As for the raven, it just isn't very fussy; it will eat almost anything at all.

The insects have special relationships with the mammals, both large and small. Mosquitoes draw the blood they must have in order to reproduce, from the caribou, musk ox, wolves and foxes, attacking these animals on the lips, ears, around the eyes and muzzle, on any bare patches of skin rubbed free of fur during the annual moult. Mites and lice use lemmings and mice

as living hosts; fleas breed in the thick, soft coats of the Arctic hare. Worms, spiders, midges, flies find food in the droppings of the smaller mammals and find breeding places in their burrows and nests. The blowfly utilizes the carcasses of lemmings and mice as a principle breeding ground, wherever no carcasses of the larger mammals can be found. In one recorded instance well over two hundred blowflies emerged from the tiny carcass of one dead lemming.

Warble flies begin life as eggs deposited on the legs or rump of the caribou by the parent in the months of July and August. The eggs develop into larvae which immediately burrow in under the skin of the animal and make their way along the back. Over the winter they live in the fat beneath the skin, growing in size until about as big as a bumble bee. The following June they burrow out through the hide to drop on the ground of the caribou range where they pupate to emerge a few weeks later as warble flies, that immediately lay more eggs on more caribou. Warble flies are the scourge of the caribou of the tundra; one animal can have as many as 350 larvae living within its flesh.

Operating in a wider cycle of parasitic life is the tiny tapeworm, *echinococcus granulosis*, which begins life as one of millions of tiny eggs deposited in the intestines of dogs, foxes or wolves by the adult tapeworm. The eggs are dropped onto the feeding range of the caribou in the faeces of the host, where they may lie for many months, later to be picked up and ingested by caribou browsing over the range. In the caribou the eggs hatch into larvae which migrate to the liver and other parts of the body where they form into cysts; in the brain or lungs such cysts bring death to the host animal.

Along the food chains of the tundra biome energy flows from the plants to the insects, to the birds, to the mammals. So long as all links of the chain remain intact the flow continues; life is born, it multiplies, it dies, in an endless cycle that has almost no beginning and almost no end. From sun to plant to insect, bird and mammal, the energy flows in seemingly inexhaustible supply; numbers of individuals multiply, more than enough to replace those dying of old age or accident, disease or predation. Certain species multiply slowly towards an optimum number that is seldom reached over the immense range of their tundra home. But others multiply and multiply, until suddenly there comes a year when there are too many individuals on the range and, over specific areas of the tundra biome, there occur great dyings-off of these species and their predators. One year the land teems with hares or lemmings; the next there will be almost none. Foxes are abundant for a year or two and then there will be almost none for a while. These regular cycles of plenty and scarcity are an ever-recurring phenomenon of the Arctic coast region; for most Arctic mammals the tundra biome is a vast land under constant alternation between plenty and want, a land of feast or famine.

The cycle of scarcity–plenty has been accurately plotted over many years for certain species of mammals and birds. The best documented is that of the fox, for fox skins are a staple item of trade at all Arctic posts and careful records are kept of the numbers of pelts handled each year. Everywhere on the Arctic coast there is a regular cycle in the numbers of foxes; they build to a peak population every four years, followed immediately by a rapid decline. The phases of the cycle do not match all across the Arctic; scarcity in one sector coincides with plenty in others; but the cycle occurs regularly everywhere, year after year after year, the direct result of a break in the links of a basic food chain.

Lemmings eat tundra vegetation; foxes and snowy owls eat lemmings—a simple food chain. Lemmings have one or more litters, of from four to six kits each, during the year, consequently they multiply rather quickly. But the tundra is wide and there is a lot of food in it for lemmings. In addition, the increase in their food supply stimulates the sex glands of the lemming predators, the snowy owl and the fox, in ways that are not yet clearly understood. In the owl it seems that the simple fact of excess visual sightings of lemmings stimulates areas of the brain that control secretions of the pituitary gland that controls the degree of sexual activity and the number of eggs produced by the female bird—the more lemmings seen by the snowy owls means the higher the production of snowy owls which will eat more lemmings. Similarly, in times of lemming abundance the foxes increase the numbers born in each litter, and there is usually a migration movement of foxes from other areas into the region of plenty, all helping to swell the numbers of the predators.

But it is the lemmings which increase the fastest. Despite the

Lemmings live on sun-nourished vegetation and, in turn, themselves become food for the Arctic fox and the snowy owl, to complete a simple food chain.

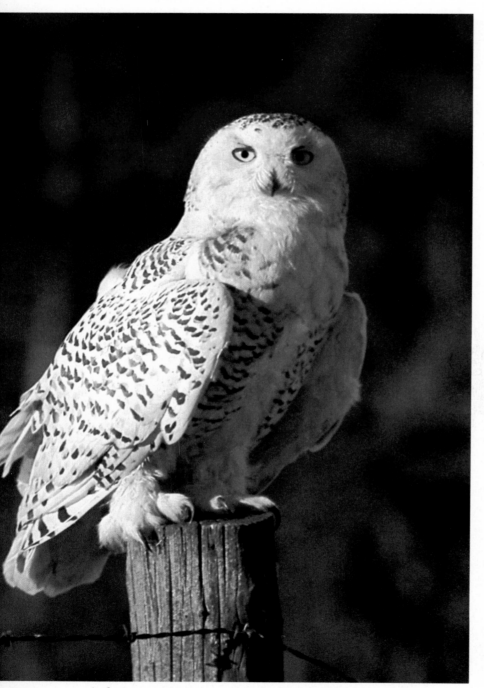

A shortage of lemmings, a basic food of the snowy owl, can drive the beautiful birds far south of their normal range.

ever-intensifying predation lemmings increase much faster than they die or are killed off. Three years after the time when lemmings were scarce on the land, the region teems with them. Because they live on a restricted range all their lives the pressure on the food supply in the area becomes prohibitive, as does the pressure of overcrowding on the lemmings themselves. Lemmings scurry everywhere across the tundra, preyed upon by owls, jaegers, foxes, wolves, dogs, even bears. Frantically they begin to leave their home range; almost blindly they swarm over the tundra, swimming across lakes and swift flowing rivers to leave hundreds drowned along the banks. In some sectors of the tundra biome, principally in Scandinavia and Alaska where the number of litters born to a single female in one year can be as high as eight, at the peak of the cycle millions of lemmings stream en masse across the tundra, swimming lakes and rivers, sometimes swimming to their deaths in ritual parade out into the open sea. Starved for food, frustrated into a state of nervous exhaustion through overcrowding, they die in their thousands. Next year the tundra is almost empty of lemmings, and of the foxes and owls which depend on them as food. Many foxes have died, others have migrated to different sectors of the tundra where lemmings are not yet in short supply. The snowy owls abandon their tundra range in the winter to appear far south in the woods and fields of southern Canada, searching for the food they cannot find in their far north home.

Shortage of food undoubtedly plays a major role in the dying-off of the lemmings. But overcrowding plays an equally important role. It is well known that simple overcrowding among humans and rodents causes stress to develop within the individual of the species with its typical effect on the nervous system, on the sex and the adrenal glands. When overcrowded, lemmings develop swollen adrenal glands and shrunken sex glands. The shrunken sex glands means that the male produces less sperm, the female produces fewer eggs; the mating urge decreases and fewer young will be conceived; of those conceived, more will die in the uterus, fewer will survive the first days after being born due to a shortage of milk from the mother. Because the hormones secreted by the adrenal cortex reduce inflammation and because inflammation is a defence mechanism of the body against infection, a lemming with an overactive adrenal gland is much more liable to invasion by bacteria and viruses, thus increasing greatly the possibility of its succumbing to infectious diseases. The effect of stimulation of the adrenal cortex is cumulative; if the stress developed through overcrowding is continued indefinitely, the adrenal gland becomes exhausted and the ability of the lemming to resist any adverse situation is drastically reduced; excess heat, excess cold, simple food shortage will very quickly cause death. And death comes quickly to the thousands and thousands of lemmings.

They die because they have eaten up most of the food on their range; they die by predation under attacks of the birds and mammals; they drown in their hundreds. They die of disease, excess heat, excess cold. And because they die their predators die, or they migrate away, and the land over which they fled and fought becomes empty almost overnight. A few lemmings remain, just enough to begin the cycle all over again.

Only one other mammal invades the tundra biome in numbers to match the lemming—the barren ground caribou. The caribou of the Arctic is a link in another simple food chain; caribou eat the mosses, lichens and grasses; wolves (and hunting man) eat the caribou. Unlike the lemming which lives on a restricted home range until driven from it by the pressures of overpopulation, the caribou roams the Arctic tundra constantly, for it is a big animal and they are many; their food supply does not grow tall and it grows again but slowly. To stay alive the caribou must spend its life on the move. Two species live on the Arctic coast—the barren ground caribou of the mainland and lower Arctic islands and the Peary caribou of the high Arctic islands, smaller than its southern cousin, white in general colour rather than brown with splashes of white.

Although most of the barren ground caribou migrate in great herds south into the trees for the winter, other mainland groups, and all those of the Arctic islands, remain on the tundra all winter, protected from the cold by their winter pelage of dense, erect hollow-stemmed hair which covers almost every part of the animal. The extremities of the caribou are short and the body stocky which gives it a short circulation course with minimum cooling of the blood and minimum body surface exposed to the biting winds. The cloven hoofs are round in outline, unlike those of southern deer which are always pointed; the hoofs splay out to form a wide snowshoe somewhat larger than a man's hand with fingers extended, which provides excellent support on the snow. Sharp edges on the hoofs give the caribou good traction on every type of surface except glare ice and provide it with efficient digging tools for scraping down through the hard packed winter snow cover to get at the moss and lichen on which it feeds. In the caribou, unlike southern deer, both sexes have antlers which differ from those of deer to the south by having a brow tine—a long, shovel-like projection that extends down over the forehead between the eyes.

On the mainland tundra the first thaw of spring usually comes late in April or early in May. By that time the herds of barren ground caribou, that have spent the winter in the forests to the south, have started to move northward on the return portion of their long migration move back to the tundra. First come the cows, those pregnant as a result of unions with bulls on the southward march of the previous autumn, now filled out with calf; the bulls follow far behind. Caribou in their thousands flow over the land heading north, diverted from their path only by exceptionally deep snow or by a particularly bad storm. Five or six miles an hour is their speed; thirty miles a day their average move. The herds follow traditional routes, land deeply grooved along its surface with meandering, parallel paths worn deep into the turf and soil by constant pounding of thousands of hoofs, year after year. In the spring the caribou often travel over the frozen surfaces of the lakes and rivers; in the summer they tend to follow the heights of land, crossing rivers and lakes at the same places every year. Along the way many die of accidents; drowned by waves from high winds on the lakes, swept over rapids and waterfalls on the rivers, of broken legs suffered running among the rocks trying to escape from wolves.

Early in June the lakes and rivers of the mainland tundra are beginning to break up and the caribou are nearing their summer calving grounds. The herds split up, pregnant cows scatter far and wide over the hills, the remainder to browse on the new forage of the river valleys and the lake shores. By mid-June most of the calves have been born and by the end of the month the herds have come together again—bulls, cows, yearlings, new calves, to wander for the rest of the summer wherever wind, weather, mosquitoes and food supply may take them.

In August a new restlessness comes over the herds; they usually break up into smaller groups, sometimes making a brief

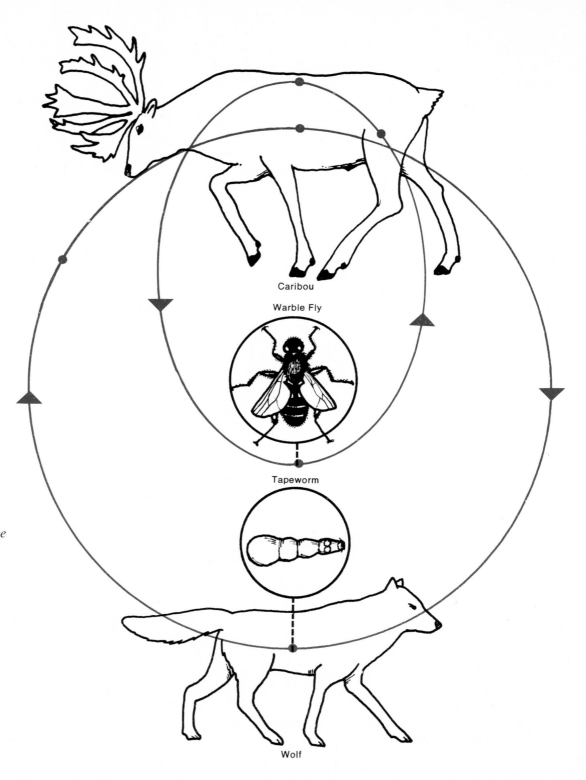

TWO MAJOR PARASITES — SCOURGE OF THE CARIBOU

In the summer months, warble flies deposit their eggs in the rump of a caribou; the eggs develop into larvae and work their way up the animal's back by burrowing under the skin. Once there, as many as 350 can feed and grow over the winter. They burrow back out and drop to the ground the following summer, to pupate and emerge as warble flies. A tapeworm begins life as a tiny egg, deposited in the intestines of a wolf, fox or dog. The eggs are later dropped in the faeces of the host animal, and may then be picked up and ingested by a browsing caribou. Once inside the caribou, they are hatched into larvae and migrate to other parts of the body where they form into cysts; in the brain or lungs such cysts can bring death to the caribou. The illustration points out the continuing cycle of these parasitic life forms.

Caribou

Warble Fly

Tapeworm

Wolf

130

dash southward into the edge-of-the-tree country and then back out onto the tundra again. The first sign of approaching winter and the groups come together and drift southward, gradually gathering together into great herds. By the end of September the bulls are sparring with one another in preparation for the mid-October rut; by the first week in November the rut is over and the scrawny, depleted bulls leave the females and gather into separate herds shedding their horns as they move. All during this time there has been much fighting and erratic movement of the individuals, but the main southward movement of the herds has continued. By December the main herds are feeding in the northern bush; behind they have left the smaller groups to winter on the open tundra.

In their ceaseless flow of movement north and south across the immense length and breadth of their tundra range the caribou have not been alone. Travelling with the herds have been groups of tundra wolves, the "villains" of the world of nature in the tundra biome. Tundra wolves are usually off-white or light grey in colour as opposed to the darker grey of the timber wolves to the south. On the winter feeding grounds in the bush the timber wolves have moved with the caribou herds but they rarely penetrate far onto the open tundra with the herds in the spring. The tundra wolves remain north of the tree line all winter, feeding on the herds of caribou left behind, on the musk ox, on the ground squirrels and lemmings if they cannot get caribou. These huge, white wolves are well adapted to the life of a carnivore in the tundra biome; they are big animals, weighing in at 125 pounds and more; long-legged for fast movement across the open plains; deep-chested for staying power when they have to travel fast and far; big-footed for superb traction on the chase over the snow. Their heavy coat of long, off-white fur provides ample protection from the cold wind and low temperature. The tundra wolf is a predator, superbly designed and built for its task.

Wolves kill caribou; however, the wolf hardly seems deserving of its image as a bloodthirsty killer, bent on the destruction of all wildlife in its area. The wolf usually operates as a deadly, efficient meat-gathering machine; along with the caribou it has existed on the wide range of the tundra for centuries past. Caribou eat vegetation; wolves eat caribou; a simple food chain. Many biologists consider that the wolf assists the caribou by helping keep their numbers in balance, eliminating possible overgrazing of the range. By killing off diseased and inferior animals from the herd, the wolf assists it to maintain group health and alertness, allowing no degenerative units to survive. At times wolves do kill more caribou than they can eat up immediately, but this usually occurs during the months of April, May and June, immediately prior to the whelping period for which the wolves need a good store of meat handy to the den in order to feed the bitch and the growing pups. It is interesting to note that the wolf bitch drops its cubs about the same time as the caribou cow drops its calf; thus both hunter and hunted are tied up in the cycle of birth at the same time, usually far distant from each other at just the time when the caribou needs most to be free of the association with the wolf. Could this be an adaptation to the realities of life in this land?

The best hunting for wolves is around the large herds of caribou as they move north and south across frozen land and lake. The wolf moves with the herd and the herd knows that the wolf, or wolves are there. So long as no overt movement is made by the wolf in the direction of the herd, peace reigns. Wolves can pass within fifty to one hundred yards of a large herd of caribou and not disturb the animals one whit. But when the wolf needs food it moves with precision and purpose. Rushing straight at the herd it will have picked out the animal it wishes to kill. Immediately the herd goes on the alert; those distant from the wolf do not move but they watch the proceedings with great care. Those closer to the wolf, but out of the line of its attack, are slightly uneasy but not terrified; they usually trot along, angling slightly outward to keep clear of a possible change in the direction of the attack. Those directly in front of the wolf are in full flight; quickly the gap between the hard driving wolf and the fleeing deer closes. The victim senses that it is the one and redoubles its efforts to escape. As the wolf moves in close, the other caribou angle away from the victim, leaving it alone in its flight. With a rush the wolf leaps for the neck or the throat; down goes the deer under the tremendous power of the hurtling wolf. In a moment the caribou is dead on the snow, throat cut and mangled, or head nearly torn from its body. The wolf enjoys its meal of raw meat; the rest of the caribou can settle down to feed in peace; the tundra food chain consisting of moss-caribou-wolf is now complete.

13 HUNTING MAN

No one knows why man, creature of warmth, first moved into the Arctic environment of the north polar region. Perhaps he was driven there by relentless pressure from new and more powerful groups of mankind emerging out of the heartland areas of Africa and Asia, until, eventually, certain groups found themselves facing out over the ice of the Asian Arctic seas. Perhaps he drifted north, after becoming adapted to life in a cold land in earlier times when the encroaching ice of the Pleistocene glaciers first inundated the hunting grounds of northern Europe and Asia, forcing certain groups of men who were reluctant to move far south away from the lands in which they had been born, into refugia along the outer edges of the ice. We do not know; we may never know. But, whatever the historical incentive may have been, the fact is that hunting man, at some point in his long development, met and successfully adapted to life in a land in which the dominant physical feature was ice—land under the control of cold.

The Arctic plants, insects, birds, and most of the mammals adapted to life in the cold through changes in their basic processes, their physical features, and their instinctual behaviour patterns. Man did none of these things; he used his brain and his hands to devise special ways of meeting the challenges imposed upon him by his world of ice. Hunting man had no heavy coat of fur; he took the coat of the caribou and from it fashioned warm clothing for his naked body, clothing so well designed and of such excellent insulating material that it has remained the best winter clothing ever produced, so far unduplicated for warmth and comfort while working and travelling in the Arctic winter. From the heavier, but more waterproof, skins of the sea mammals he made clothing that kept him warm and dry during the spring and summer as he hunted and travelled over the melting ice or on the open water of the sea. From the skins of the sea mammals he made lashings for his sleds; his summer shelters were made from sealskin, as were the coverings of his ingenious boats, the kayak and the umiak. Bone and ivory gave him materials he needed for his weapons—the special spears for the fish; the distinctive harpoons for the seals, the walrus and the small whales. From soft soapstone he carved his cooking pots, and the half-moon shaped oil lamps in which he burned the fat of the sea mammals to give him heat and light in his winter house made of sod and stone, or from blocks of snow.

Hunting man learned to use the cold of his far north land to his own advantage. The hard packed snow of the Arctic coast made an excellent building material, firm enough to be cut into building blocks with a bone knife, yet full of tiny air pockets

Lance head

Lance handle

Lance joint

In order to kill the elusive seal, the Eskimo hunter devised special weapons that were light enough to be wielded from his kayak, but still deadly enough to kill his prey on the first strike.

that provided excellent insulation against the severe cold. A thin film of ice on the runners of his sled made it slide more easily over the dry Arctic snow. In the central Arctic, where wood was a very scarce commodity, he often used cold to help him build his winter sled. Laying frozen Arctic char end to end and wrapping them tightly in a wet sealskin which was then allowed to freeze, he fashioned "fish and skin" plank runners for a small sled. Lashed together by skin lines and crossbars of antler or bone, such a sled could be used by one man and his family to haul their meagre possessions over the snow. It also served as an emergency food supply whenever hunting failed and he was unable to secure fresh meat.

Hunting man was the ultimate predator of the Arctic coast biome. Over land and ice and water he roamed constantly, killing in order to feed himself, his family and his dogs. Herbivorous and carnivorous, equipped with the ability to observe, to think and to reason, hunting man in the Arctic lived as a kind of super-mammal, preying on everything that came his way. He watched the caribou, studied their ways; he fashioned bows and arrows of bone and sinew to kill them and devised the techniques needed to trap them at the water crossings on the lakes and rivers, or in the long, rocky valleys that he studded with piles of rocks in imitation of men to force the caribou into the path of his primitive weapons. He made nets of sinew to trap flocks of small birds in winter; snares to catch Arctic hares;

stone traps to catch foxes and wolves; even small, stone corrals into which he would drive the flightless, moulting geese so that he could kill them with stones or clubs. He gathered eggs; he ate, and considered a great delicacy the larvae of the warble fly of the caribou.

Using his hunting kayak on the open sea he stalked and killed the swimming seals, walrus and whales with harpoons made of wood and bone and ivory. He crept up on the seals as they lay on the ice dozing in the spring sun, always in full view of the seal, moving ahead while it slept, moving about when it awoke in imitation of the seal, trying to make the seal believe that he was just another seal until he could get close enough to rush it for the kill. He hunted baby seals as they lay in their caves beneath the snow on the sea ice, breaking in the roofs of the aglos in imitation of the hunting technique of the polar bear. And for the seals under the thick ice cover, he devised an elaborate and highly successful technique for seeking out the breathing holes and harpooning the seals as they rose up to take a breath of air.

Hunting man on the Arctic coast spent his life in killing. But he was not a savage for he killed with compassion. Not the sentimental, sometimes maudlin compassion of today, but a compassion born of the belief that all the animals he killed had souls, just like himself. A man's soul was a little man; the soul of a seal was a little seal. He believed that you couldn't kill the

Three-pronged spear

Caribou arrow

Caribou spear
(for use in water)

Caribou provided the major source of food and clothing for inland Eskimos. The weapons illustrated above were devised by the primitive Eskimo hunter to kill the mighty animal.

Eskimo hunters killed only to meet the needs of the day as they believed the soul of a dead seal would return to seek vengeance.

soul and because of this there was great danger in the killing of all animals; once the soul was set free by the death of the body it could seek vengeance on the hunter. Especially was he vulnerable if he had failed to live up to the rules of life, the laws laid down by the wisdom of his ancestors in days long ago, the precepts we call taboos. Taboos belonged to the world of his gods who dwelt far off in the sky, beneath the land, at the bottom of the sea, in a supernatural world that was as real to the Eskimo hunter as the natural world he could see all about him.

> "Nuliakjuk, great god of mankind,
>   Send us the seals,
>   Send us the bears,
>   Send us the walrus;
>   So that we may have food
>   And fat
>   And clothing;
>   Beasts of the sea
>   Come offer yourself,
>   In the cold, clear light of the morning."

The Eskimo hunter was not a conscious conservationist; sometimes he killed great numbers of caribou, far more than he could use; sometimes he blocked a river completely and fished it to near extinction, completely unaware of what was taking place. To him the thought that the animals he hunted could be killed off to extinction just did not exist; there had always been animals in his land and, despite their cyclic appearances and disappearances, they would always be there. With his primitive weapons he lacked the ability to kill on a scale grand enough to decimate animal species over their entire range; his own numbers could never grow so many as to pose a threat to the continued existence of the game on which he depended for his life, except in a short term, very local way. Besides, hunting and fishing was hard work, often dangerous work; the Eskimo hunter usually killed only to meet the needs of the day.

Today in the Arctic coast region of Canada there are a few Eskimo hunters still able to follow the mammals in the manner of their forefathers of long ago; hunters willing to wait for hours over a small hole in the winter ice, hunters able to kill caribou with bow and arrow, hunters not afraid to seek out the polar bear while armed only with the short, bone-tipped spear. Today, there are a few old people living out their lives on the shores of Chantry Inlet and Pelly Bay who still carry with them the vivid memories of their younger days, when the Eskimo hunter reigned supreme, the virtual ruler of all this far northern land.

Virtual ruler, but not absolute. For all his skill and ingenuity in adapting to the cold climate of his Arctic land, the Eskimo hunter remained a predatory mammal, one link in a simple food chain, condemned to spend his life locked into an unchanging cycle of movement from hunting area to hunting area, a tyranny of timetable even more rigid than the tyranny of the time-clock and punch-card of today. At the peak of its development his culture was a bone and stone society, locked irrevocably into a pattern of alternate feast and famine, the basic cycle of scarcity and plenty of an Arctic land. The hunter was totally dependent on the mammals of land and sea; so long as they fell beneath his spears and arrows and harpoons, he remained happy and well fed, able to live and travel throughout his land. But, when they died off, or disappeared from his area, when the herds of caribou failed to come to the water crossings; when the seals failed to come to the breathing holes; when the fish failed to swim up the rivers in the fall, then hunting man died; died of starvation and cold in the vast white emptiness of his wilderness home. His folk tales tell of such horror on the land.

"One winter, many years ago, hunting was a failure and nobody had anything to eat. People died of hunger, and the quick lived on the dead. Day after day the few remaining hunters stood over the few seal holes they were able to find by themselves, for their dogs had long since been eaten. But the seals had gone, no one knew where. Hour after hour the hunters waited, with their bellies empty and the cold pecking at their bones. Back at their snow houses they knew that their families were dying, slowly, first the old people, then the very young, then the healthy ones. Without food, without heat, without light, their lives flickered and were gone."

Such was the fortune of the high Arctic hunter—to live or to die, always unto himself, making no mark, leaving almost no record that he once passed this way. He lived in harmony and in balance with his Arctic environment, but such harmony had its dreadful price. Often he was called upon to pay.

14 THE DESTROYERS

For thousands of years the Arctic coast of Canada was known only to the primitive humans from Asia who had spread in successive waves across the top of North America, and on into Greenland. Around 1000 A.D. the early Norse began to settle the west coast of Greenland and make voyages to Baffin Island, but all records of these voyages were lost to Europe until recent times when contact between Europe and Greenland was cut off late in the fourteenth century. As recently as five hundred years ago darkness shrouded European knowledge of the Arctic world that lay beyond the vast expanse of the north Atlantic Ocean. Out beyond that shadowy horizon lay unknown lands "wherein nature breeds perverse, all monstrous, all prodigious things, worse than fables yet conceived, gorgons, Hydras, and chimeras dire, all peopled with strange infidels whose like was never seen, read nor heard before."

It wasn't until the beginning of the fifteenth century that the darkness began to lift. In quick succession came the rediscovery of the earth as a sphere; came the development of sailing vessels capable of traversing the open ocean far from land; came the discovery of the miracle of the magnetic compass. The eyes of Europe turned westward, seeking new routes to the enchanted land of Cathay—Cathay, described by Marco Polo as a form of Christian Heaven, where highways were paved in gold; a land of incense and perfume, and enough rare spices and herbs to whet the greed of every man.

Instead of Cathay western man came to the shores of northern North America, and the Arctic coast appeared to him in a much different light than it had to the earlier migrants from the east. The newcomers were as fearful of the strange land they found as they were of the fires of Hell. The "civilized" Europeans were disgusted with the primitive Eskimo, " a brutish people . . . link between Saxons and seals—hybrids, putting the seal's body into their own and then encasing their skins in the seals'." They were terrified of the winter darkness, "dark, dark, dark . . . without all hope of day." They lived in fear of the power of the ice on the sea. "No water was to be seen around our ship . . . from day to day we hoped for the hour of our deliverance; at first we expected it hourly, then daily, then from week to week, then after the seasons of the year, then at the changes in the new year. But, alas, that hour never came, never again were we destined to see our vessel in water; we were prisoners of the pack." They were awestruck by the bleak, treeless, and seemingly lifeless land under their feet, "snow and rock and broken ice surrounded us on every side. A more desolate place could not be found on earth than the land we walked on." Even today, in mid-twentieth century, with very few exceptions Canadians are afraid of their Arctic coast region; only about one tenth of one percent of Canada's population lives there, and of this miniscule proportion it is quite probable that at least one-third would rather be anywhere but where they are.

The early explorers were sea captains, hired by the businessmen of Europe to seek out new trade routes along which they could conduct their enormously profitable trade in spices, incense and jewels with the countries of the Far East. These men neither expected nor desired to find new lands between them and their goal, but when land was found they moved quickly to exploit any wealth it might contain.

The first of the European sea captains to penetrate the eastern Arctic was Martin Frobisher who, outbound from England in 1576 in his tiny ship the *Gabriel,* came to the shores of southern Baffin Island and sailed into his bay. For Frobisher the discovery of the Northwest Passage to the Orient was "the only thing of the world left undone whereby a notable mind might be made famous and fortunate." He made three voyages to the bay that now bears his name, sponsored by the newly formed Cathay Company, favoured by the interest and financial support of Queen Elizabeth who called the new land *Meta Incognita* – worth unknown – a somewhat prophetic name in view of future events. Although Frobisher started out to find a passage to the Orient he was diverted from his task by a chance discovery. "The Captain and six of his men landed on a small island where they found many strange flowers and grasses among the stones . . . one of the men found a piece of black stone by the weight of which seemed to be some kind of metal or mineral . . . they came to a place where all the sands and rocks did glisten so that all seemed to be gold."

Gold! The quest for the Northwest Passage was all but forgotten. "Upon this island was found a good store of the ore,

whereupon it was thought best to load here than to seek further. Setting the miners to work, our Captain showed a good precedent of painful labour himself, whereupon every man, both better and worse, willingly laid their helping hands . . . with the hold of the ship full of ore we set sail for home."

Alas! Frobisher's gold turned out to be iron pyrites. The Cathay Company was bankrupt; the ore so laboriously hauled across the Atlantic was dumped into the harbour at Bristol, England, where four hundred years later it would cause considerable damage to a dredge working at deepening the harbour. Northern North America's first mine came into production in the Arctic coast region of Canada; its open pit scars the landscape of Kadloonak Island today.

Very quickly did the merchants of western Europe adapt to the newly discovered facts about the geography and natural history of the Arctic coasts of the world. Out from the sea ports of Spain, France, Holland and England came huge fleets of whaling vessels, hundreds of ships employing thousands of men, all seeking the great whales that swam in uncounted numbers in the waters off the Arctic coasts; the huge Greenland "right" whale, its body larded with tons of blubber that could be rendered down into oil for the lamps of Europe and Asia, its mouth a mass of thin, parallel plates of baleen, a unique substance in the animal world, light, tough and flexible, able to be split along its entire length into strips of any desired thinness, ideal material to help shape the form and figure of the ladies of the courts at St. James and The Hague; and the sperm whale, equally well-laden with blubber, without baleen but having in its massive head an enormous reservoir of spermaceti, basis for cosmetics and perfumes. In the seventeenth century, whales from Arctic waters lighted Europe, greased its wheels, provided its soap, and kept its ladies in trim.

As the prices for whale oil and baleen increased – in 1775 the products from a single whale brought about $3,000 at the port of Dundee but by the early 1900's this had increased to as much as $10,000 per whale – whaling became one of the biggest extractive industries of the western world. It brought fortunes to many and, in the disputes it generated, it brought nations to the brink of war. The risks of whaling were high; between 1772 and 1852 eighty ships from a single port were lost at sea or crushed in the ice. On a single day, June 19th, 1830, nineteen

WHALERS – LONG THE SCOURGE OF THE ARCTIC SEAS

In the three hundred years between 1600 and 1900 the Arctic whales were hunted relentlessly by vast fleets of ships. The voyages often lasted three years and the conditions on board these ships were so incredibly harsh that they provided material for several novels on the nineteenth century. The whales provided lamp oil, axel grease, soap and whalebone for Europe and North America. The illustration depicts the normal whaling operation during this bloody period.

A Whale is ordinarly about 60 foote longe

When the whale comes aboue water ye shallop rowes towards him and being within reach of him the harpoiner darts his harpingiron at him out of both his hands and being fast they lance him to death

When the whale is killed hee is in this mann' towed to the shipps by twoe or three shal: lops made fast one to another.

The whale is cut up as hee lyes floting crosse the stearne of a shipp the blubber is cut from the flesh by peeces 3 or 4 foote long and being rased is rowed on shore towards the copers

The peeces of blubber are towed to the shore side by a shallop and drawne onshore by a crane or caried by twoe menn on a barrowe to ye twoe cutters wch cutts them the breadt of a trencher and very thine & by twoe boyes are caried wth handhookes to ye choppers

They place 2 or 3 copers on a rœ and ye chopping boate on the one side and the cooking boate on the other side to receiue ye oyle of ye copers, the chopt blubber being boyled is taken out of the copers and put in wiker baskets or barowes wthrowg wch the oyle is dreaned and runes into ye cooler wich full wt water out of wch it is convaied by troughs into butts or hogsheads

No one questioned the wisdom of destroying so valuable a source of oil, baleen and spermaceti, so long as sale profits kept pouring in.

ships of the Hull whaling fleet were crushed against the land-fast floe and destroyed, leaving over one thousand men stranded on the sea ice of Melville Bay. But, high as the risks were, the chance of profit was even higher; there was rarely a shortage of money to outfit new vessels, nor a shortage of men to act as their eager crews.

Little has been written about this black period in the history of men on the sea. Arctic waters were far from the centres of civilization; the high seas were anyone's domain. So long as the oil and the baleen and the spermaceti poured into the warehouses, and the profits from their sale poured into the pockets of seamen, merchants and princes alike, no one questioned the ultimate wisdom of destroying so valuable a resource of the open sea. Out of sight, out of mind, seemed to have been the order of the day.

For over three hundred years the whalers were the scourge of the Arctic seas. Through the seventeenth century they destroyed the herds of whales in the coastal waters of the Greenland and Norwegian Seas. By the eighteenth century dwindling catches along the coast forced them onto the open sea where they killed whales with relentless ferocity. Following hard on the heels of the explorers, in cases even preceding them, they moved into the more distant waters of Davis Strait and Baffin Bay, into the inlets of the eastern Arctic islands, until, by the late nineteenth and early twentieth century, they had penetrated deep into Hudson Bay. In the west they moved north from the

Great numbers of walrus were also included in the indiscriminate destruction by the whalers, who expected to profit by the ivory tusks.

Pacific through Bering Strait into the Chukchee and Beaufort Seas. Early in the twentieth century, from the whaling base at Herschel Island, American whalers hunted the big whales as far east as the waters of Amundsen Gulf and north into the Arctic Ocean. Until the invention of substitutes for whalebone in the year 1906, which brought about the complete collapse of the whaling industry in northern waters in the space of a single year, the whaler was despotic king of the Arctic seas.

No one knows the numbers of whales destroyed through three centuries of unrestricted killing; the total count would probably stagger the imagination. So many were killed that the large whales virtually disappeared from Arctic waters; where they once swam and fed and blew in their hundreds, they appear now only rarely, usually as single animals, at most two or three. It is quite likely that the large whales are gone forever from the waters of the Arctic coast region of Canada, too few in number to perpetuate their kind.

The destructiveness of the whalers did not end with the killing off of the whales. They also killed great numbers of walrus and polar bears; walrus for their ivory tusks, polar bears for their luxuriant white coats, both valuable items of trade in the marketplaces of Europe and Asia. And, at their wintering-over places on the Arctic coasts, at Fullerton on the northwest coast of Hudson Bay, at Herschel Island off the mouth of the Mackenzie, at various locations on the east coast of Baffin Island, the whalers hunted out over the land, or encouraged the local Eskimos to hunt for them, killing thousands upon thousands of caribou, hundreds of musk ox to keep themselves supplied with fresh meat. As with the whales in the sea, no one knows how many animals were slaughtered over the years but the total number must have been as equally enormous as those butchered on the sea.

"One winter fifteen vessels wintered at Herschel Island and I am reliably informed that these vessels each used from 10,000 to 20,000 pounds of caribou meat an aggregate of over 300,000 pounds in one winter, principally the saddles; at the head of Franklin Bay, in the winter of 1897-98, four ships used of the same kind of meat about 90,000 pounds, and at Cape Bathurst, in 1898-99, one vessel used in the neighbourhood of 40,000 pounds." Small wonder that a government report, compiled long after the whaling ships and their rapacious crews had passed from the scene, concluded that "the whaling fleet at the commencement of this century was a primary factor in the serious reduction of these herds (of caribou) along the western Arctic coast."

For thousands of years life in the tundra biome of North America, and in the waters and on the ice of the seas along the Arctic coasts, had co-existed within a stable ecological unit that embraced within its borders a delicately balanced world of plants and animals, including hunting man, all especially adapted to life in a land under the control of cold. Then, in the short space of three hundred years, this world was shattered and laid waste by the predations of western man, creature of warmth, moving as an itinerant visitor and intruder into what he considered to be a disordered land. The early explorers ended the isolation of the Arctic coast from the rest of the world; the whalers followed, first to systematically kill off much of the big game of land and sea, then to become dealers in ivory and fur. For when whaling died many whalers remained on the Arctic coast as independent traders. Both as whalers and traders they encouraged the local Eskimo groups to change their way of life from that of a free-roaming hunter, intent only on obtaining food for himself and his family, into that of a hunt-and-trap-for-profit businessman who killed caribou and musk ox for sale to the ship's crews; who killed polar bears, foxes and wolves for their fur, walrus and small whales for their ivory, all of which he traded for rifles and ammunition, pots and pans, clothing of wool and cotton, trinkets of glass and brass, all items that

The harsh natural environment frequently took its revenge on the rapacious whaling fleets.

only added weight to his equipment and nothing at all to his ability to survive as a hunter in a cold land.

Whalers of the seventeenth and eighteenth centuries were at least partly responsible for the disappearance of the Thule Eskimo culture for, although change in Arctic coast climate was undoubtedly a basic factor in the dwindling away of the Thule culture from the north coast of Canada, the killing off of the large whales probably contributed much to the destruction of this advanced hunting society; even without the increasing severity of the weather the slaughter of the big whales would have eventually brought about its demise. There is no doubt that the whalers destroyed, or at least planted the seed that would destroy, the society of the modern Eskimo hunter of the Arctic coast; directly by killing off groups of people through strange diseases they introduced, indirectly by so changing the mores and habits and thinking of the remaining indigenous inhabitants that a high Arctic culture, the like of which the world will never see again, began to slip away into oblivion in a process that has continued unabated down through the first half of the present century, and continues in its last stages today.

The whalers of the Arctic coast have passed into history; the last of the Arctic hunters will very soon be but a memory as western technology moves ever deeper into the Arctic coast region. On the land, herds of caribou still roam the tundra, much reduced in numbers and haunted by the spectre of extinction through excessive predation, disease, reduction of range due to fire, poor calf crops due to inclement weather at calving time, but still a viable element of the tundra biome that, with good management and some luck, will survive and thrive in future generations. Musk ox, now completely protected, are increasing in numbers after being nearly wiped out through excessive killing by explorers, whalers and Eskimos alike. In the sea the big whales are nearly gone, but seals and walrus still swim along the coasts or sleep on the ice in the spring sun, polar bears still roam the icefields, all being killed in ever-increasing numbers but being studied and watched so that it is quite probable that their future well being is assured. And, although we western humans still tend to look upon the Arctic as a distant land of ice and snow, we are beginning to study it, to learn from it, to adapt our technology to its unique conditions.

But we cannot be complacent about the future in the natural

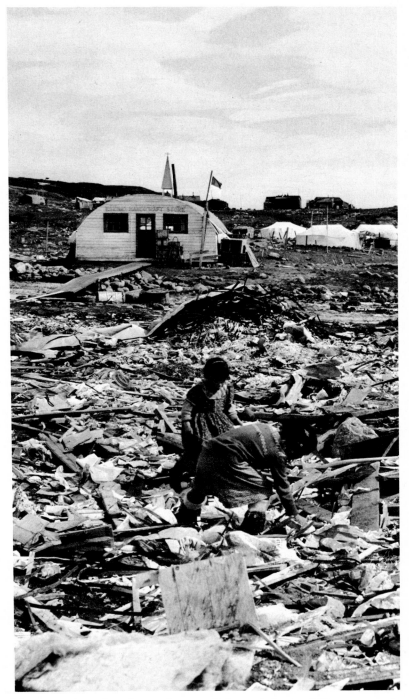

Western culture has almost destroyed the native way of life.

history of the Arctic coast region. Although any repeat of the mass slaughter of earlier years is unlikely, the Arctic is still a long way from southern Canada; what goes on there often seems to be quite remote, quite separate from life in the south. In today's world nothing could be further from the truth. The world has become a global village in which all events concern all peoples, no matter where they may be. Nowhere is this better illustrated than by what some scientists have come to call "the new caribou problem."

Lichens stand at the bottom of an Arctic food chain, deriving their sustenance from the sun and from the fall-out of natural materials in the air. Until the explosion of the first atomic bomb in 1945 lichens absorbed only the harmless fall-out of dust and other wind-blown materials; today they absorb the radioactive fall-out resulting from the nuclear explosions in the atmosphere of the world. Lichens are extremely efficient garnerers of materials from the air and they grow very slowly, storing up in their exposed, edible parts the fall-out particles of many years. Over the years lichens of the Arctic coasts have built up a high degree of radioactive contamination.

Caribou eat lichens, commonly called caribou moss, as a primary food and, as a result, caribou (and reindeer) of Canada, Alaska, Scandinavia and Russia have begun to show excessive ⸱levels of contamination by radioactive elements, principally Strontium-90 and Cesium-137. In some cases the levels are far above that recommended as being "safe" for man. On the Arctic coasts man eats caribou meat, often as a primary food. Although data is scarce as yet, what little there is seems to indicate that radioactive contamination of humans feeding on caribou and reindeer meat is much higher than that in humans feeding on other meats. Thus it would seem that the entire food chain of lichen-caribou-man, in sections of the Arctic coast regions of the world, is becoming excessively contaminated by radioactive materials.

This problem was first noted in 1959; since that time there has been little additional research and almost no publicity. Yet it is a problem that affects all life in an area that comprises almost one third of Canada; on the world stage it affects an area that makes up almost one-fifth of the land in the northern hemisphere. There is little doubt that if a similar situation existed in southern Canada, in the grass-cattle-man food chain,

reaction would be immediate and violent. But the Arctic coast is a long way off, lichens are an unfamiliar plant, the caribou is a strange animal. Except to a few scientists the problems of the lichen-caribou-man food chain seem no closer to most of us today than did the problem of the whales seem to the average man and woman of the eighteenth century.

This thinking must change. Here in Canada we have gone from a stage of not thinking about our Arctic at all to a situation in which we think about it quite a bit, but usually in the romantic sense—the land of the Eskimo, of Eskimo Art, the true north strong and free. Or we think about it in the economic sense; we talk about oil and gas beneath the land of the high Arctic islands, copper, iron and nickel under the rocks of the Shield. We see visions of northern development, with new mines, new towns, new people with new thoughts building new empires out beyond the northerly limit of the trees. And so we should, for we are Canadians; our land stretches north to within some 450 miles of the true North Pole.

But as we dream our northern dreams we should remember that, even with the most optimistic development of the resources beneath the land, we would still be utilizing only a tiny fraction of the land area of the tundra biome. Our new mines and town-sites and airfields would be but pin-pricks on this vast land. All about would still be the enormous areas of land and sea on and in which live the cold-adapted plants, insects, birds, mammals, each one a resource, each one tied inextricably into a basic food chain of an Arctic land, each slow to grow and slow to reproduce, and thus easily destroyed if the system is thrown out of kilter by unmanaged, exploitive use of one or more elements in the vital chain.

Remote from the rest of Canada, sparse in human population, meagrely represented in the power structure of government, the natural world of the Arctic coast must rely for its future well-being on the continuing interest of science, on the understanding and vociferous pleading of a special few, and, ultimately, on the understanding and co-operation of millions of people in southern Canada who will never see the Arctic, who will always consider it to be a disordered land, but who care enough about all parts of their country to make sure that the Arctic coast will remain forever as a living symbol of the great wilderness that was once our entire world.

GEOLOGIC TIME SCALE

TIME (MILLIONS OF YEARS)	ERA	PERIOD	EPOCH	THE ASCENT OF LIFE:
	CENOZOIC	QUATERNARY	PLEISTOCENE	
		TERTIARY	PLIOCENE	
			MIOCENE	
			OLIGOCENE	
			EOCENE	
50			PALEOCENE	
100	MESOZOIC	CRETACEOUS	UPPER / LOWER	
150		JURASSIC	UPPER / MIDDLE / LOWER	
200		TRIASSIC	UPPER / MIDDLE / LOWER	
250	PALAEOZOIC	PERMIAN	UPPER / MIDDLE / LOWER	
300		PENNSYLVANIAN		
350		MISSISSIPPIAN		
		DEVONIAN	UPPER / MIDDLE / LOWER	
400		SILURIAN		
450		ORDOVICIAN	UPPER / MIDDLE / LOWER	
500		CAMBRIAN	UPPER / MIDDLE / LOWER	
550				

THE ASCENT OF LIFE: 1, protozoan; 2, jellyfish; 3, crinoid; 4, cephalopod; 5, climatius; 6, shark; 7, brachiopod; 8, seed fern; 9, dimetrodon; 10, brontosaurus; 11, plesiosaur; 12, tyrannosaurus; 13, taeniolabis; 14, diatryma; 15, hyracotherium; 16, brontotherium; 17, oxydactylus; 18, pliohippus; 19, mastodon; 20, man.

SHORT LIST OF ROCKS, PLANTS AND ANIMALS

The lists on the following pages have been compiled as a basic guide for amateur naturalists intending to explore the wealth of natural history of the Arctic Coast region. These selected summaries cannot possibly cover all species — there are many thousands of insects alone — but an attempt has been made to include the common life forms and the natural phenomena peculiar to this region. Readers should find it useful to study the lists touching on their sphere of interest, checking off items they have observed during field trips. Those wishing to extend their search will find an extensive Bibliography on pages 153-5; references listed there contain more detailed information on specific subjects.

ROCKS

CENOZOIC ERA

TERTIARY PERIOD
Carbonized wood
Gypsum
Lignite
Mudstone
Sand
Sandstone
Shale

MESOZOIC ERA

CRETACEOUS PERIOD
Black shale
Clay
Coal
Diabase
Ironstone
Sandstone
Shale
Siltstone
Volcanic breccia

JURASSIC PERIOD
Coal
Conglomerate
Dolomite
Phosphatic nodules
Sand
Sandstone
Shale

TRIASSIC PERIOD
Limestone
Sandstone
Siltstone
Shale

PALAEOZOIC ERA

MISSISSIPPIAN AND PENNSYLVANIA PERIOD
Basalt
Chert
Conglomerate
Greywacke
Gypsum
Lignite
Limestone
Phyllite
Sandstone
Shale
Liltstone
Tuff

DEVONIAN PERIOD
Coal
Conglomerate
Coralline Limestone
Dolomite
Sandstone
Sandy shale
Siltstone
Slate

SILURIAN PERIOD
Argillite
Black limestone
Black shale
Gypsum
Mudstone
Sandstone

ORDOVICIAN PERIOD
Anhydrite
Dolomite
Gypsum
Limestone
Sandstone
Shale

CAMBRIAN PERIOD
Dolomite
Gypsum
Limestone
Sandstone

PRECAMBRIAN PERIOD
Argillite
Dolomite
Gneisses
Greenstone
Limestone
Marble
Paragneiss
Quartzite
Quartz-mica schist
Sandstone
Shale
Siltstone
Slate

MINERALS

The minerals listed are those most likely to be found in the regions named.

BAFFIN ISLAND
Altlanite
Antimony
Apatite
Asbestos
Coal
Cobalt
Columbite
Copper
Cordierite

Diopside
Fluorite
Garnet
Graphite
Gypsum
Hematite
Iron
Lapis Lazuli
Lazurite
Magnetite
Marble
Mica
Native sulphur
Nickel
Phosphorous
Platinum
Pyrite
Quartz
Seapolite
Serpentine
Sillimanite
Silver
Soapstone
Spinel
Steatite
Tourmaline

MACKENZIE DISTRICT

Chromite
Cobalt
Copper
Gold
Nickel
Pentlandite
Pitchblende
Silver
Soapstone
Sphalerite

HIGH ARCTIC ISLANDS DISTRICT

Agate
Chalcedony
Copper
Jasper
Pentlandite
Sphalerite

KEEWATIN DISTRICT

Amethyst
Arsenic
Chalcopyrite
Chromite bearing minerals
Copper
Fluorite
Gold
Jasper
Molybdenite

Pentlandite
Pitchblende
Platinum
Pyrite
Pyrrhotite
Quartz
Silver

WESTERN ARCTIC ISLANDS

Copper
Pyrite
Serpentine

UNGAVA

Asbestos
Chalcopyrite
Copper
Galena
Garnet
Graphite
Hematite
Iron
Jasper
Jaspilite
Magnetite
Pyrite
Pyrrhotite
Quartz
Silver
Soapstone

FOSSILS

Southern Baffin Island

SILURIAN

Corals
Calapoecia borealis
Halysites catenularia
Halysites catenulatus
Heliolites megastoma
Gastropods
Loxonema sp.
Hormotoma sp.
Lophospira sp.
Cephalopods
Endoceras sp.
Cyrtoceras sp.
Huronia sp.

ORDOVICIAN

Stromatoporoids
Stromatocerium
Corals
Calapoecia anticostiensis
Zaphrentis sp.

Gastropods
Maclurites sp.
Lophospira sp.
Eotomaria sp.

Cephalopods
Armenoceras richardsoni
Endoceras proteiforme
Actinceras sp.
Trocholites ammonius

Tribolites
Ogygites canadensis

Grinnell Peninsula
(Devon Island)

PERMIAN

Foraminifera
Schubertella kingi
Pseudofusulinella utahensis
Schwagerina paralinearis
Corals
Caninia ovibos
Lithostrotion grandis
Roemeripora wimani
Brachiopods
Lingula arctica
Streptorhynchus kempei
Muirwoodia mammatus
Stenoscisma plicatum
Cephalopods
Pseudogastrioceras fortieri
Metalegoceras sp.

Banks, Victoria and
Stefansson Islands

CRETACEOUS

Plankton
Cyclonocephalum distinctum
Deflandrea acuminata
Hystrichosphaeridium complex
Pelecypods
Nucula athabaskensis
Psilomya elongatissima
Beudanticeras affine
Arctica limpidiana

DEVONIAN

Foraminifera
Schubertella sp.
Brachiopods
Gypidula pseudogaleata
Nervostrophia sp.
Pelecypods
Paracyclas robusta

SILURIAN

Corals
Favosites sp.
Syringopora sp.
Brachiopods
Atrypella scheii

ORDOVICIAN

Corals
Receptaculites sp.
Cephalopods
Gonioceras sp.
Brachiopods
Pholidops trentonensis

Ellesmere Islands

TERTIARY

Ferns
Lycopodium sp.
Laevigatosporites albertensis
Gleichenia concavisporites
Osmundacidites primarius
Gleichenia concavisporites
Conifers
Pinus strobipites
Picea grandivescipites
Taxodium hiatipites
Larix sp.
Angiosperms
Betula sp.
Corylus sp.
Carya sp.
Myrica sp.

LOWER AND MIDDLE ORDOVICIAN

Gastropods
Liospira sp.
Hormotoma sp.
Turritoma sp.
Cephalopods
Spyroceras sp.
Gonioceras sp.
Trilobites
Bathyurus sp.
Isotelus sp.

LOWER ORDOVICIAN

Brachiopods
Lingulella sp.
Cephalopods
Euconia quebecensis
Clarkoceras holtedahli
Trilobites
Hystricurus ravni
Hystricurus longicephalus

MIDDLE CAMBRIAN
Trilobites
Glossopleura expansa
Glossopleura longifrons
Glossopleura walcotti
Clavaspidella sp.

LOWER CAMBRIAN
Brachiopods
Acrothele pulchra
Trilobites
Paedeumias borealis
Bonniopsis rostrata
Bonniopsis nasuta

Western Queen Elizabeth Islands

TERTIARY
Tree pollen
Pine
Spruce
Hemlock
Birch
Alder
Hazel
Poplar

CRETACEOUS
Plant microfossils
Alisporites
Abietaepollenites
Gleecheniidites
Stenozonotriletites
Ammonites
Beudanticeras affine
Lemuroceras belli

UPPER JURASSSIC
Pelecypods
Buchia piochii
Buchia fischeri
Buchia blandjordiana
Buchia bronni
Buchia keyserlingi
Vertebrates
Plesiosaur
Elasmosaur
Ichthyosaur

PERMIAN
Pelecypods
Plicatula hekiensis
Gryphaea arcuatiformis
Monotis ochotica
Protocardia striatula

Cephalopods
Dactylioceras commune

PENNSYLVANIAN
Corals
Chaetetes radians
Brachiopods
Muirwoodia mammatus
Linproductus cora
Echinoconcus punctatus
Productus longispinus
Choristites fritschi
Diclyoclostus gruenewaldti
Streptorhynchus kempei

DEVONIAN
Corals
Spongophyllum sp.
Cystiphylloides sp.
Disphyllum sp.
Brachiopods
Atrypa independensis
Reticularia curvata
Lingula melvillensis
Camarotoechia lettiensis
Schizophoria sp.
Pelecypods
Nuculana sp.
Cephalopods
Bactrites sp.
Crustaceans
Estheria canadensis
Fish
Bothriolepis sp.

SILURIAN
Brachiopods
Atrypa reticularis
Gastropods
Styliolina sp.
Tentaculites sp.

ORDOVICIAN
Graptolites
Tetragraptus quadribrachiatus
Didymograptus extensus
Didymograptus uniformis
Isograptus gibberulus
Climacograptus bicornis
Petalograptus palmeus
Monograptus regularis
Corals
Coenites sp.
Brachiopods
Conchidium alaskense

PLANTS

LICHENS
Polyblastia hyperborea
Sphaerophorus globosus
Placynthium asperellum
Psoroma hypnorum
Solorina crocea
Nephroma arcticum
Peltigera aphthosa
Peltigera scabrosa
Lecidea melinodes
Lecidea tesselata
Lecidea dicksonii
Rhizocarpon chionophilum
Rhizocarpon jemtlandicum

Reindeer moss
Cladonia pyxidata
Cladonia alpestris
Cladonia rangiferina
Cladonia mitis
Cladonia bellidiflora
Cladonia unicialis
Shrubby lichen
Stereocaulon alpinum
Stereocaulon arcticum
Omphalodiscus virginis
Gyrophora proboscidea
Gyrophora hyperborea
Gyrophora arctica
Sporostatia testudinea
Pertusaria oculata
Pertusaria coriabea
Lecanora epibryon
Lecanora verrucosa
Haematomma ventosum
Skull lichen
Parmelia saxatilis
Iceland moss
Cetraria islandica
Cetraria nivalis
Cetraria cucullata
Dactylina arctica
Dactylina ramulosa
Cornicularia divergens

Rock tripe
Rinodina roscida
Physcia musigena
Thamnolia vermicularis

MOSSES
Sphagnum songstromii
Sphagnum capillaceum
Andreaea rupestris
Fissidens exiguus
Ditrichum flexicaule

Horn-tooth moss
Ceratodon purpureus
Distichium capillaceum
Wind-blown moss
Dicranum elongatum
Dicranum groenlandicum
Dicranum fuscescens
Extinguisher moss
Encalypta rhabdocarpa
Tortella fragilis
Didymodon recurvirostris
Pottia heimii
Tortula ruralis
Grimmia apocarpa
Rhacomitrium lanuginosum
Tetraplodon mnioides
Hapladon wormskjoldii
Pohlia cruda
Pohlia nutans
Leptorbryum pyriforma
Hair cap moss
Polytrichum alpinum
Bryum pendulum
Bryum obtusifolium
Bryum calophyllum
Mnium affine
Cinclidium subrotundum
Campylium stellatum
Aulocomnium acuminatum
Meesea uliginosa
Bartramia ithyphylla
Conostomum boreale
Philonotis tomentella
Timmia austriaca
Orthotrichum speciosum
Amphidium lapponicum
Myurella apiculata
Myurella julacae
Abietinella abietina
Campylium stellatum
Drepanocladus uncinatus
Calliergon turgescens
Tomenthypnum nitens
Carpet moss
Hypnum revolutum

Stair-step moss
Hylocomium splendens

HORSETAILS
Common horsetail
Equisetum arvense
Variegated horsetail
Equisetum veriegatum
Scouring rush
Equisetum scirpoides

FERNS
Rusty woodsia
Woodsia ilvensis
Alpine woodsia
Woodsia alpina
Smooth woodsia
Woodsia glabella
Fragile bladder fern
Cystopteris fragilis
Fragrant shield fern
Dryopteris fragrans

SEDGES
Tall cotton grass
Eriophorum angustifolium
Cotton grass
Eriophorum scheuchzeri
Needle spike-rush
Eleocharis acicularis
Kobresia myosuroides
Kobresia hyperborea

RUSHES
Bog rush
Juncus castaneus
Juncus biglumis
Woodrush
Luzula wahlenbergi
Luzula nivalis
False asphodel
Tofieldia pusilla

GRASSES
Holygrass
Hierochloe odorata

Sweetgrass
Hierochloe alpina
Foxtail
Phippsia algida
Bentgrass
Agrostis borealis
Reed-bentgrass
Calamagrostis purpurascens
Hairgrass
Deschampsia pumila
Short-hairgrass
Deschampsia brevifolia
Bluegrass
Poa alpigena
Arctic bluegrass
Poa arctica
Mountain bluegrass
Poa alpina
Semaphore grass
Pleuropogon sabenei
Marshgrass
Dupontia fisheri
Goosegrass
Puccinellia angustata
Meadow-grass
Puccinellia bruggemanni
Puccinellia poacea
Sheathed meadowgrass
Puccinellia vaginata
Northern fesscue
Festuca baffinensis
Wheatgrass
Agropyron latiglume
Lyme-grass
Elymus arenarius
Buckwheat
Koenigia islandica

HERBS
Alpine bistort
Polygonum viviparum
Mountain sorrel
Oxyria digyna
Arctic sourdock
Rumex arcticus
Knotweed
Polygonum viviparum
Eskimo rhubarb
Polygonum alaskanum
Purslane
Montia lamprosperma
Chickweed

Stellaria longipes
Stellaria humifusa
Stellaria crassifolia
Mouse-ear chickweed

Cerastium alpinum
Cerastium arcticum
Cerastium regelii

Pearlwort
Sagina caespitosa
Sagina nodosa
Sagina intermedia
Sea-beach sandwort
Arenaria peploides
Sandwort
Arenaria humifusa
Arenaria rubella
Arenaria rossii
Arenaria sajanensis
Moss-campion
Silene acaulis
Arctic bladder-campion
Melandrium arcticum
Common campion
Melandrium affine
Wild bladder campion
Melandrium triflorum
Marsh marigold
Caltha palustris
White water-buttercup
Ranunculus trichophyllus
Pallas' buttercup
Ranunculus pallasii
Lapland buttercup
Ranunculus lapponicus
Snow buttercup
Ranunculus nivalis
Dwarf buttercup
Ranunculus pygmaeus
Arctic poppy
Papaver radicatum
Papaver keelei
Scurvy grass
Cochlearia officinalis
Tansy mustard
Descurainia sophioides

Whitlow grass
Draba alpina
Draba belli
Draba nivalis
Draba lactea
Draba subcapitata
Draba glabella
Draba groenlandica

Bitter cress
Cardamine bellidifolia
Rock cress
Arabis arenicola
Wallflower
Erysimum pallasii
Braya arctica
Braya purpurascens
Yellow mountain saxifrage
Saxifraga aizoides
White mountain saxifrage
Saxifraga aizoon
Tufted saxifrage
Saxifraga chespitosa
Nodding saxifrage
Saxifraga cernua
Spider plant
Saxifraga flagellaris
Yellow marsh saxifrage
Saxifraga propinqua
Alpine saxifrage
Saxifraga nivalis
Purple saxifrage
Saxifraga oppositifolia
Brook saxifrage
Saxifraga rivularis
Prickly saxifrage
Saxifraga tricuspidata
Golden saxifrage
Chrysosplenium tetrandrum
Grass-of-Parnassus
Parnassia kotzebuei

Cloudberry (baked apple)
Rubus chamaemorus
Arctic cinquefoil
Potentilla hypartica
Beautiful cinquefoil
Potentilla pulchella
Cinquefoil
Potentilla rubricaulis
Potentilla vahliana
Mountain avens
Dryas integrifolia

Milk-vetch
Astragalus richardsoni
Alpine milk-vetch
Astragalus alpinus
Liquorice-root
Hedysarum alpinum
Crowberry (curlewberry)
Empetrum nigrum
Willow herb
Epilobium arcticum
Water-milfoil
Myriophyllum exalbescens
Mare's-tail
Hippuris vulgaris
Nodding wintergreen
Pyrola secunda
Large flowered wintergreen
Pyrola grandiflora

Labrador tea
Ledum decumbens
Arctic white heather
Cassiope tetragona
Lapland rosebay
Rhododendron lapponicum
Billberry
Vaccinium uliginosum
Primrose
Primula stricta
Leadwort
Armeria maritima
Jacob's ladder
Polemonium boreale
Richardson's phlox
Phlox richardsoni
Lungwort
Mertensia maritima
Lapland lousewort
Pedicularis lapponica
Labrador lousewort
Pedicularis labradorica
Woolly lousewort
Pedicularis lanata
Hairy lousewort
Pedicularis hirsuta

Butterwort
Pinguicula vulgaris
Bellflower
Campanula rotundifolia
Aster
Aster pygmaeus
Fleabane
Erigeron grandiflorus
Everlasting
Antennaria glabrata
Antennaria angustata
Antennaria ekmaniana
Antennaria compacta
Wild chamomile
Matricaria ambigua
Chrysanthemum
Chrysanthemum integrifolium
Wormwood
Artemisia hyperborea
Northern wormwood
Artemisia borealis
Richardson's wormwood
Artemisia richardsoniana
Sweet coltsfoot
Petasites frigidus
Yellow arnica
Arnica alpina
Marsh-fleabane
Senecio congestus
Dandelion
Taraxacum lacerum
Taraxacum hyparcticum
Taraxacum pumilum
Taraxacum phymatocarpum
Hawk's beard
Crepis nana

SHRUBS

WILLOWS
Wideleaf dwarf willow
Salix herbacea
Tundra dwarf willow
Salix arctophila
Salix pulchra

Richardson's willow
Salix richardsonii
Netvein dwarf willow
Salix reticulata
Salix alexensis
Salix niphoclada
Ungava willow
Salix cordifolia
Tundra birch
Betula glandulosa
Dwarf birch
Betula nana

COMMON EDIBLE PLANTS

Rock tripe (tripe-de-roche)
Gryophora
Reindeer Moss
Cladonia rangiferina
Cladonia sylvatica
Cladonia alpestris
Cetraria islandica

SEAWEED
Rhodymenia palmato
Laminaria spp.

HERBS
Lousewort
Pedicularis lanata
Arctic lousewort
Pedicularis arctica
Hairy lousewort
Pedicularis hirsuta
Fernweed
Pedicularis sudetica
Mountain sorrel
Oxyria digyna
Eskimo rhubarb
Polygonum alaskanum
Arctic sourdock
Rumex arcticus
Sweet coltsfoot
Petasites frigidus
Marsh-fleabane
Senecio congestus
Seabeach-sandwort
Arenaria peploides
Round-leaved saxifrage
Saxifrage punctata

Marsh marigold (cowslip)
Caltha palustris arctica

ROOTS
Liquorice-root
Hedysarum alpinum
Alpine bistort
Polygonum viviparum
Scurvy grass
Cochlearia officinalis

FRUITS and BERRIES
Crowberry
Empetrum nigrum
Baked apple
Rubus chamaemorus
Billberry
Vaccinium uliginosum

ANIMALS

SPIDERS
Erigone psychrophila
Pardosa glacialis
Tarantula exasperans
Xysticus deichmanni
Minyriolus pampia
Microphantidae
Collinsia spitsbergensis
Crab spider
Tegenaria destabilis

MITES
Cocceupodes curviclaua
Haemogamasus alaskensis
Laelaps alaskensis
Hirstionyssus isabellinus
Protereunetes borneri
Nanorchestes collinus
Liochthonius sellnicki
Brachychthonius scalaris
Fuscozetes sellnicki
Oribita lucasii
Tectocepheus velatus
Trichoribates polaris
Springtails
Collembola

Anurida sp.
Hypogatrura viatica
Hypogatrura humi
Agrenia bidenticulata
Folsomia bisetosa
Folsomia regularis
Folsomia diplophthalma
Folsomia fimitaria
Isotomurus palustris
Isomata viridis
Isomata violacea
Isomata olivacea
Onychiurus groenlandicus
Onychiurus debilis
Neelus minimum
Smimthurides malmgrini
Smimthurides aquaticus
Archisotoma besselsi
Neogastrura tullbergi
Proisotama mackenziana

INSECTS
Aphids
Homoptera
Mealybug
Pseudococcus (trionymus) sp.
Caddis fly
Apatania zonella

MOTHS and BUTTERFLIES
Tussock moth
Gynaephora rossi
Plusia moth
Sungrapha parilis
Tiger moth
Parasemia parthenos
Looper moth
Pheumaptera hastata
Psychophora sabini
Gynoephora groenlandica
Sulphur butterfly
Colias boothi
Pink-edged sulphur butterfly
Colias interior
Common sulphur
Colias hecla

Bog fritillary
Boloria eunomia
Polaris fritillary
Boloria polaris
Arctic fritillary
Boloria chariclea
Arctic blue
Pelbeius aquilo
American copper
Lycaena phloeas

BEETLES
Water beetle
Agabus moestus
Ground beetle
Amara alpina
Fungus beetle
Lathridius minimus
Tortoise beetle
Metriochemus obscuripes

WASPS, SAWFLIES and BEES
Bumble bee
Bombus polaris
Bombus hyperboreus
Ichneumon wasps
Mesoleius sp.
Ichneumon lariae
Ichneumon amauroplis
Ichneumon erythomelas
Ichneuman erythomelas

TWO-WINGED FLIES
Crane fly
Tipula arctica
Nephrotoma arcticola
Chironomidae
Sandfly
Ceratopogon sp.
Mosquito
Culicidae
Aedes impiger
Aedes nigripes
Hover fly
Syrphidae
Helophilus borealis
Sericomyia sexfasciatus
Metasyrphus chillcotti
Phalacrodira nigropilosa
Calliphoridae
Carrion fly
Borealius atriceps
Northern blowfly
Phormia terraenovae

Arctic midge
Chironomus polaris
Trichotanypus posticalis
Protanypus caudatus
Diamesa arctica
Cricotopus alpicola
Diplocladius bilobatus
Psectrocladius barbatimanus
Chaetocladius adsimilis
Lymnophyes borealis
Smittia polaris
Microspecta insignilobus

Blood-sucking midges
Ceratopogonidae
Forcipomyia sp.
Tachinid fly
Tachinidae
Spoggosia gelida
Peleteriopsis aenea
Dung fly
Muscidae
Scatophaga multisetosa
Scatophaga apicalis
Scatophaga nigripalpis
Cabbage maggot
Anthomyiinae
Hylemya fasciventris
Pegomyia arctica
Pegomyia tunicata
Muscoid fly
Limnophorinae
Spilgona almquisti
Spilgona deflorata
Spilgona dorsata
Spilgona obsoleta
Spilgona tundrae

BLACKFLIES
Gymnopais sp.
Prosimulium ursinum
Cnephia eremites
Cnephia borealis
Seal louse
Lepidophthirius macrohini

Louse
Hoplopleura acanthopus
SEA ANEMONES
Hacampa arctica
Bunodactis stella
Tapeworm
Echinococcus granulosus
Roundworm
Trichinella spiralis
Sea worm
Nemertina
Amphiporus angulatus
Marine worm
Priapulida
Priapulus caudata
Scale worm
Polychaeta
Harmothoe imbricata
Lug worm
Arenicola marina

MOLLUSCS
Clams
Pelecypods
Thin nut shell
Nucula tenuis
Sulcate nut shell
Nuculana tenuisulcata
Stout nut shell
Nuculana buccata
Mya-like yoldia
Yoldia myalis
Arctic yoldia
Yoldia arctica
Iceland scallop
Chlamys islandicus
Prickly jingle shell
Anomia aculeata
Blue mussel
Mytilus edulis
Horse mussel
Volsella modiolus

Smooth discord musculus
Musculus discors
Wrinkled musculus
Musculus corrugatus
Black musculus
Musculus niger
Faba crenella
Crenella faba

Glandular crenella
Crenella glandula
Fragile spoon shell
Periploma fragilis
Conrad's thracia
Thracia conradi
Large pandora
Pandora glacialis
Rostrate dipper
Cuspidaria rostrata
Black clam
Arctica islandica
Waved astarte
Astarte undata
Striate astarte
Astrate striata
Northern heart shell
Venericardia borealis
Iceland cockle
Clinocardium ciliatum
Northern dwarf cockle
Cerastoderma pinnulatum
Greenland cockle
Seripes groenlandicus
Venus shell
Liocyma fluctuosa

Little macoma
Macoma balthica
Chalky macoma
Macoma calcarea
Stimpson's surf clam
Spisula polynyma
Dwarf turton clam
Turtonia minuta
Long-neck clam
Mya arenaria

Short clam
Mya truncata
Arctic saxiclave
Hiatella arctica
Northern propeller clam
Cyrtodaria siliqua
Great piddock
Zirphaea crispata
Common shipworm
Teredo navalis

SNAILS

Tortoise shell limpet
Acmaea testudinalis
Little puncturella
Puncturella noachina
Cup-and-saucer
Cricibulum striatum
Northern rosy top shell
Margarites costalis
Smooth top shell
Margarites helicinus
Wavy top shell
Margarites groenlandica
Ladder shell
Epitorium groenlandicum
Waller's aclis
Aclis walleri
Iceland moon-shell
Amauropsis islandica
Greenland moon-shell
Lunatia groenlandica
Arctic natica
Natica clausa
Common velvet shell
Velutina laevigata
Cap shell
Capulus ungaricus
Orb shell
Skenea planorbis
Common periwinkle
Littorina littorea
Smooth periwinkle
Littorina obtusata
Northern rough periwinkle
Littorina saxatilis
Common Atlantic chink shell
Lacuna vincta
Pale chink shell
Lacuna pallidula
American pelican's foot
Aporrhais occidentalis

Atlantic dogwinkle
Thais lapillis
Trophon
Trophon clathratus
Trophon scalariformes
Rock purple
Thais lapillus

Common northern whelk
Buccinum undatum
Stimpson's spindle shell
Colus stimpsoni
Common northern neptune
Neptunea despecta
Kroyer's plicifusus
Plicifusus kroyeri
Noble bela
Lora nobilis
Common northern admete
Admete couthouyi
Needle shell
Turritellopsis acicula
Brown's barrel-bubble
Cylichna alba
Arctic barrel-bubble
Retusa obtusa

CRUSTACEANS
Common rock barnacle
Balanus balanoides
Northern ridged barnacle
Balanus balanus
Notched acorn barnacle
Balanus crenatus

ECHINODERMS
Polar starfish
Leptasterias polaris
Blood sea-star
Henrica sanguinolenta
Green sea urchin
*Strongylocentrotus
    droebachiensis*
Sea squirt
Tunicata
Ascidia callosa

FISHES

LAMPREYS
Entosphenus japonicus

STURGEONS
Lake sturgeon
Acipenser fulvescens
Atlantic sturgeon
Acipenser oxyrhynchus

HERRINGS
Pacific herring
Clupea harengus

SALMONS and TROUTS
Brook (char) trout
Salvelinus fontinalis
Arctic char
Salvelinus alpinus
Lake trout
Salvelinus namaycush
Atlantic salmon
Salmo salar
Lake whitefish
Coregonus clupeaformis
Broad whitefish
Coregonus nasus
Round whitefish
Prosopium cylindraceum
Cisco (lake herring)
Coregonus artedii
Inconnu
Stenodus leucichthys
Smelts
Osmeridae
Capelin
Mallotus villosus

SHARKS
Greenland shark
Somniosus microcephalus
Atlantic prickly skate
Raja radiata
Spiny dogfish
Squalus acanthias

PIKES

Northern pike
Exos lucius

SUCKERS

Longnose sucker
Catostomus catostomus

Northern redhorse
Moxostoma macrolepidotum

MINNOWS

Emerald shiner
Notropis atherinoides

Spottail shiner
Notropis hudsonius

LANTERN FISH

Glacial lanternfish
Benthosema glaciale

CODS

Burdot
Lota lota

Arctic cod
Boreogadus saida

Saffron cod
Elginus navaga

Atlantic cod
Gadus morhua

Pacific tomcod
Microgadus proximus

Greenland cod
Gadus ogac

Rough-head grenadier
Macrourus berglax

STICKLEBACKS

Threespine stickleback
Gasterosteus aculeatus

Ninespine stickleback
Pungitius pungitius

Brook stickleback
Eucalia inconstans

WOLF FISH

Anarhichas denticulatus

SNAKEBLENNY

Fourline snakeblenny
Eumesogrammus praecisus

Spotted snakeblenny
Stichaeus punctatus

Stout eelblenny
Lumpenus medius

Slender eelblenny
Lumpenus fabricii

EELPOUT

Pale eelpout
Lycodes pallidus

Arctic eelpout
Lycodes reticulatus

Polar eelpout
Lycodes turneri

SANDLANCE

Arctic sandlance
Ammodytes hexapterus

Dubius sandlance
Ammodytes dubius

ROSEFISH

Sebastes marinus

SCULPINS

Hookeye sculpin
Artediellus uncinatus

Arctic staghorn sculpin
Gymnocanthus tricuspis

Twohorn sculpin
Icelus bicornis

Fourhorn sculpin
Myoxocephalus quadricornis

Arctic sculpin
Myoxocephalus scorpioides

Shorthorn sculpin
Myoxocephalus scorpius

Slimy sculpin
Cottus cognatus

Mailed sculpin
Triglops nybelini

Ribbed sculpin
Triglops pingelii

SEAPOACHER

Alligator fish
Aspidophoroides monopterygius

Arctic seapoacher
Aspidophoroides olrikii

Sturgeon-like seapoacher
Agonus acipenseringus

LUMPSUCKER

Lumpfish
Cyclopterus lumpus

Leatherfin lumpsucker
Eumicrotremus derjugini

Spiny lumpsucker
Eumicrotremus spinosus

Gelatinous seasnail
Liparis koefoedi

RIGHTEYE FLOUNDERS

Greenland halibut
Reinhardtius hippoglossoides

Arctic flounder
Liopsetta glacialis

Smooth flounder
Liopsetta putnami

Starry flounder
Platichthys stellatus

BIRDS
Found in Summer only

Common loon
Gavia immer

Yellow-billed loon
Gavia adamsii

Arctic loon
Gavia arctica

Red-throated loon
Gavia stellata

Fulmar
Fulmarus glacialis

Whistling swan
Olor columbianus

Canada goose
Branta canadensis

Brant goose
Branta bernicla

Black brant
Branta nigricans

White-fronted goose
Anser albifrons

Snow goose
Chen hyperborea

Blue goose
Chen caerulescens

Ross's goose
Anser rossii

Pintail
Anas acuta

Oldsquaw
Clangula hyemalis

Common eider
Somateria mollissima

King eider
Somateria spectabilis

White winged scoter
Melanitta deglandi

Red-breasted merganser
Mergus serrator

Rough-legged hawk
Buteo lagopus

Golden eagle
Aquila chrysaetos

Peregrine falcon
Falco peregrinus

Sandhill crane
Grus canadensis

Ringed plover
Charadrius hiaticula

Semipalmated plover
Charadrius semipalmatus

Golden plover
Pluvialis dominica

Blackbellied plover
Squatarola squatarola

Ruddy turnstone
Arenaria interpres

Whimbrel
Numenius phaeous

Eskimo curlew (possibly extinct)
Numenius borealis

Harlequin duck
Histrionicus histrionicus

Knot
Calidris canutus
Purple sandpiper
Erolia maritima
Pectoral sandpiper
Erolia melanotos
White-rumped sandpiper
Erolia fuscicollis
Baird's sandpiper
Erolia bairdii
Dunlin
Erolia alpina
Stilt sandpiper
Micropalama himantopus
Semipalmated sandpiper
Ereunetes pusillus
Buff-breasted sandpiper
Tryngites subruficollis
Hudsonian godwit
Limosa haemastica

Sanderling
Crocethia alba
Red phalarope
Phalaropus fulicarius
Northern phalarope
Lobipes lobatus
Pomarine jaeger
Stercorarius pomarinus
Parasitic jaeger
Stercorarius parasiticus
Long-tailed jaeger
Stercorarius longicaudus
Glaucous gull
Larus hyperboreus
Iceland gull
Larus glaucoides
Great black-backed gull
Larus Marinis
Herring gull
Larus argentatus
Thayer's gull
Larus thayeri

Ivory gull
Pagophila eburnea
Black-legged kittiwake
Rissa tridactyla
Ross's gull
Rhodostethia rosea
Sabine's gull
Xema sabini
Arctic tern
Sterna paradisaea
Short-eared owl
Asio flammeus
Horned lark
Eromophila alpestris
Wheatear
Oenanthe oenanthe
Water pipit
Anthus spinoletta
Hoary redpoll
Acanthis hornemanni
Common redpoll
Acanthis flammea
Savannah sparrow
Passerculus sandwichensis
Tree sparrow
Spizella arborea
White-crowned sparrow
Zonotrichia leucophrys
Lapland longspur
Calcarius lapponicus
Snow bunting
Plectrophenax nivalis

BIRDS

Found all year around

Gyrfalcon
Falco rusticolus
Willow ptarmigan
Lagopus lagopus
Rock ptarmigan
Lagopus mutus
Thick-billed murre
Uria lomvia
Dovekie
Plautus alle
Black guillemot
Cepphus grylle
Snowy owl
Nyctea scandiaca
Common raven
Corvus corax

LAND MAMMALS

SHREWS
Masked shrew
Sorex cinereus
Arctic shrew
Sorex arcticus

HARES
Arctic hare
Lepus arcticus

SQUIRRELS
Arctic ground squirrel
Citellus parryi

BEARS
Barren ground grizzly
Ursus arctos

Polar bear
Thalarctos maritimus

MICE
Red-backed vole
Clethrionomys rutilus
Tundra vole
Microtus oecoromus
Collared lemming
Discrostonyx groenlandicus
Brown lemming
Lemmus trimucronatus

WOLVES and FOXES
Arctic fox
Alopex lagopus
Arctic wolf
Canis lupus

WEASLES, FERRETS and MINKS
Ermine
Mustela erminea
Least weasel
Mustela rixosa
Wolverine
Gulo gulo

DEER
Barren-ground caribou
Rangifer arcticus

Peary's caribou
Rangifer tarandus

CATTLE
Musk ox
Ovibos moschatus

SEA MAMMALS

WHALES, DOLPHINS and PORPOISES
Right and bowhead whales
Balaenidae
Greenland bowhead whale
Balaena mysticetus
Finback whales
Balaenopteridae
Common finback
Balaenoptera physalus
Lesser rorqual
Balaenoptera acutorostrata
Blue whale
Sibbaldus musculus
Humpback whale
Megaptera novaeangliae
Killer whale
Orcinus orca
Harbour porpoise
Phocoena phocoena
White whale
Delphinapterus leucas
Narwhal
Monodon monoceros

SEA LIONS and SEALS
Ringed seal
Phoca hispida
Harbour seal
Pusa vitulina
Hooded seal
Cystophora cristata
Bearded seal
Erignathus barbatus
Atlantic walrus
Odobenus rosmarus
Harp seal
Pagophilus groenlandica

REGIONAL MAPS AND INFORMATION

Large-scale maps and other information on the Arctic coast region can be obtained at moderate cost from: Government of Canada, Department of Energy, Mines, and Resources, 601 Booth Street, Ottawa, Ontario; Information Service, Government of the North West Territories, Yellowknife, N.W.T.; Department of Indian Affairs and Northern Development, Ottawa, Ontario. A selection of film strips and slides is available from: National Film Board, P.O. Box 6100, Montreal 3, P.Q.

BIBLIOGRAPHY

REGIONAL

BAIRD, P. D.
The Polar World.
New York: Wiley and Sons, 1964.

BIRKET-SMITH, KAJ.
The Eskimos.
London: Methuen & Co., 1959.

DUNBAR, M. and GREENAWAY, K. R.
Arctic Canada from the Air.
Ottawa: Queen's Printer, 1956.

FREUCHEN, PETER.
Book of the Eskimos.
New York: World Publishing, 1961.

HEARNE, SAMUEL. (J. B. Tyrell, ed.)
A Journey from Prince of Wales's Fort to the Northern Arctic Ocean.
Toronto: Champlain Society, 1911.

KIMBLE, G. H. T. and GOOD, D. (eds.)
Geography of the Northlands.
New York: Wiley and Sons, 1955.

MACDONALD, R. ST. J. (ed.)
The Arctic Frontier.
University of Toronto Press, 1966.

MIRSKY, J.
To the Arctic.
New York: Alfred A. Knopf, 1948.

NANSEN, FRIDTJOF.
In Northern Mists.
London: W. Heinemann, 1911.

PIKE, W.
The Barren Ground of Northern Canada.
London: Macmillan, 1892.

PIRIE, A.
Fallout.
London: MacGibbon & Kee, 1958.

SETON, E. T.
The Arctic Prairies.
New York: Scribner's, 1912.

SMITH, I. N. (ed.)
The Unbelievable Land.
Ottawa: Queen's Printer, 1964.

STEFANSSON, VILHJALMUR.
The Friendly Arctic.
London: Macmillan, 1943.

WILKINSON, DOUG.
Land of the Long Day.
Toronto: Clarke, Irwin, 1955.

WILSON, J. TUZO.
The Year of the New Moons.
New York: Knopf, 1961.

CLIMATE

GEIGER, R.
The Climate near the Ground.
Cambridge: Harvard University Press, 1950.

RAE, R. W.
Climate of the Canadian Arctic Archipelago.
Ottawa: Queen's Printer, 1951.

SUTTON, O. G.
Understanding the Weather.
London: Penguin Books, 1960.

THOMAS, M. K.
Canadian Arctic Temperatures.
Ottawa: Dept. of Transport, Meteorological Branch, Circular 3334, 1960.

THOMPSON, H. A.
The Climate of the Canadian Arctic.
Ottawa: Queen's Printer, 1967.

WILSON, H. P., MARKHAM, W. E., DEWAR, S. W., and THOMPSON, H. A.
Weather in the Canadian Arctic.
Ottawa: Dept. of Transport, Meteorological Branch, Circular 2387.

PERIODICAL

HARE, F. K. and MONTGOMERY, M. R.
"Ice, Open Water and Winter Climate in the Eastern Arctic of North America."
Arctic (Montreal), Volume 2, 1949.

GEOLOGY

BLACKADAR, R. G.
Geological Reconnaissance North Coast of Ellesmere Island.
Ottawa: Geological Survey of Canada, Paper 53-10, 1954.

CHAPMAN, SYDNEY.
The Earth's Magnetism.
London: Methuen & Co., 1951.

CRAIG, B. G. and FYLES, J. G.
Pleistocene Geology of Arctic Canada.
Ottawa: Geological Survey of Canada, Paper 60-10, 1960.

DUNBAR, C. O.
The Earth.
London: Weidenfeld & Nicholson, 1966.

DUNBAR, C. O.
Historical Geology. (2nd ed.)
New York: Wiley and Sons, 1960.

FLINT, R. F.
Glacial and Pleistocene Geology.
New York: Wiley and Sons, 1957.

FORTIER, Y. O., MCNAIR, A. H. and THORSTEINSSON, R.
Geology and Petroleum Possibilities in Canadian Arctic Islands.
Bulletin American Ass'n. Petroleum Geology, Volume 38, No. 10, 1954.

JEFFREYS, H.
The Earth.
Cambridge University Press, 1959.

LAND, A. H.,
Prospecting in Canada.
Ottawa: Queen's Printer, 1960.

MOORE, E. S.
Elementary Geology for Canada.
Toronto: J. M. Dent & Sons, 1944.

SABENA, A. P.
Rock and Mineral Collecting in Canada.
Ottawa: Queen's Printer, Vol. 1,
Yukon, Northwest Territories and British Columbia, 1965.

STOCKWELL, C. H.
Geology and Economic Minerals of Canada.
Ottawa: Queen's Printer, 1957.

STONMEN, C.
The Polar Aurora.
Oxford, Clarendon Press, 1955.

THORSTEINSSON, R. and TOZER, E. T.
Summary Account of Structural History of the Canadian Arctic Archipelago since Precambrian Times.
Ottawa: Geological Survey of Canada, Paper 60-7, 1960.

TYRNELL, J. W.
Across the Sub-Arctic of Canada, A Journey of 3,000 Miles by Canoe and Snowshoe through the Barren Lands.
London: T. Fisher Unwin, 1898.

ICE

KING, T.
Water, Miracle of Nature.
New York: Macmillan, 1953.

MACKAY, J. R.
The Mackenzie Delta Area, N.W.T.
Ottawa: Queen's Printer, 1963.

MULLER, FRITZ.
Preliminary Report 1961-62 of the Axel Heiberg Island Research Project.
Montreal: McGill University Press, 1963.

NANSEN, F.
Farthest North.
New York: Harper Bros., 1897.

PAPANIN, I. D.
Life on an Ice Floe
New York: Messner, 1939.

PEARY, R. E.
The North Pole.
London: Hodder & Stoughton, 1910.

WRIGHT, G. F.
The Ice Age in North America.
New York: Appleton & Co., 1889.

PERIODICALS

BILELLO, M. A.
"Formation, Growth and Decay of Sea Ice in the Canadian Arctic Archipelago."
Arctic (Montreal), Vol. 14, No. 1, 1961.

FLINT, R. F.
"The Ice Age in the North American Arctic."
Arctic (Montreal), Vol. 5, No. 3, 1952.

KOENIG, L. S., GREENAWAY, K. R., DUNBAR, M., and HATTERSLY-SMITH, G.
"Arctic Ice Islands."
Arctic (Montreal), Vol. 5, No. 2, 1952.

RAY, L. L.
"Permafrost."
Arctic (Montreal), Vol. 4, No. 3, 1951.

SHARP, R. P.
"Glaciers in the Arctic."
Arctic (Montreal), Vol. 9, Nos. 1 and 2, 1956.

TEDROW, J. C. F. and CANTLON, J. E.
"Concepts of Soil Formation and Classification in Arctic Regions."
Arctic (Montreal), Vol. 11, No. 3, 1958.

PLANTS

BESCHEL, R. E.
Botany, and Some Remarks on the History of Vegetation and Glacierization.
Montreal: McGill University Press, 1961.

Flora, Fauna and Geology.
Ottawa: Dept. of Northern Affairs and National Resources, 1954.

POLUNIN, NICHOLAS.
Circumpolar Arctic Flora.
Oxford University Press, 1959.

POLUNIN, NICHOLAS.
Botany of the Canadian Eastern Arctic. Parts 1 and 2.
Ottawa: Queen's Printer, 1947-48.

PORSILD, A. E.
Illustrated Flora of the Canadian Arctic Archipelago.
Ottawa: Queen's Printer, 1964.

SAVILLE, D. B. O.
*Botany of the Northwestern
Queen Elizabeth Islands.*
Ottawa: Dept. Mines & Tech. Surveys,
Geography Branch, Memoir 3, 1961.

PERIODICAL

BLISS, L. C.
"Adaptations of Arctic and Alpine
Plants to Environmental Conditions."
Arctic (Montreal), Vol. 15, No. 2, 1962.

ANIMALS

ANDERSON, R. M.
Catalogue of Canadian Recent Mammals.
Ottawa: National Museum of Canada,
Bulletin 102.

BANFIELD, A. W. F.
*Preliminary Investigation of
the Barren Ground Caribou.*
Ottawa: Queen's Printer, 1954.

CLARKE, C. H. D.
*A Biological Investigation of the
Thelon Game Sanctuary.*
Ottawa: National Museum of Canada, 1940.

DUNBAR, M. J.
Eastern Arctic Waters.
Ottawa: Fisheries Res. Board,
Bulletin 88, 1951.

GODFREY, W. E.
The Birds of Canada.
Ottawa: Queen's Printer, 1966.

HARINGTON, C. R.
Denning Habits of the Polar Bear.
Ottawa: Canadian Wildlife Service,
Paper No. 5, 1968.

KELSALL, J. P.
*Barren Ground Caribou Movements
in the Canadian Arctic.*
Washington: Wildlife Management
Institute, 1955.

KELSALL, J. P.
*The Migratory Barren Ground
Caribou of Canada.*
Ottawa: Queen's Printer, 1968.

MANSFIELD, A. W.
Seals of Arctic and Eastern Canada.
Ottawa: Queen's Printer, 1964.

PEDERSON, A.
Polar Animals.
London: Harrap & Co., 1962.

SETON, E. T.
The Arctic Prairies.
Toronto: Wm. Briggs, 1911.

SCHOLANDER, P. F., HOCK, R.,
WALTERS, U., and IRVING, L.
*Adaptations to Cold in Arctic and Tropical
Mammals and Birds in Relation to Body
Temperature, Insulation and Basal
Metabolic Rate.*
Ottawa: Biological Bulletin, 99: 259-271.

SNYDER, L. L.
Arctic Birds of Canada.
University of Toronto Press, 1957.

SYMINGTON, F.
Tuktu.
Ottawa: Queen's Printer, 1965.

TENER, J. S.
Muskoxen in Canada.
Ottawa: Queen's Printer, 1965.

PERIODICALS

BUTLER, L.
"The Nature of Cycles in Populations
of Canadian Mammals."
Canadian Zoology (Toronto), Vol. 313, 1953.

FAY, F. H.
"Carnivorous Walrus and Some
Arctic Zoonoses."
Arctic (Montreal), Vol. 13, No. 2, 1960.

HOHN, E. O.
"Lemmings, Hares and Hormones."
The Beaver (Winnipeg), Winter, 1961.

HOHN, E. O.
"Birds in the Arctic."
The Beaver (Winnipeg), Summer, 1959.

IRVING, L. and KROG, J.
"Body Temperature of Arctic and
Sub-Arctic Birds and Mammals."
Journal of App. Phys., Volume 6, 1954.

LOUGHERY, ALAN G.
"The Polar Bear and its Protection."
Oryx (Washington), Vol. 3, No. 5, 1956.

PRUITT, W. O.
"A New Caribou Problem."
The Beaver (Winnipeg), Winter, 1962.

PRUITT, W. O.
"Snow as a Factor in the Winter
Ecology of the Barren Ground Caribou."
Arctic (Montreal), Vol. 12, No. 3, 1954.

RAND, A. L.
"The Ice Age and Mammal
Speciation in North America."
Arctic (Montreal), Vol. 7, No. 1, 1954.

TWINN, C. R.
"Studies of the Biology and Control
of Biting Flies in Northern Canada."
Arctic (Montreal), Vol. 3, 1950.

INDEX

ACKNOWLEDGEMENTS

The author wishes to acknowledge with gratitude the advice and assistance given unstintingly throughout twenty years of itinerant contacts in offices in southern Canada, and in snowhouses, tents and ships' cabins in Arctic Canada, of the following individuals: Dr. R. Thorsteinsson, Dr. T. Tozer, and Dr. Y. O. Fortier, of the Geological Survey of Canada – on geology and minerals; Dr. F. Mueller of the Dept. of Geography, McGill University, Dr. G. Hattersley-Smith of the Defence Research Board, Dr. Vilhjalmur Stefansson (deceased), Commodore O. C. S. Robertson (ret.) R. C. N. and Miss Moira Dunbar of the Defence Research Board – on ice; Dr. M. J. Dunbar, Fisheries Research Board – on the subject of the sea; Singeetuk (deceased) of Rankin Inlet, Idlouk (deceased) of Resolute Bay, Itteemangnak of Pelly Bay and Attungala of Baker Lake, Dr. J. S. Tener, C. R. Harington, J. P. Kelsall and A. Loughery of the Canadian Wildlife Service – on animals; Dr. D. B. O. Saville, Dept of Agriculture, Dr. A. E. Porsild (ret.), National Museum of Canada, Kidlak (deceased) of Pond Inlet – plants; Dr. D. R. Oliver, Dept. of Agriculture – on insects; Dr. W. E. Taylor, Jr., National Museum of Canada, Graham Rowley, Dept. of Indian Affairs and Northern Development, Akomalik (deceased) of Pond Inlet – on Eskimo history; Alex. Stevenson, Dept. of Indian Affairs and Northern Development, Patrick Baird, McGill University, Henry Larsen (deceased), R. C. M. P., P. E. C. Nichols, Hudson's Bay Company, Father F. van de Velde, O.M.I., Oblate Missions and Canon J. James, Anglican Missions, on the Arctic.

PICTURE CREDITS

Order of appearance in the text of pictures listed here is left to right, top to bottom.

Cover/National Film Board
1/Fred Bruemmer
2-21/Doug Wilkinson
22/National Air Photo Library
23/National Film Board
24-31/Doug Wilkinson
40/John de Visser
45-53/Doug Wilkinson
57-71/Fred Bruemmer
72/John de Visser, Dr. G. Peck,
  Dr. Donald R. Gunn
73/Dr. G. Peck, Fred Bruemmer,
  Dr. R. R. Tasker, Barry Ranford
74/Dr. D. R. Gunn, Dr. G. Peck,
  Dr. D. R. Gunn
75/Fred Bruemmer
79/Ernest Kuyt
93-97/Dr. G. Peck
98/Fred Bruemmer, Dr. G. Peck
99/Dr. G. Peck, Barry Ranford,
  Dr. G. Peck, Dr. G. Peck
100-107/Fred Bruemmer
108/Fred Bruemmer, S. D. MacDonald,
  Fred Bruemmer, Fred Bruemmer,
  Fred Bruemmer
109/E. Kuyt, John de Visser,
  National Film Board
110-113/Fred Bruemmer
119/John de Visser
120/Doug Wilkinson, John de Visser,
  John de Visser,
  National Film Board
121/John de Visser
122/Fred Bruemmer
125/John de Visser
128/Dr. G. Peck
132/Glenbow Archives Calgary
133/Geological Survey of Canada
134/National Film Board
137-140/Toronto Public Libraries
141/Doug Wilkinson

This book was produced entirely in Canada by:
Mono Lino Typesetting Co. Limited / *Typesetting;* Herzig Somerville Limited / *Film Separation;*
Ashton-Potter Limited / *Printing;* T. H. Best Printing Co. Limited / *Binding.*
Typefaces: Times New Roman and Helvetica. Paper: 65 lb. Georgian Offset Smooth.

PRINTED IN CANADA